T0329938

A Research Agenda for Organisational Continuity and Change

A Research Agenda for Organisational Continuity and Change

Edited by

TOR HERNES
Centre for Organization and Time, Department of Organization, Copenhagen Business School, Denmark

MIRIAM FEULS
Centre for Organization and Time, Department of Organization, Copenhagen Business School, Denmark

Elgar Research Agendas

Cheltenham, UK • Northampton, MA, USA

Published by
Edward Elgar Publishing Limited
The Lypiatts
15 Lansdown Road
Cheltenham
Glos GL50 2JA
UK

Edward Elgar Publishing, Inc.
William Pratt House
9 Dewey Court
Northampton
Massachusetts 01060
USA

A catalogue record for this book
is available from the British Library

Library of Congress Control Number: 2023943175

This book is available electronically in the **Elgar**online
Business subject collection
http://dx.doi.org/10.4337/9781802200164

ISBN 978 1 80220 015 7 (cased)
ISBN 978 1 80220 016 4 (eBook)

Printed and bound in Great Britain by
TJ Books Limited, Padstow, Cornwall

To the late Andy Van de Ven for his tireless efforts to accommodate novel views into studies of organisational continuity and change.

Contents

Figures

Tables

Contributors

Jeremy Aroles is Senior Lecturer in Organisation Studies at the University of York, UK. Before joining the University of York, he worked at Durham University and at the University of Manchester, where he obtained his PhD in 2016. His research currently focuses on the exploration of new ways of working, the management of cultural institutions, and the intricate relation between fiction and organizational worlds. His research has notably been published in *Organization Science, Organization Studies, Work, Employment and Society, Organization, Management Learning* and *New Technology, Work and Employment.*

Nicolas Bencherki is an Associate Professor of organizational communication at Université TÉLUQ and an affiliate professor at Université du Québec à Montréal, in Canada. His research focuses on the intersecting roles of communication and materiality in constituting authority, membership, and strategy in community-based organizations. His work has appeared in the *Academy of Management Journal, Organization Studies, Human Relations,* and the *Journal of Communication.* He co-edited the *Routledge Handbook of the Communicative Constitution of Organization,* published in 2022.

Frans Bévort is an Associate Professor at the Copenhagen Business School, Denmark. His research focuses on HRM, professions, identity, narrative and paradox. Recent research projects: (1) the effect of AI on professional judgement and, (2) how the Nordic model of HRM influences organisational resilience. He has (co-)authored 10+ books and has published articles in journals such as *International Journal of HRM* (in press), *German Journal of HRM, Journal of Professions and Organization, International Studies of Management and Organization.* His latest book is *Navigating Leadership Paradox* with De Gruyter (2023, co-authored).

Blagoy Blagoev is Professor of Organization at Technische Universität Dresden. His research draws on a temporal lens to examine the interplay of organizations and society in the context of current technological, ecological, and cultural changes. His main research interests include organizational change, business sustainability, emerging technologies, and new forms of working and organizing. His research has been published in *Administrative Science Quarterly, Academy of Management Journal, Journal of Management Studies, Organization Studies, Organization* and *Scandinavian Journal of Management*.

Are Branstad is an Associate Professor at University of Southeast Norway with a PhD in entrepreneurship. Are is currently researching the dynamics between digital technology and work organizations, economic clusters and networks, and consumer adoption. He has also done research in marketing and consumer culture, public–private partnerships, and innovative procurement processes. His current research includes implementation of digital health logistics systems in hospitals and regional development in the Norwegian healthcare industry.

Anders Buch (MA in philosophy, PhD in Education) is a Senior Associate Professor (docent) and head of research programme at the Research Centre for Quality of Education, Profession Policy and Practice at VIA University College, Aarhus, Denmark. His empirical research area is focused on technological expert cultures, organizations, education, professions, and professionalism. His theoretical approach is primarily inspired by science & technology studies, practice theory, and pragmatism. He has published articles and books on knowledge, learning, education, professionalism, and the professional development of engineers.

Miriam Feuls is an Assistant Professor at the Department of Organization and Co-Director of the Centre for Organization and Time at Copenhagen Business School, Denmark. Miriam's research draws on insights from organization studies, process studies, and cultural and social studies to advance understanding of processes of organizational continuity and change and their interrelation. Empirically, she is engaged in the study of time and temporality, innovation and creativity, and environmental and social sustainability.

Raghu Garud is Farrell Chair in Innovation and Entrepreneurship, and Professor of Management & Organization, Pennsylvania State University. Raghu's research explores the emergence of novelty and its adoption. Specifically, he explores how new ideas emerge, are valued, and become institutionalized. Towards this end, Raghu has been researching and writing about the role time plays in constituting innovation processes, with concepts such as synchrony, diachrony, serendipity, and the plasticity of time. His work was recognized by the TIM Division of the Academy of Management as its distinguished scholar for 2020.

Tor Hernes is currently Professor of Organization Theory at Copenhagen Business School and Adjunct Professor at University of Southeast Norway. He is director of the Centre for Organization and Time based at Copenhagen Business School. Tor works with theories of time and temporality from process philosophy. His empirical research focuses on dynamics between continuity and change in organizations. Tor won the George R. Terry Book Award in 2015 for his book *A Process Theory of Organization* (Oxford University Press, 2014).

Anthony Hussenot is a Full Professor in Organization Studies at the Université Côte d'Azur, France. His research and teaching focus on the new or alternative ways of working and organizing, and the relation between work and society. His research has notably been published in several academic journals such as *Organization Studies*, *M@n@gement*, *International Journal of Organizational Analysis*. His recent book *Pourquoi travailler?* (in French, EMS, 2022) deals with the role and status of work in our society.

Astrid Jensen (PhD) is Associate Professor of Organizational Communication at the Department of Language, Culture, History and Communication, University of Southern Denmark. Her research interests include various aspects of organizational cognition and communication. Recent work combines theories of narratives in organizational change, culture, and identity.

Jacob A. Klopp is a PhD candidate at The Pennsylvania State University Smeal College of Business. Jacob's research investigates how the process of entrepreneurial innovation unfolds in the face of cultural, technological, and institutional challenges. His work is exploring new directions for integrating qualitative methods and natural language processing of large text corpora.

Henrik Koll is Associate Professor of Organizational Communication at the Department of Language, Culture, History and Communication at University of Southern Denmark. His research interests include organizational change management, time and temporality in organization and management studies, and Bourdieusian social theory.

Waldemar Kremser is Professor and Head of the Institute of Strategic Management at Johannes Kepler University, Linz. In his research, he is combining a routine dynamics perspective on organizations with insights from complexity theory and other fields like strategy and organization design. He is most interested in open strategy processes, self-managing forms of organizing, self-reinforcing dynamics and radical innovations. Waldemar has published his work in international top journals, including *Administrative Science Quarterly*, *MIS Quarterly*, *Organization Science*, and *Organization Theory*.

Ann Langley is Emerita Professor at HEC Montréal, and Distinguished Research Environment Professor at University of Warwick. Her research deals with strategic processes and practices in complex organizations with an emphasis on qualitative research methods. She is Deputy Editor for qualitative research at *Academy of Management Journal* (2022–25), and co-editor with Haridimos Tsoukas of the book series Perspectives on Process Organization Studies published by Oxford University Press.

Ansgar Ødegård is an associate professor (senior lecturer) at The University of Southeast Norway. He is currently researching on the post-reform within the Norwegian electricity industry from a temporal perspective and the relation between society and business when it comes to sustainability. He has also done research on how multinational companies conduct responsible business when locating in distanced local communities.

Mie Plotnikof is Associate Professor of Public Governance and Organization, Danish School of Education, Aarhus University, Denmark. Her research explores issues and micro-politics of discourse, subjectivity, temporality, difference, dis/organization and power/resistance in everyday work – often within educational and other social sectors. She has published in journals such as *Organization, Gender Work and Organization, ephemera*, and *Organization Studies*, and in international edited volumes as well as in Danish outlets. She is part of the editorial collective of ephemera: theory and politics in organization, and associate editor in *Gender Work & Organization*.

Kätlin Pulk (PhD, MA, MBA) is an Associate Professor at Estonian Business School. After receiving her PhD from Copenhagen Business School, her research focus has stayed on time and temporality and their connection to various organizational phenomena like organizational change, outsourcing, backsourcing, innovation, commitment and continuity.

Majken Schultz is Professor of Management and Organization Studies at Copenhagen Business School and member of the Centre for Organization and Time based at Copenhagen Business School. Her current work explores how organizational actors construct their temporality, which she has applied in studies of organizational identity reconstruction, strategic transformation and the use of history for future change. She is chair of Carlsberg Foundation and PI of the research project "Making Distant Futures Actionable".

Iben Sandal Stjerne is Associate Professor at Technical University of Denmark (DTU), Department of Engineering Technology. Iben does ethnographic work on how time and temporality organize managerial and strategic practices. She has investigated this in various settings where time is an inherent key organizing principle, that is, the selection processes in the search for a future fit, connecting actors towards a shared future SDG, the shadows of past and future in and between temporary organizations, and agile organizing of time.

Matthias Wenzel is Professor of Organization Studies at the Leuphana University of Lüneburg. He examines the interplay between organizing and strategizing through a practice lens as well as the societal implications of this interplay. Matthias also serves as co-editor for media innovations of the *Strategic Management Journal*, *Strategic Entrepreneurship Journal* and *Global Strategy Journal*, and as member of the Editorial Board of *Organization Studies* and *Strategic Organization.*

1 Introduction: suggestions for a framework of organizational continuity and change

Miriam Feuls and Tor Hernes

The interwoven yet uneasy relationship between organizational continuity and change

To understand the workings of contemporary organizing and organizations, it is crucial to develop a richer understanding of the dynamics between organizational continuity and change. We intentionally put continuity before change in the previous sentence to challenge the dominance of change over continuity in organizational research. A number of works have privileged change over continuity in some form or other, thereby underestimating the primordial role of continuity in enabling change. As pointed out by Blagoy and Kremser in this volume (chapter 9), the "stickiness" of routines and structural couplings between actors and their persistence through time is primordial for organizational continuity *and* change (see also Howard-Grenville, 2005). Most of the time, actors in organizations enact a sense of continuity even when their enactment is dressed up as change or interpreted as change.

While continuity and change have been studied as separate phenomena, whether opposed to one another or complementary to one another, their dynamic interplay has been overlooked in organization and management research. In this introduction, we first take continuity and change research back to its roots. Drawing on process-oriented thinking, we then develop a framework that explains the relationship between change and continuity as mutually constitutive processes, that is, the continuity of change and the change of continuity (see also chapters by Hussenot & Aroles, chapter 5, Plotnikof & Bencherki, chapter 6, and Branstad & Ødegård, chapter 10, this volume). Several process-oriented researchers contribute to this volume to explore how continuity and change can be understood through mutual interplay rather than through mutual exclusion. At the end of the introduction, we introduce each chapter and outline its contribution to the research agenda on organizational continuity and change.

The interplay between continuity and change ranges arguably among the most overlooked research foci in organization and management research. The oversight stems in part from entrenched assumptions among scholars about continuity and change as the antitheses of each another. Continuity and change have long been seen as mutually exclusive phenomena, leading to axioms such as, if there is continuity, there cannot also be change, and if there is change there cannot also be continuity. The assumption may be traced back to Newtonian physics and its linear assumptions about time and space according to which an object either moves or stays still, irrespective of the position of the observer. But Newtonian thinking is not a very useful tool for understanding the dynamics of contemporary organizations. On the contrary, it can be shown how organizations undergoing disruptive change may *also* maintain a high degree of continuity (see Hussenot & Aroles, chapter 5, and Stjerne et al., chapter 7, this volume).

In recent years, organization and management researchers have sought to break with Newtonian worldviews (Chia & Tsoukas, 2003) to theorize the gap between continuity and change. These researchers have engaged in process-oriented theorizing to dismantle dichotomies in the field, such as those between continuity and change. But as, for example, argued by Schultz and Hernes in this volume (chapter 2), it is possible to extend their notion of continuity and change from a purely situated, micro-level view. Over the last 20 years, temporal research has brought to light additional aspects of time, which enable richer and more nuanced theorizing of the relationships between continuity and change than was done previously. These added aspects enable continuity to take on a richer meaning. For example, whereas continuity has been understood as an unbroken process, it may also be understood as the "joining together" (Chambers, 1988) of temporally separate events or periods. In fact, as Hernes et al. (2021) point out, an event might signify a change in temporal trajectory compared with some other events on that trajectory while it marks continuity compared with other events on that same trajectory. Developing this thought further, we argue that research should address the relationships between change and continuity as explicitly mutually constitutive processes along the temporal trajectory of an organization (Hernes & Feuls, 2022). Addressing the continuity of change and the change of continuity is important for understanding some of the more profound temporal challenges facing contemporary organizations.

Dismantling the continuity–change dichotomy is not a theoretical project disconnected from managerial practice. The assumption of continuity and change being antitheses to one another does not hold for the world of contemporary management practices (see, for example, Koll & Jensen's discussion of narration, practices, and habitus, chapter 8, this volume). From our research into managerial practices and from hundreds of hours of teaching managers, it is clear to us that continuity and change are closely intertwined in people's practices, although they are not always aware of it. Here lies a paradox that extends to change more generally. Managers are fed the idea that change is the opposite of continuity or stability. This view, partly fuelled by Lewin's (1947) famous "unfreeze, change and refreeze" model, underpins ideas and techniques, such as burning platforms, radical innovations, and disruption. A common idea among these and multiple other trends is that only a radical departure from the current state of affairs can save the organization. However, we have serious doubts about such assumptions. Hernes (2022, p. 151) makes the point as follows:

> Change management scholars might well argue that in order to confront disruptive change actors should become something else. All the actor needs is a bold vision of disrupting the present and of suppressing the past that did not deliver on change. All they need to do is cut the moorings from the past and, by some Houdinian feat, escape the shackles of the present. Unfortunately, that is neither practically nor theoretically feasible. A hotel cannot become a version of Airbnb by forgetting its past, even if that might seem strategically advantageous in the long run.

In implementing change, managers enact continuity amidst change or even enact change as a form of continuity. For example, managers may choose to keep some existing technologies while changing others or they may choose to keep the more seasoned staff on the payroll because they have other competencies needed in the future organization. For some, such enactments are about mobilizing aspects of the organization to harness future change. For others, such measures are about making sure the potential of ongoing practices is not being lost for the future. However, this is not how change tends to be prescribed, nor does it always correspond to how managers explain the ways they enact change. In her study of technology-based organizational change, Orlikowski (1996) found that managerial action intentionally triggered change by introducing the new technology, but that the use of the technology over time, during which organizational actors innovated, improvised, or made changes to existing solutions and routines, was critical for change to take place. According to Orlikowski, rather than result of managerial intentions, strategies and plans, change emerged out of their "accommodations to and experiments with the everyday contingencies, breakdowns, exceptions, opportunities, and unintended consequences" (1996, p. 65).

To explore the paradoxical relationship between continuity and change and to resolve the dichotomy, we discuss four views of the relationship between continuity and change. The first three views (dominance, alternating, and interdependence views) include many influential works in organization and management research. The fourth view (integrative) is one that is predominately addressed in this volume. It is a view that is currently emerging but remains novel and perhaps radical to many scholars, students and practitioners. Still, as we will argue below, an integrative view actually offers a novel and alternative view to the situations in which practitioners find themselves than the other three views, which have largely dominated the field over the past couple of decades.

Four views of the relationships between continuity and change

The history of organization and management research has followed a path of changing relationships between organizational change, on the one hand, and organizational stability or continuity, on the other. Views of change and continuity have proliferated since the inception of organizational research around seven decades ago. We can distinguish four main views, which we discuss below. In this volume, we foreground the notion of continuity to propose and extend what we call an integrative view of continuity and change. The chapters in the book consider in different ways how we may arrive at a more integrative view than that which has existed until now. To accomplish this task, the chapters take time and temporality into consideration. It is through the lens of time that the integration between continuity and change becomes particularly visible. When, for example, a company engages in a transformation to become 100 per cent sustainable within five years, that is manifestly a process of change. New technologies will be put in place, new people will be recruited, new systems will be put in place and new business models may be developed as part of the process. But, as Weik (2011) points out, nothing emerges "ex nihilo nihil", meaning nothing springs out of nothing. If the change process is not connected to a trajectory of continuity, such change may not be possible. And, as shown by the different chapters, continuity may be enacted across different spans of time, enabling different forms and degrees of change to emerge (see, for example, Branstad & Ødegård, chapter 10, this volume). Continuity may be enacted through the ongoing process of interacting during a meeting, which constitutes situated continuous change (Orlikowski, 1996; Tsoukas & Chia, 2002), or it may be enacted as a connection between events or periods that lie years, decades or even centuries apart (Stjerne et al., chapter 7, this volume).

In what follows, we will discuss the four main views of organizational continuity and change (see also Table 1.1).

Table 1.1 Summary of main views of organizational continuity and change

View of continuity – change	Main features	Origin and role in research	Role of continuity
Dominance view	Focus lays on either change or continuity or stability	Originally organizations as predominately stable systems. Less common but influential since the 1990s change as dominant	Either as dominant, usually as a stable state, or as a stable background against which change takes place (exception: continuous change)
Alternating view	Periods of relative continuity or stability are interspersed with periods of change	Emerged from the biology-inspired punctuated equilibrium views in the 1980s	Mainly routine dominated and enduring periods of relative stability interrupted by change
Interdependence view	Continuity (or stability) and change are seen as duality, i.e. as separate but interdependent processes	Influenced by views of stability and change in systems theory since 2010	Continuity (or stability) as predictable process enabling change as coping with uncertainty
Integrative view	Continuity and change are mutually constitutive processes	Inspired by process theory and the philosophy of time and recently emerging	As effortful accomplishment alongside change

A dominance view

Past decades of organization and management research have witnessed a swing of the pendulum from seeing organizations as predominately stable of continuous systems, on the one hand, to continuously changing systems, on the other. During the early period (i.e. the 1960s to 1970s), works aimed to establish organizations as predominately stable systems with their own systemic identity (Emery & Trist, 1965; Lawrence & Lorsch, 1967; Thompson, 1967). This view enabled the identification of structural features of organizations that distinguished them from other organizations and their external environment more generally (Emery & Trist, 1965). Later works considered organizations as quasi-stable symbolic and cultural systems (Schein, 1985; Meyerson & Martin, 1987). Martin et al.'s study of The Body Shop, for example, shows how Anita Roddick, the founder, maintained a compelling story about its history through-out the time she led the company. In this view, when organizations changed, their change was considered an adaptation to a changing environment (Burns, 1958; Burns & Stalker, 1961). In any case, the works may be described as con-sidering stability to be dominant, with change being the exception.

Whereas strategic views emerging in the 1980s and 1990s would emphasize change (e.g. Porter, 1996), they considered change more as a consequence of strategy than a driving force of strategy. Later currents would take a more active view of organizational adaptation. For example, new institutionalist scholars (e.g. Meyer & Rowan, 1977) studied how organizations would decou-ple and shelter parts of their structures from external influence. From these and several other perspectives, organizations were still considered quasi-stable systems. When organizations changed, their change was considered to take place as a result of external influence(s) (DiMaggio & Powell, 1983) or gradual adaptation to external and internal demands. For example, theorizing the institutional dimensions of organizations, which has been very influential in organizational research, has traditionally operated from assumptions of stabil-ity or continuity as dominant forces of organizing, only recently beginning to focus on the micro-processes of institutional change (Micelotta et al., 2017).

Continuity or stability has not been considered the only dominant form of organizing. Some works have argued for organizations as being in a con-stant state of change. Brown and Eisenhardt (1997) introduced the concept of continuous change in their study of multi-product innovations in the fast-changing and high-velocity computer industry. They defined continuous change as the sequential stringing together of changes over time. For example, they pointed out how the frequency of change may vary depending on the occurrence of new product development cycles. They discussed what they call "rhythmic transition processes" (1997, p. 3) from one process of change to the next, but without specifying how such transitions may constitute acts of continuity that are enacted to enable certain forms of change.

Other scholars have discussed continuous change from a somewhat different viewpoint. We have mentioned above how Orlikowski (1996) defines change as the micro-level adaptations and improvisations that go on all the time in organizations. Orlikowski's views are theorized further by Tsoukas and Chia (2002) in drawing upon foundational ideas by philosophers of time, notably Bergson (1911) and James (1909). The radical idea posited by Tsoukas and

Chia is that change "is all there is" (2002, p. 576), and organization is but a temporary glimpse of intractable flows emerging in situated settings. Their theorizing has been influential in process-oriented organization and management research and has also influenced the emerging integrative view, as we will outline below.

An alternating view

A view of organizations as dominated by stability or continuity became gradually displaced by the need to understand change and especially intentional, programmed change. Lewin's (1947) famous "unfreeze, change and refreeze" model of change began to take hold and is still a dominant view of change. A reason for its popularity may be that change and continuity or stability are seen as feeding off one another through time. For instance, Kotter's (1996) well-known model of eight stages of successful change processes reflects how periods of stability are followed by periods of change. During the 1990s, a number of scholars adhered to a punctuated equilibrium view of change, which saw change as a shift from one equilibrium state to another. These scholars built on Lewin's model of change to emphasize step-by-step phases of change in-between two stable processes (unfreezing and refreezing). In a punctuated equilibrium view, change happens during a concentrated period to disrupt a state of equilibrium, for a new state of equilibrium to then emerge. Papers by Romanelli and Tushman (1994) and Gersick (1991) advocated this view of change broadly as an interruption of stability (see also Tushman & Romanelli, 1985), leading to a different state of affairs. For several years, change had an ideal antithesis in stability, closely associated with equilibrium; hence scholars could identify change as a more or less radical departure from stability. In this view, change is seen as rare and episodic as opposed to continuous change (Weick & Quinn, 1999).

An alternating view implies that periods of continuity or stability become interspersed or interrupted by periods of change. There may be several explanations for such a view. One explanation is empirical and suggests that organizations have limited resources making them unable to cope with too much change within a given period of time, forcing them to try and achieve periods of stability. Change places demands on scarce resources, especially on time and attention, as argued by March (1991). One reason is that functions in organizations are invariably interconnected, and a change in one or more functions requires that others adjust, as well. Another explanation is that as different parts of the organization adjust, unexpected consequences arise, requiring that further adjustments be made, even sometimes resulting in the entire change initiative needing to be revised. Thus, multiple scholars have followed in the wake of March's (1991) distinction between exploration and exploitation of organizations, which he drew to alert scholars and practitioners to dilemmas posed to managers about how to use resources when confronted with the need to change. We note nevertheless March's (1996) suggestion that "The achievement of an effective mixing of continuity and change is made possible by […] a tension between the delights of exploitation and the delights of exploration" (p. 287).

An interdependence view

Although an alternating view explains how change and stability or continuity succeed one another, it does not explain well *how* transitions take place. Nor does it explain how continuity and change interact when enacted in parallel with one another. Complex organizations have multiple processes running in parallel, some of which may be more geared towards continuity and others which are more geared towards change. Schultz and Hernes (2020) show from their longitudinal study of continuity and change at Carlsberg how the company initiated different change processes over time. However, Carlsberg succeeded only when they were able to connect sustainable strategic change processes with the enactment of the company's identity, which formed a basis of continuity over long time spans.

Other works have brought to light the complex relationships that arise when change emerges from continuity (or stability) or vice versa (Farjoun, 2010). Farjoun argues that it is problematic to keep continuity and change separate from each other and that we need to think of continuity and change as interacting dialectically through time. His framework addresses how stability enables change as well as how change enables stability. For instance, he argues that routines and formalization help manage nonroutine processes in organizations, such as innovation. On the other hand, he points out that change also enables stability. For instance, he argues that change leads to uncertainty, which motivates actors to search for continuity.

Although an interdependence view moves continuity and change closer to one another than the dominance and the alternating views do, there is a bias towards change as more dynamic and risk-taking than continuity. For example, Farjoun suggests continuity be associated with "reliability, predictability, low variance, and regularity", and change be associated with "variation, adaptability, new knowledge, flexibility, and innovation" (2010, p. 204). Such an assumption views change as open-ended and uncontrollable, while it relegates continuity to the status of controllable processes (Huy, 2002). However, as we will argue below, making such distinctions has more to do with the particular ontological assumptions scholars make about organizational behaviour than with the actual challenges that practitioners face in their work. It is on this basis that we introduce an integrative view of continuity and change.

An integrative view

An integrative change view is underpinned ontologically by works in process philosophy and the philosophy of time. The core idea of a process ontological view is of the world as ever emerging, the world is perpetually "on the move" (Hernes, 2014). This idea may appear overly abstract to many readers. However, emergence, in the form of ongoing streams of ideas, actions, people, solutions, technologies, trends, etc., surrounds actors and calls for reflection and action to be able to keep things on track, not to speak of changing things. The ongoing streams, some of which remain mere potentialities, others of which form actualities, form part of the ever-emerging reality in which actors find themselves.

If we accept this ontological assumption, it has important implications for how we understand continuity and change. In a world on the move, continuity cannot be taken as a given. On the contrary, creating a sense of continuity in such a world requires effortful activity because multiple continuit*ies* are available to actors. This point is borne out by Langley et al.'s (2013) argument, that "Much more active work is required to maintain practices, organizations, and institutions than most management scholars would admit" (p. 10) (see also Van de Ven & Poole, 2021). Managers are well acquainted with the dilemmas created by the effortful nature of continuity and having to choose between different directions that continuity may take in the future (Howard-Grenville et al., 2017; Pentland & Goh, 2021). For example, they may choose between opting for an old and proven technology or a technology that has been recently developed. If we look closer at this situation, both choices imply continuity *and* change. In other words, both continuity and change imply effortful processes.

An integrative view of continuity and change differs from the above views by considering acts or processes of continuity as effortful and with uncertain outcomes, much the same as acts or processes of change. In fact, as argued by Van de Ven and Poole (2005), depending on the perspective of the observer, continuity (or stability) may refer to the same processes: "In this view, stability and change are explained in the same terms: stability is due to processes that maintain the organization so that it can be reified as the same thing by some observer(s), while change occurs when the processes operate in a manner that is reified by observer(s) as changing the organization" (p. 1380).

The chapters in this volume correspond in different ways and to different degrees to what we here call an integrative view of continuity and change. To locate the chapters within the integrative view, we define such a view as characterized by four distinct aspects.

1. *Continuity and change both require effort and both harbour uncertainty.* For instance, projecting a known technology onto an uncertain future constitutes continuity in the sense of tying past and future events together by using the technology. However, such continuity carries uncertainty because the consequences cannot be known beforehand. Projecting a known technology onto an uncertain future is inevitably also an act of change because the future is likely to be different from the past. Pulk (chapter 3, this volume) offers an intriguing account of how change as backsourcing may be seen as a reversal of processes, which poses particular demands on continuity. Additionally, because the world is assumed to be in an ever-emergent state rather than in an accomplished state, various actors may appear, reappear and disappear, and new technologies may be developed, abandoned or retrieved as time goes by. Achieving continuity and change under such conditions requires that actors engage in temporal practices, including communication (Plotnikof & Bencherki, chapter 6, this volume) and the use of artefacts (Hussenot & Aroles, chapter 5, this volume), through which they enact the events. But for such practices to address continuity and change requires effortful activity in the present to combine past and future events in novel ways, regardless of whether the connecting of events is expressive of continuity or change. Moreover, continuity and change may be expressed through different forms of processes, such as discourse, communication, narrative, ongoing practices or routines (see, for example, Plotnikof & Bencherki, chapter 6, Hussenot & Aroles, chapter 5, Stjerne et al., chapter 7, and Blagoev & Kremser, chapter 9, this volume). Finally, attaching uncertainty to continuity demands that continuity, such as the reproduction of order over time, become a critical research topic, alongside change as a research topic, as pointed out by Langley in chapter 12 of this volume.

2. *Continuity and change are both same and different.* Hussenot and Missioner (2016) argue from their study of change at a bank that continuity and change could be seen as two sides of the same coin (see Van de Ven & Poole, 2005 and Pulk, chapter 3, this volume). By this they imply that activities may connect the same past and future events yet signify both continuity and change (see also Garud & Klopp, chapter 4, this volume). We may assume that change without continuity is impossible and that continuity without change is equally impossible. We agree with Farjoun (2010) that a sense of predictability makes it possible for actors to engage

in change processes. We stress a *sense* of predictability, based on the idea that continuity engenders uncertainty, as pointed out above. Nevertheless, actors may stake out a different future on the assumption that their journey into the future entails continuity as well as change. We take Farjoun's point one step further, by positing that the ways that continuity is pictured or enacted give shape to the type of change envisaged. For example, implementing a new strategy driven by in-house innovation may demand that the identity of the organization provide a sense of continuity (Schultz & Hernes, 2020) through stories and narratives (Bartel & Garud, 2013; see also Koll & Jensen, chapter 8, and Bévort, chapter 11, this volume) or routines (Blagoev & Kremser, chapter 9, this volume); see also Langley, chapter 12, in this volume for a methodological discussion.

3. *Continuity and change take place through situated activity.* Situated activity takes place at all the myriads of encounters throughout organizations. Participants' experiences of being in a meeting consist of retrieving and retranslating previous interactions while anticipating other interactions forward through time (see also Plotnikof & Bencherki, chapter 6, as well as Hussenot & Aroles's, chapter 5, discussion of practices and materiality, this volume). They may connect things that were said at the beginning of the meeting to the anticipated ending of the meeting. The temporal experience unfolds, like a shuttle on a weave, moving back and forth between various gestures and utterances from various moments of the meeting to produce an emerging pattern. The collective sense of this movement back and forth between things said and done creates a sense of continuity in the meeting, since without it, conversations would have to start afresh every time. The sense of continuity thus created also makes for change during the meeting, as members gain new insights and understandings and generate novel solutions together (Schultz & Hernes, chapter 2, this volume). Actors also try and create threads of continuity *between* encounters. For instance, members create continuity between meetings by connecting insights or views gathered at the various meetings, while also reckoning change takes place between meetings, as meetings deal with different issues or problems.

4. *Continuity and change emerge through recursive processes of connecting past and future in the present.* As people enact continuity and change during encounters, they also try and connect different encounters and events taking place in the past or the future. Whereas mainstream views of continuity and change assume that the past leads to the future, an integrative view advocates understanding the present-past-future as evolving as actors connect iteratively past and future in the present (Reinecke & Ansari, 2017). By switching their attention back and forth between past and future, past and future become effectively mutually constitutive through the processes

of connecting and reconnecting. Reconnective processes between past and future may be expressive of continuity when actors recognize that past and future events form an intelligible whole (Ricœur, 1984). For example, organizations may continuously reconnect to accounts of a forgotten past that may become future identity referents (Howard-Grenville et al., 2013; see also Bévort, chapter 11, this volume). Reconnective processes between past and future may be expressive of change when actors define as change the differences between past and future events or periods. It is important, however, not to give the same ontological status to present, past, and future. The present is open-ended and indeterminate as it unfolds and as past and future are connected iteratively. The past has taken place; it has been experienced and lingers in evocative practices (see Koll & Jensen, chapter 8, as well as Branstad & Ødegård, chapter 10, and Blagoev & Kremser, chapter 9, this volume), whereas the future is imaginary, potential, and virtual to be actualized in the shaping of the present (see also Stjerne et al., chapter 7, this volume). An integrative view thus does not reject movement from past to future but assumes that every future anticipation is conditioned by – and conditions in turn – the view of the past.

Organization of chapters

The aim of this edited volume is to inspire others – scholars and practitioners – to explore the relationships between continuity and change. We believe that an integrative view, as outlined above, has the potential to inform new and exciting research on the topic. Therefore, we invited the authors of the chapters to explore different ways to integrate continuity and change in their respective fields of research. The chapters of the volume provide variations of an integrative view which, taken together, provide substance to the above-mentioned aspects and investigate their interrelations.

Two chapters (Schultz & Hernes, and Langley) address more generally the integrative dynamics between continuity and change, whereas the remaining 9 chapters may be related more specifically to the four aspects discussed above. Schultz and Hernes develop in their chapter (chapter 2) what they call the organizational change diamond by introducing a temporal view to the organizational change literature. They argue that applying a temporal view furthers an understanding of continuity and change as inextricably interconnected. The organizational change diamond displays the reconfiguration of the connections between change and continuity in four forms: episodic change, continuous change, ongoing continuity, and episodic continuity. Schultz and Hernes draw on studies in organizational change research such as Weick and Quinn (1999), Tsoukas and Chia (2002), and Hernes et al. (2021) to develop the notion of *episodic continuity*. Episodic continuity aims to connect events and periods from across temporal trajectories, connecting past, present, and future through recursive dynamics. For example, Schultz and Hernes show how through situated activity actors can weave sources from the past into continuity strands that reach into a near or distant future (see also Branstad & Ødegård, chapter 10, this volume). They then discuss how the enactment of episodic continuity interacts with the other forms of organizational change and outline their contribution to an integrative view of continuity and change.

Whereas Schultz and Hernes offer a theoretical discussion and potential framework for a future research agenda on an integrative view of continuity and change, Langley discusses the methodological implications of such a view in her chapter (chapter 12). She writes from a similar understanding of the continuity-change relationship to an integrative view by calling the relationship a co-constructed duality. She suggests three different research foci exploring the linkage between change and continuity. Studies focusing on *change* often undertake longitudinal studies, thereby realizing the importance of continuity as its counterpart. Studies focusing on the continuous production and *reproduction* of activities and practices are helpful to theorize the continuity of activities, smaller changes within continuous activities, as well as their endogenous capability for change. Whereas in these research foci either change or continuity are dominant, their interconnectedness is also implied. Studies with a *narrative* research focus then make the interconnectedness explicit, showing how narratives may integrate continuity and change. Langley gives several examples of studies that make her chapter illustrative and methodologically useful for scholars and practitioners to study continuity and change and their relations in different contexts.

Continuity and change both require effort and both harbour uncertainty

This aspect of an integrative view raises an endless set of questions about who does what, when, and how when addressing distant change as the enactment of continuity. Addressing the more distant events may, for instance, take place during periods or situations of crisis, such as when the imminent future appears highly uncertain, or there is a risk of loss of organizational identity (Schultz & Hernes, 2020), or both. Moreover, experimenting with the past in the present may move the company towards the distant future, as Hernes et al. (2020) show in their discussion of how Carlsberg brewery sought to reproduce beer from the 1880s using strains of yeast found in old bottles. It later turned out that 130-year-old barley seeds could be reused as a basis for ecologically brewed beer, which would form part of the company's distant future pledge to become carbon neutral. Two contributions in this edited volume address some of the potential questions in relation to their areas of study (chapters 3 and 4). Both chapters draw on an empirical study of organizational change, a study that reveals not only the temporal complexity but also the various actors involved in continuity–change interrelations.

In her chapter (chapter 3), Pulk discusses outsourcing and backsourcing in the context of finance and accounting in a multinational company with a global divisional structure. Backsourcing is a relatively little investigated phenomenon in organizational research, yet in practice it is as challenging as outsourcing, as attempts are made to "bring once outsourced activities back in-house to restore full ownership and control" (Pulk, this volume, p. 46). In discussing the interdependence of organizational activities and their embeddedness in the organizational context, Pulk shows how acts of change are also acts of continuity and vice versa. She states, for example, that "it is hard to make a clear-cut distinction between continuity and change" (p. 47). For example, by transferring activities to a different organization, these activities will change as they are adapted to a new context while still maintaining their continuity with those of the initial organization. The activities' variations, as well as their persistence, may, however, harbour unforeseen and unintended consequences, as they are brought into interaction with other activities, leading in the worst case to uncontrollable change. Pulk also points out the paradoxical nature of the interplay between continuity and change, by arguing that substantial change may take place amid very stable practice, just as small variations in practices, which enable a high degree of continuity, may lead to substantial change.

Garud and Klopp's chapter (chapter 4) shifts our attention to internal dynamics, which unfold in the emergence of Post-it Notes at 3M. The authors discuss how prior literature on innovation has followed an alternating view on continuity and change and suggest a view that goes "beyond a view of continuity and change as contradictions" (Garud & Klopp, this volume, p. 80) expands our understanding of *innovation as process*. By exploring several episodes during the emergence of Post-it Notes, the authors show how the same phenomenon may be simultaneously experienced as continuity and change, depending on the context and temporal orientation of the actors involved. The authors explain that actors cultivate serendipitous moments through ongoing activity and endow them with meaning by narrating their past-present-future connection. Such a view emphasizes the entanglement of continuity and change, where "continuity and change can always be seen inside one another"

(p. 82). In conceptualizing continuity and change as embodying each other, Garud and Klopp offer an additional and exciting way to understand the relationships between continuity and change.

Continuity and change are both same and different

This aspect of an integrative view allows for a richer understanding of the interrelatedness of continuity and change. Enacting continuity implies also enacting change when, for instance, an organization addresses past or potential future solutions in the present along its temporal trajectory. As different past and future solutions are enacted in the present, the continuity to be accomplished is that of the organization as a complex yet intelligible whole of past and future events. Taking this view seriously implies understanding the whole of events as expressive of a sense of continuity, while also being expressive of change. Chapters 5 and 6 of this volume provide an empirical and theoretical account of these implications for research.

Hussenot and Aroles develop in their chapter the notion of *boundary events* to account for how some events can be experienced as either a mere continuity or a radical change (chapter 5). Boundary events are characterized by how they are experienced differently by different actors, leading to different forms of continuity. Boundary events provide a "spatiotemporality" as they materialize different temporalities (i.e. a shared narrative made of past, present, and future events) By exploring the adoption of teleworking in France in the context of the COVID-19 pandemic as a boundary event, the authors conclude that "people can experience continuity and change simultaneously" (p. 97). This means the same organizational phenomenon can be experienced either as continuity or as change. The authors argue that simultaneous experience is made possible through the enactment of different temporalities (e.g. when experiencing teleworking in a local context). Advancing a process ontological view of time, the authors conclude that change is always in a state of becoming continuity, as events are enacted and become tangible through situated activity.

The chapter by Plotnikof and Bencherki offers another illustration of continuity and change as mutually constitutive processes. They argue that continuity and change are "becoming together" in communicative practices (chapter 6). The authors focus on the organizational discourse studies (ODS) and communicative constitution of organization (CCO) literature and identify three ways continuity and change have been addressed in the literature: (1) strategic versus resisting communication and discourse, (2) text/conversation dynamics, and (3) interactional approaches. Illustrating these approaches by drawing on the case of the United Nations' Sustainable Development Goals (SDGs) and the Canadian electoral campaign in 2021, the authors show how continuity and change emerge in "entangled and open-ended relations" (Plotnikof & Bencherki, this volume, p. 116). In particular, actors' performance in everyday activities reveals the micro-temporalities of talk that are "crucial to study as it is through such situatedness that multiple temporalities interweave in constituting various organizational times" (p. 112). While these findings add to an integrative view of continuity and change, they also allow for more temporally sensitive theorizing within ODS and CCO.

Continuity and change take place through situated activity

This aspect of an integrative view brings forward the effortful and creative work as well as the simultaneous enactment of continuity and change as situated activity. Through situated activity, near and distant pasts and futures are continuously enacted in the present (Hernes & Schulz, 2020). Hernes and Schultz (2020, p. 1) emphasize how through situated activity "actors may combine different temporalities" which enables them to "go beyond, and potentially transform, the temporal structures within which they operate". For example, when companies have made binding commitments to distant future goals such as becoming carbon neutral, they perform change and continuity by translating between what they imagine may be possible in the future and at present. Even disruptive change can be a great act of continuity. Three contributions to this volume investigate such great acts of continuity in the form of *imaginary practices* (Stjerne et al., chapter 7), *narrative habitus* (Koll & Jensen, chapter 8), and *enacted history* (Blagoev & Kremser, chapter 9).

Stjerne et al. explore in their chapter (chapter 7) continuity and change through a practice theory lens. From this perspective, continuity emerges through the performance of practices that reproduce social life, whereas change emerges through small variations in the situated performance of practices. The authors extend this perspective by drawing on American pragmatism, notably John Dewey's work to introduce the concept of *imaginary practices*, and explain how actors may break with the continuity of current practices and produce alternative futures through their practices. The authors illustrate the imaginary practices in the case of the Dogma 95 movement in the Danish filmmaking industry. They show how actors can engage with a situation's possibilities and realize what could be, guiding the direction for actions as they are "holding situated potentials to disrupt established nexuses of practices" (Stjerne et al., this volume, p. 141). The authors conclude that imaginary practices hold the potential to illustrate a close connection between continuity and change, as they describe how actors can practice continuity and break with practice by "enacting futures that differ significantly from the past" (p. 142).

In their chapter (chapter 7), Koll and Jensen explore how actors enact the past in the present with the help of narratives "pertaining to the fields of practice in which they are invested and socialized" (Koll & Jensen, this volume, p. 151). Drawing on the work of Bourdieu, the authors argue that a habitual aspect that they call *narrative habitus* is at play when actors enact the past, which offers them a sense of direction towards the future. At the same time, they emphasize, some pasts become possible in the present, just as other pasts become impossible as a basis for narrating their trajectory through time. They emphasize narration as an embodied and embedded process. They summarize their argument nicely as follows: "... the way actors enact the past, which past events that emerge as significant to them, which narratives they construct about these events, and their ability to appropriate these narratives, is not merely a product of conscious and deliberate engagement with the past" (p. 146). Giving examples of a study of how a Scandinavian telecommunications company changes from a monopolistic working culture to a more business-oriented and performance-driven working culture, Koll and Jensen illustrate the necessity of engaging in a practice over time in order to narrate change.

The chapter by Blagoev and Kremser (chapter 9) takes a similar view by suggesting that history in organizations is not only a narrated memory of the past but is also enacted in the present, what the authors call *enacted history*. Puzzled by the question of how certain pasts persist over time, Blagoev and Kremser go beyond thinking of the past as a resource to make sense of the present and suggest a more structural approach that understands "history [...] as a specific and non-random pattern of interdependence among multiple socio-material patterns of action enacted in the present" (p. 166). Combining research on routine dynamics, structural couplings, and interactionist role theory, the authors develop a compelling argument to explain "those 'sticky' aspects of the present that actors seem to be unable to narrate away" (p. 176). Providing examples from cooking routines and service routines, they show how these routines are structurally coupled enacting each other's past and thus produce and reproduce (historically conditioned) continuity. Every variation of their performance, however, generates change in continuity.

Continuity and change emerge through recursive processes of connecting past and future in the present

This aspect emphasizes that an integrative view is not so much about stretching the present, but about creating an intelligible and complex whole between present, past, and future that may be expressive of change and/or continuity. Intelligible wholes are temporal and may take the form of immanent trajectories (Hernes et al., 2021; Hernes & Obstfeld, 2022) that are expressive of an organization's temporal identity. Scholars drawing upon Ricœur's (1984) work on narrative and time also refer to temporal wholes of, for instance, events as narrative. Ricœur discussed the combinatory work of connecting events and actors into intelligible wholes that evolve over time to guide social action while being addressed through social action in turn. Two contributions included in this volume take on a similar view by outlining the different roles of the past in the organization's future (chapters 10 and 11).

In their chapter (chapter 10), Branstad and Ødegård tell the fascinating story of how two energy companies, in the wake of a market liberalization reform, initially rejected their recent past as public electricity providers. Branstad and Ødegård refer to *nostophobia* to explain their reaction to the recent past. However, with time the two companies developed different relationships with their increasingly distant past. One company reconnected with it to form a sense of continuity with previous practices, which the authors explain as a form of *reflective nostalgia*. The other company, on other hand, distanced itself even more from their similar distant past, extending their sense of nostophobia. Branstad and Ødegård's chapter brings new knowledge about the effects of moving through time by explaining the ways that organizations enact continuity and change. The authors conclude: "Taking a temporal perspective on organisational change, we found that the time that passes between events matters in terms of what those events mean. The main benefit gained from analysing the development of two organisations over this extensive period has been to observe how the past played different roles along the timeline of our study" (Branstad & Ødegård, this volume, p. 196).

In his chapter (chapter 11), by drawing on narrative theory, in particular Ricœur's work, Bévort shows the ongoing efforts of actors in creating continuity and change. Bévort argues how a narrative creates a sense of continuity while simultaneously stimulating new ideas to enact change as a novel future. Importantly, narrative supports both the perception of continuity in the face of change and the perception of change, as it is contextualized in continuity. He argues that "the use of organisational narrative can provide a way to connect what is and what was with what could/should be and thus balance continuity and change processes" (Bévort, this volume, p. 208). Bévort illustrates his argument by drawing on the case of a small Danish retail bank. The bank first changed its narrative by distancing itself from its past, but then, in a series of change efforts, returned to the past or elements of it, to narrate its future. In this sense, a narrative provides a comprehensive image that shows both organizational continuity and its potential for change, and thus their interconnectedness when actors move through time.

Moving forward: connecting with practice

The chapters in this book show new directions for understanding the dynamics between continuity and change that have been left underdeveloped in organizational research. They also offer new ways for practitioners to understand issues at stake when they stake out a course for the future (and for the past). We suggest some issues that research as well as teaching may address to offer new understanding to practitioners.

First, new futures involve continuity even if they appear distinctly different from the present. The chapters in this volume offer some ideas about the *form* of continuity that may support a different future. Narrating, for example, is one way to facilitate change amid continuity. Second, new futures that are distinctly different from the present may involve substantial change. Sometimes companies persist in pursuing solutions that eventually become important for entire fields of organizations. Third, disruptive change, which is expressive of what takes place when actors envisage and plan for a qualitatively different future, may require a stronger sense of continuity than if less disruptive change is experienced or envisaged. Fourth, the past may represent a changing or even a surprising source of continuity and change. Although one's history may be known, the past includes many events that may be reinvented as actors perform searches into their past for cues of how to move into the future. Their discoveries may offer novel ways to connect past and future events into a trajectory of continuity and change. Fifth, as actors connect past and future events, practices, processes or patterns may reveal themselves as novel ways to move towards the future.

To this end, this volume brings together stimulating yet instructive chapters that advance a future research agenda for organizational continuity and change and attune us to a temporally sensitive theorizing of continuity and change to navigate the challenges of managing contemporary organizations.

References

Bartel, C. A., & Garud, R. (2013). The role of narratives in sustaining organizational innovation, *Organization Science*, 20, 107–17.

Bergson, H. (1911). *Creative Evolution*, New York: Macmillan and Co.

Brown, S. L., & Eisenhardt, K. M. (1997). The art of continuous change: linking complexity theory and time-paced evolution in relentlessly shifting organizations, *Administrative Science Quarterly*, 42(1), 1–34.

Burns, T. (1958). The idea of structure in sociology, *Human Relations*, 11(3), 217–28.

Burns, T., & Stalker, G. M. (1961). *The Management of Innovation*, London: Tavistock.

Chambers (1988). Continuously, in C. Schwarz et al. (eds), *Chambers English Dictionary*, Cambridge: Chambers.

Chia, R., & Tsoukas, H. (2003). Everything flows and nothing abides, *Process Studies*, 32(2), 196–224.

DiMaggio, P. J., & Powell, W. W. (1983). The iron cage revisited: institutional isomorphism and collective rationality in organizational fields, *American Sociological Review*, 48(2), 147–60.

Emery, F. E., & Trist, E. L. (1965). The causal texture of organizational environments, *Human Relations*, 18, 21–32.

Farjoun, M. (2010). Beyond dualism: stability and change as a duality, *Academy of Management Review*, 35(2), 202–25.

Gersick, C. J. C. (1991). Revolutionary change theories: a multilevel exploration of the punctuated equilibrium paradigm, *Academy of Management Review*, 16, 10–36.

Hernes, T. (2014). *A Process Theory of Organization*, Oxford: Oxford University Press.

Hernes, T. (2022). *Organization and Time*, Oxford: Oxford University Press.

Hernes, T., Feddersen, J., & Schultz, M. (2020). Material temporality: how materiality does time in food organising, *Organization Studies*, 42(2), 351–71.

Hernes, T., & Feuls, M. (2022). From continuity of becoming to becoming of continuity: extending continuous change by the concept of temporal folds, paper presented at the 2nd Colloquium on Philosophy and Organization Studies, Rhodes, Greece.

Hernes, T., Hussenot, A., & Pulk, K. (2021). Time and temporality of change processes: integrating episodic and continuous change from an event-based view, in M. S. Poole & A. van de Ven (eds), *Oxford Handbook of Organization Change and Innovation*, 2nd edition (pp. 731–50), New York: Oxford University Press.

Hernes, T., & Obstfeld, D. (2022). A temporal narrative view of sensemaking, *Organization Theory*, 3(4), https://doi.org/10.1177/26317877221131585.

Howard-Grenville, J. (2005). The persistence of flexible organizational routines: the role of agency and organizational context, *Organization Science*, 16(6), 618–36.

Howard-Grenville, J., Metzger, M. L., & Meyer, A. D. (2013). Rekindling the flame: processes of identity resurrection, *Academy of Management Journal*, 56(1), 113–36.

Howard-Grenville, J., Nelson, A. J., Earle, A. G., Haack, J. A., & Young, D. M. (2017). "If chemists don't do it, who is going to?" Peer-driven occupational change and the emergence of green chemistry, *Administrative Science Quarterly*, 62(3), 524–60.

Hussenot, A., & Missonier, S. (2016). Encompassing novelty and stability: an events-based approach, *Organization Studies*, 37, 523–46.

Huy, Q. N. (2002). Emotional balancing of organizational continuity and radical change: the contribution of middle managers, *Administrative Science Quarterly*, 47, 31–69.

James, W. (1909). *A Pluralistic Universe*, Lincoln: University of Nebraska Press.

Kotter, J. P. (1996). *Leading Change: Why Transformation Efforts Fail*, Boston, MA: Harvard Business Press.

Langley, A., Smallman, C., Tsoukas, H., & Van de Ven, A. H. (2013). Process studies of change in organization and management: unveiling temporality, activity, and flow, *Academy of Management Journal*, 56, 1–13.

Lawrence, P. R., & Lorsch, J. W. (1967). Differentiation and integration in complex organizations, *Administrative Science Quarterly*, 12(1), 1–47.

Lewin, K. (1947). Frontiers in group dynamics: concept, method and reality in social science; social equilibria and social change, *Human Relations*, 1, 5–41.

March, J. G. (1991). Exploration and exploitation in organizational learning, *Organization Science*, 2, 71–87.

March, J. G. (1996). Continuity and change in theories of organizational action, *Administrative Science Quarterly*, 41(2), 278–87, https://doi.org/10.2307/2393720.

Meyer, J. W., & Rowan, B. (1977). Institutionalized organizations: formal structure as myth and ceremony, *American Journal of Sociology*, 83(2), 340–63.

Meyerson, D., & Martin, J. (1987). Cultural change: an integration of three different views, *Journal of Management Studies*, 24, 623–47.

Micelotta, E., Lounsbury, M., & Greenwood, R. (2017). Pathways of institutional change: an integrative review and research agenda, *Journal of Management*, 43(6), 1885–910.

Orlikowski, W. J. (1996). Improvising organizational transformation over time: a situated change perspective, *Information Systems Research*, 7, 63–92.

Pentland, B., & Goh, K. (2021) Organizational routines and organizational change, in A. Van de Ven & M. S. Poole (eds), *The Oxford Handbook of Organizational Change and Innovation* (pp. 339–63), Oxford: Oxford University Press.

Porter, M. E. (1996). What is strategy? *Harvard Business Review*, 74(6), https://hbr.org/1996/11/what-is-strategy.

Reinecke, J., & Ansari, S. (2017). Time, temporality and process studies, in A. Langley & H. Tsoukas (eds), *The Sage Handbook of Process Organization studies* (pp. 402–16), London: SAGE Publications.

Ricœur, P. (1984). *Time and Narrative*, Chicago, IL: University of Chicago Press.

Romanelli, E., & Tushman, M. (1994). Organizational transformation as punctuated equilibrium: an empirical test, *Academy of Management Journal*, 37(5), 1141–66.

Schein, E. H. (1986). *Organizational Culture and Leadership*, San Francisco, CA: Jossey-Bass.

Schultz, M., & Hernes, T. (2020). Temporal interplay between strategy and identity: punctuated, subsumed and sustained modes, *Strategic Organization*, 18(1), 106–35.

Thompson, J. D. (1967). *Organizations in Action: Social Science Bases of Administrative Theory*, New York: McGraw-Hill.

Tsoukas, H., & Chia, R. (2002). On organizational becoming: rethinking organizational change, *Organization Science*, 13(5), 567–82.

Tushman, M., & Romanelli, E. (1985). Organizational revolution: a metamorphosis model of convergence and reorientation, *Research in Organizational Behavior*, 7, 171–222.

Van de Ven, A. H., & Poole, M. S. (2005). Alternative approaches for studying organizational change, *Organization Studies*, 26(9), 1377–404.

Van de Ven, A. H., & Poole, M. S. (2021). Introduction: central issues in the study of organizational change and innovation, in A. Van de Ven & M. S. Poole (eds), *Oxford Handbook of Change and Innovation*, 2nd edition (chapter 1), Oxford: Oxford University Press.

Weick, K. E., & Quinn, R. (1999). Organizational change and development, *Annual Review of Psychology*, 50, 361–86.

Weik, E. (2011). In deep waters: process theory between Scylla and Charybdis, *Organization*, 18(5), 655–72.

2 Integrating the missing link of episodic continuity into change theorizing

Majken Schultz and Tor Hernes

Introduction

A search for definitions of change reveals that 'change' entails that something becomes different, modified, or altered from what it was before. In that sense, organizational change is a movement from one state to another involving organizational actors, as exemplified by Poole and Van de Ven's definition of change as 'a difference in form, quality or state over time in an organizational entity' (2004, p. xi). Assuming it is possible to distinguish between a before and after, change happens across time as actors move from a situation at one point in time to another. Such a notion of change underpins models of succession between different stages, such as Lewin's classic 'unfreeze, change and refreeze' model (e.g., Lewin, 1947) and models of 'punctuated equilibrium' (e.g., Romanelli & Tushman, 1994). Here, change is conceived as the antithesis to stability, closely associated with equilibrium, raising questions of how change may be a more or less radical deviation from stability.

However, from a different ontological stance, change is happening in time, as actors move through time (Hernes, Feddersen and Schultz, 2021). In this view, change is not observed in terms of different states at different points in time, but as a continuous movement *in* time, without stops and starts. We may call this 'changing in time' or 'through time' rather than changing 'across time'. Taking such a 'through-time view' of change implies that the analytical focus shifts from an external to an internal focus because how change happens through time cannot be readily observed from the outside. When you observe a team working together on a project or a sports team playing a match, it is hard for you, as an external observer, to see the change taking place in time. As an external observer, you may be able to observe how the activity of the team differs between two points in time, such as between the beginning of a match and, say, its halfway point. However, the team members and the players that are performing the activity experience the change quite differently. They may, like the external observer, see differences in their activity between two points in time. But in addition, they *experience* ongoing change *as they move through time* on a moment-to-moment basis, where the movement from moment to moment is a mixture of change and continuity.

Both changing through time and changing across time ontologies are in our view needed and may be further advanced by taking a more comprehensive view of change and continuity in relation to time. In this chapter, we apply such a view by focusing on how actors experience and connect past(s) and future(s) as they move through time, thereby enacting both continuity and change. Our argument concerns how changing across time may also provide a sense of continuity to actors. Such a view has been largely overlooked in organizational research because of the tendency of organizational researchers to separate continuity from change and treat them as separate phenomena, then leave continuity as a stable background against which change takes place. This tendency is evident from important works on continuity and change, where change and continuity (or stability) are held as separate, as dualities, although they are acknowledged to interact with one another (e.g., Farjoun, 2010).

Practising change and continuity

Take a few moments to read and reflect on the following extract from a paper based on a study of how members of a sustainability strategy team at a global consumer goods company prepare for developing packaging solutions towards distant future sustainability goals (Feuls et al., 2021). Then think about the following question. Do these discussions address change or continuity?

[Member 1]: I'm wondering, how did that twist suddenly happen without our involvement, and this promise that makes me really scared? And that was why I was just pointing out to you, those things we need to do to deliver on our Key Performance Indicators (KPIs), they are not necessarily delivering [net-zero emission goals], and that was the whole reason why we needed to bring our strategy around.

[Member 2]: […] But the purpose of the discussion was much more to get direction on the overall ambition level and to have everyone sit and nod and say we agree, sustainability is super important. And it's super important that we deliver on our current commitment, and we should go beyond that when it makes commercial sense. […]

[Member 1]: What I'm interested to understand now is concretely what this means for us in terms of next steps and plans, because if the bulk of the message from EMT [Executive Management Team] was that we need to be more concrete about […] the existing KPI and the existing roadmap, what concretely does that mean? What do we need to do in the next couple of months that is on top of our existing strategy, considering how much has gone into that existing strategy already?

We can observe how this brief exchange, like much social interaction in organizations, reflects how the boundaries between change and continuity are shifting and fluid. We can nevertheless recognize the contours of change and continuity at two different levels of time. First, change and continuity are found in the movement between *topics* of the conversation as it unfolds through time. The conversation changes by shifting from a concern about existing KPIs to situating those KPIs within the broader framework of the existing company strategy. But although the perspective on KPIs is changing during the exchange, KPIs also form a line of continuity as they are brought up and referred to at different points of time during the conversation. The KPI example illustrates another point about the dynamics between change and continuity, namely that the repeated focus on KPIs *enables* the perspective taken of KPIs to change during the conversation. In other words, the continuity of KPIs makes the change in talking about them possible.

Second, change and continuity are expressed in the temporal *focus* of the conversation. To take change first, the members of the team move between the current situation of packaging and the possible future state of packaging represented by net-zero emission goals. The present is represented by what they may be doing in the next couple of months, and they are focused on how to get from the present situation, which is represented by plans, to a distant future goal scenario to be reached through a sustainability strategy. This is what Weick and Quinn (1999) refer to as episodic change, that is, systemic change that is anticipated to take place between two different points in time. But as with the ongoing conversation above, there is also continuity in what the team projects towards the distant future. For example, there is a connection tentatively drawn between existing strategies stretching into the past, their current commitments, short-term goals, and the distant future scenario. What we mean by continuity here is the (implicit) description of a trajectory of interconnected events that make sense to the members as a holistic narrative. And as with the conversation level, it is easy to see how the longer-term change and continuity are intertwined with each other to the extent that they may even be hard to distinguish from one another. For instance, when team members compare the distant future with the present situation, they express a need for grand-scale change to move closer to the future goals. However, when they seek to connect the present and future into a holistic narrative of the trajectory from the present towards the distant future, it makes more sense to speak of continuity than of change. Such a holistic narrative, in our view, is an example of what we argue constitutes 'episodic continuity'; the connecting of past and future events into a meaningful whole.

The missing link of episodic continuity

In this chapter, we discuss four forms of change and continuity that we could infer from the brief conversation: episodic change, continuous change, ongoing continuity, and episodic continuity. As mentioned above, episodic change, taken from Weick and Quinn (1999), signifies the more classic definition of change as anticipated or observed differences in the system between different points in time. We will refer to the shifting of perspectives or focus during the conversation above as 'continuous change', an expression taken from Weick and Quinn (1999) and from Tsoukas and Chia (2002). But equally important for our chapter is the continuity expressed through the holistic trajectory imagined between interconnected events in the past and the future, which we label episodic continuity.

Of the four forms of change and continuity, episodic continuity represents a missing link in organization and management research. However, as we will show in this chapter, it is a form of continuity that underlies much of the work that goes into creating change in organizations because it offers a way for organizational members to discover and commit to a longer view of continuity and change. We extend Tsoukas and Chia's (2002) theory of indivisible continuity (which we refer to as ongoing continuity) to include episodic continuity, which we define as the ongoing or occasional connecting of different events from across time. Pulk (chapter 3 in this volume) advances a similar argument by illustrating empirically the importance of organizations being able to enact continuity across larger timespans. In particular, we argue that 'episodic continuity' shows the importance of past events, as actors weave together multidirectional threads of continuity to enable change. By expanding the theorizing of continuity, we can move further towards understanding change and continuity, not as opposing or even separate, phenomena, but as coexisting (see also Hernes, Hussenot, & Pulk, 2021).

In this chapter, we aim to advance a temporal view of organizational change and continuity in three ways. First, we elicit the temporal assumptions underpinning the three forms of organizational change: episodic, planned change; continuous change; and ongoing continuity. Second, we argue that a temporal view invites a fourth form of organizational continuity, which we call 'episodic continuity'. We illustrate how actors enact episodic continuity by selectively reconnecting different parts of the past and the future, thereby complementing the other forms of change. Finally, we suggest that these four forms of organizational change constitute what we label the 'organizational change diamond'. Together they expand our notion of intersections between change and continuity and suggest new opportunities for managing organizational change.

A temporal view on change and continuity

The field of organizational change and development is rich and holds numerous nuances both from managerial and from scholarly perspectives (e.g., Poole & Van de Ven, 2021; Stouten et al., 2018). Whereas the various change models are elaborate with respect to what generates organizational change and how change can be managed, they are less concerned with the intersections between organizational change and continuity. We particularly include and discuss contributions which, from different ontologies, are concerned with change, continuity, and the connections between them. In the following, we use the label 'forms of organizational change' as the overall concept for these various notions of change and continuity, because they are all addressing how change and continuity occur in the flow of time, whether through ongoing activity or as continuity and change projected onto the temporal trajectory of the organization. In doing so, we take a temporal view, which enables us to highlight the underpinning temporal assumptions of existing forms of organizational change. In the basic distinctions between episodic change, continuous change, and ongoing continuity, we particularly draw upon the contributions by Weick and Quinn (1999) and Tsoukas and Chia (2002), because they are expressive of 'ideal types' of different forms of organizational change. Last but not least, we suggest a novel conception of organizational change, which we label 'episodic continuity'. The four forms of organizational change are summarized in Table 2.1.

Table 2.1   Four forms of organizational change

Key concept	Conceptual framework	Organizational embedding	Temporal assumptions
Episodic change	• Change as discontinuity and occasional interruption • Change as adaptation or response to external environments • Change as planned and intended activity	• Strategic managerial level • Organizational-wide implications • Vertical directionality: top-down	• Discontinuity from the past in the present • Change extended into the future and occasional past • Change process within distinct stages across time (recurrent, temporary)
Continuous change	• Change as improvisations in ongoing problem-solving or modification of routines	• Operational level • Localized within the organization: units, teams, or functions	• Change happening in the present • Continuity in the present • Change process as incremental movement towards the future

Key concept	Conceptual framework	Organizational embedding	Temporal assumptions
Ongoing continuity	• Continuity as the process of connecting ongoing activity in time.	• Micro-level, nonformalized • Embedded in everyday flux among organizational actors	• Change as becoming in the present • Ongoing continuity in the present
Episodic continuity	• Continuity as episodic breaks in actors' trajectories that enable reconnections between past and future events. • Continuity through events in the making, continually redefined in terms of their meaning • Continuity and change as endogenous	• Situated and event-based • Organization-wide and localized • Vertical directionality: top-down and bottom-up	• Change as breaks in immanent temporal trajectory • Continuity as reconfiguration of connections between past and future events • Change process as the becoming of events extended into the past and the future

Episodic and continuous change

Episodic and continuous change are defined and compared by Weick and Quinn (1999). The differences between these two forms of organizational change are defined by the initiation of change (intended managerial effort vs emerging modifications or improvisation) and the directionality and comprehensiveness of the change process (top-down driven organization-wide change at the strategic level vs distributed change at the operational level).

Weick and Quinn (1999) define episodic change as centrally planned processes of defined beginnings and endings, aimed at system-wide replacement of organizational parts or processes to enable the organization to catch up with accumulated inertia and/or adapt to changes in the external environment. Episodic change is described as exogenous, macro change based on discontinuity that characterizes the more sweeping changes that are sometimes performed in organizations. Often such changes aim to replace central elements, such as technologies, or to develop novel strategies, such as in response to sustainability goals. Such changes are centrally driven, and because they involve multiple levels in the organization, they are planned in stages, each stage having explicit goals and sets of activities. The expression 'episodic change' comes from the nature of such change processes being implemented episodically with defined ends and beginnings.

In contrast, continuous change is defined as the micro-processes of adaption and improvisation that actors engage in on a continuous basis. Weick and Quinn (1999) argue that continuous changes typically emerge from improvisations in ongoing problem-solving or modifications of routines, which are localized at the more operational level of the organization. Continuous changes do not require planning or centralized orchestration, but are incremental changes, often created by individual actors or teams. Although episodic change and continuous change are readily distinguishable, there has been less discussion of the differences in temporality between them, as articulated by us in the third column of Table 2.1. Both episodic change and continuous change are happening in the present and are directed towards the future. However, episodic change is conceived as a discontinuity from the past that paves the way for redefining the present and extending it into a different future. Continuous change, on the other hand, unfolds as a process in the present with small movements towards a slightly different future. Weick and Quinn (1999), conceive episodic and continuous change as two forms of organizational change that may occur in parallel at different levels in the organization, but are less articulate with respect to the relations between them.

Other scholars have suggested how a more dynamic relationship may evolve between planned, intended, and/or anticipated change vs emergent, incremental, and/or nascent change. For example, in their development of an improvisational model of change, Orlikowski and Hoffman (1997) stress the interdependencies between what they label 'anticipated' and 'emergent' change, suggesting the pursuit of 'opportunity-based change'. We interpret opportunity-based change as a bridging construct between episodic and continuous change. As explained by Orlikowski and Hoffman (1997, p. 13): 'opportunity-based changes – changes that are not anticipated ahead of time but are introduced purposefully and intentionally during the change process in response to an unexpected opportunity, event, or breakdown' (see also Orlikowski, 1996). Referring to the relationship between episodic and continuous change, opportunity-driven change suggests how opportunities may arise in the unfolding of either one of these change processes, creating momentum for shifting between the level and scope of the change process. The relationships between these forms of organizational change and the level and scope of the change process are illustrated in Figure 2.1.

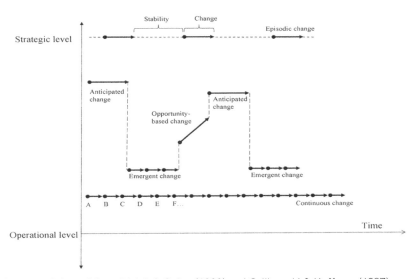

Source: Adapted from Weick & Quinn (1999) and Orlikowski & Hoffman (1997).

Figure 2.1   Episodic-, continuous-, and opportunity-based change

Other related examples are the numerous types of strategic change, developed by Mintzberg, including distinctions between intended change and emergent (strategic) change, which may come together in realized change (e.g., Mintzberg, 1987). Scholars have further elaborated how change and continuity intersect in organizational transformation, almost always including episodic change, such as the forces that 'push forward' and 'push backward' in the change process (Malhotra & Hinings, 2015).

Ongoing and episodic continuity

The concept of continuous change has been extended from an explicit process-based ontology, most significantly by Tsoukas and Chia (2002) in their suggestion of change as 'organizational becoming'. Instead of conceiving change as an attribute of organizations, which they ascribe to Weick and Quinn (1999), Tsoukas and Chia argue that 'change is all there is' (2002, p. 576; see also Chia & Tsoukas, 2004). In their discussion of continuous change, Tsoukas and Chia (2002) emphasize that it takes place against a background of what they call indivisible time. In philosophy, indivisible time is associated with the inner nature of time that we experience as individuals. This inner nature of time was described as inherently indivisible by Henri Bergson, the prominent philosopher of time. The notion of time as inherently indivisible implies that every (microscopic) change is part of an indivisible process of continuous adaptation as the underpinning of organizing, which Tsoukas and Chia (2002) discuss as indivisible continuity. We will in this chapter employ the concept of ongoing continuity as synonymous with indivisible continuity. Whereas indivisible continuity refers to the indivisible nature of time, ongoing continuity (Hernes, 2022; Pulk, chapter 3, this volume) refers to the interactive nature of the activity through which continuity is accomplished. For instance, in meetings, continuity is accomplished through patterns of micro-movements that connect backward and forward in time, such as when participants refer to utterances made earlier in the meeting to project the discussion forward in time.

The emphasis on continuity as indivisible and as patterns of micro-movements shows the importance of continuity to both large-scale and small-scale change. However, we argue that both of these process-based notions of continuity are restricted to the present. This restriction implies that current process-based conceptions of continuity do not include how actors draw upon past and/or future events characterized by significant distance from the present. Neither do they question how actors may construct a trajectory of continuity spanning a wide temporal depth (e.g., Bluedorn & Standifer, 2006; Schultz & Hernes, 2020). Drawing upon the philosophy of time (Whitehead, 1929) and organization studies (Hernes, 2022; see also Hernes, 2014), we argue that actors may connect different events from across time to form a sense of continuity as they go through change. This form of continuity we label 'episodic continuity'. The use of 'episodic' refers to Whitehead's definition of time: 'Time is sheer succession of episodic durations' (Whitehead, 1929, p. 158). Although Whitehead viewed time as a temporal experience of indivisible continuity, he did argue that the only way to understand time is as residing in epochs, such as events.

This view of time as a succession of epochs embedded in events opens a line of inquiry about how actors forge connections between past and/or future events in their construction of trajectories, making sense of why and how they are moving across time (see also Hernes, Hussenot, & Pulk, 2021). Such forging of connections between events is particularly relevant when the direction of a trajectory changes and compels actors to search for new events that may – or may not – provide an experience of episodic continuity. Episodic continuity works as 'reconstructed breaks in an immanent trajectory that signify past or future episodic change in the actors' own time' (Hernes, Hussenot, & Pulk, 2021, p. 732). This suggests that episodic continuity may be conceived as endogenous, because it is experienced 'from within', also in situations of episodic, planned, or intended change. In the following, drawing on previous work by ourselves and others, we provide examples that in our view can be reinterpreted as enactments of episodic continuity.

Enacting episodic continuity

The following examples of episodic continuity illustrate how actors forge connections between a distant past and a possible future in situations when they are compelled to enact continuity as an inherent dimension of change. Our overall argument in the chapter concerns how the various interrelations between the four forms of organizational change expand how actors may navigate and manage organizational change. Therefore, we have selected illustrations that both show how episodic continuity may occur in situations of organization-wide episodic, intended change and suggest how episodic continuity may provide a temporal depth in continuous change. Although we do not have empirical studies to support how episodic continuity is enacted through ongoing continuity, we discuss how they may enhance each other in micro-events. The illustrations below all refer to time and temporality, albeit they differ with respect to whether they use temporality as ontology or as a dimension of the phenomena studied. By the same token, they hold rather different approaches to a process-based view. However, it is beyond the scope of this chapter to further elaborate on these differences. Thus, we take a pragmatic view by focusing on what we consider to be relevant and meaningful relations between episodic continuity and the other forms of change.

Episodic continuity and episodic change

Enactment of episodic continuity may emerge in situations of organization-wide change, where organizations have deliberately aimed to change their future trajectory. Episodic continuity occurs when actors deliberately connect past events to anticipated future events, as they engage in processes of navigating change in the present. In that sense, episodic continuity can also be viewed as a dimension of temporal work, echoing the need for 'coherence' between past, present, and future, as argued by Kaplan and Orlikowski (2013, 2014). In some studies, episodic change takes place as changes in corporate strategy, where actors may search for strands of episodic continuity to show that aspects of anticipated future events are a continuation of past events – although they may appear dramatically different as defined in a new strategy. Some scholars have particularly emphasized the use of history as a resource of continuity (and discontinuity) in strategizing, as found in discussions of 'rhetorical history' (e.g., Suddaby et al., 2010.). This focus on history is illustrated, for example, by Brunninge's (2009) study of how two Swedish organizations use history to enable episodic changes in their strategies, such as changes in the manufacturing system or systematic IT implementation. However, the concept of episodic continuity differs from the notions of 'use of history' by taking an event-based view on both the past and the future and enhancing the multidirectionality between them.

One such example is found in the study of episodic strategic changes in the Carlsberg Group (Schultz & Hernes, 2020), including large-scale acquisitions and comprehensive changes in its global footprint. Here, actors constructed a narrative of episodic continuity, as they were obliged to revisit and reinterpret central passages in the will of the founder (called the 'Golden Words', dating back to 1882) to provide the changes in ownership needed to enable the strategic episodic change. The Golden Words read as follows:

> In working the brewery, it should be a constant purpose, regardless of immediate gain, to develop the art of making beer to the greatest possible degree of perfection so that this brewery as well as its products may ever stand out as a model and, through their example, assist in keeping beer brewing in this country at a high and honourable level.

Actors had to argue how the founder's stated ambitions for the Danish brewery in 1882 could be translated into a global future trajectory, which, in turn, encouraged actors to interpret the Golden Words in a new way. Whereas this enactment of episodic continuity was rather formalized, another study by Hatch et al. (2015) suggests that these episodic changes generated a search among middle managers for strands of continuity in the brewing past of Carlsberg to ensure that the purpose articulated in the Golden Words of being a 'model' brewery would not be lost in the striving to become an efficient global fast-moving consumer goods (FMCG) company. Over time, this search for episodic continuity became gradually embedded in the continuous changes that followed from the strategic episodic change, for example, in the supply-chain and corporate communication areas. Thus, episodic continuity may also drift from episodic to continuous change over time.

Other studies suggest that the enactment of episodic continuity occurs in situations of identity reconstruction, which is less surprising because organizational identity has been defined as the central, distinctive, and enduring characteristics of 'who we are as an organization' (Albert & Whetten, 1985), although a more dynamic process-based definition of identity would ask questions such as, 'who are we becoming as an organization?' However, whereas organizational identity studies assume a continuous enduring evolution of identity claims, central beliefs (e.g., Ravasi & Schultz, 2006), or long-term patterns of continuity and change (e.g., Cloutier & Ravasi, 2020), episodic continuity reconnects events that are considered central to identity construction in situations of episodic change, but may have been neglected, forgotten, or simply disconnected (e.g., Anteby & Molnár, 2012).

The importance of episodic continuity in identity reconstruction is exemplified in a study of a large-scale transformation of the LEGO Group through a sequence of increasingly discontinuous episodic changes (Schultz & Hernes, 2013). The study shows how a new team of top managers forges connections between distant, and almost forgotten, past events from the founding period and a change in the strategic trajectory of the LEGO Group. During the 1990s, LEGO's identity had become increasingly detached from the original 'construction idea' in children's play and moved towards a 'Disneyfication' driven by numerous brand extensions with few or no aspects of construction play, such as games, clothes, and thematic brick-based series. Confronted with increasing financial difficulties and market challenges, the company engaged in a year-long process of transformation underpinned by a substantial reconstruction of its organizational identity. In this process, managers deliberately searched for stories and artefacts central to the creation of LEGO's past identity as a provider of high-quality construction play experiences. The articulation of these past events was informed by the future aspiration of providing 'systematic creativity' in a play universe that combined physical and digital play, always

including dimensions of construction. Here, episodic continuity enabled identity reconstructions, which paved the way for significant episodic changes in
strategy and the related organization-wide implications in areas such as brand
architecture, communication, and global supply-chain management.

Episodic continuity and continuous change

As indicated by the Carlsberg example above, episodic continuity may also
occur in relation to continuous change, where the connections between past
and future events become embedded in the ongoing changes and patterns of
modifications taking place at the operational level in organizations. Opposed
to situations of episodic change, episodic continuity in relation to continuous
change is more dispersed and may be restricted to local units and teams.

Innovation in companies exemplifies an area where episodic continuity may
further stimulate continuous change. This is particularly relevant in industrial
sectors, such as the food industry, where episodic continuity connects past
artefacts, practices, or materials with aspirations to create more sustainable
and/or authentic food for the future. Such a role of episodic continuity is
illustrated in a study of the 'material temporality' of food innovation by
Hernes, Feddersen, and Schultz (2021) which shows how actors turn to past
epochs when innovating for the future. The authors use the notion of 'episodic
temporality', which is inspired by a conceptual foundation much the same as
that of episodic continuity. One specific example is how the innovation team
in Arla Foods, in their continuous development of new product ideas, came
across a specific type of Icelandic yogurt with a much higher level of protein
and lower fat, named 'Skyr' (https://www.arlafoods.co.uk/brands/arla-skyr/
). According to the head of innovation, the product had been consumed in
Iceland for centuries, using craft-based methods of production, but had never
been industrialized. As explained by the head of innovation cited in Hernes,
Feddersen, & Schultz (2021, p. 361):

> So, it's interesting for us to see what was done in the past. Sometimes we can make
> something for the future out of what was done. A good example for us is Skyr. It is
> interesting for us, because it was almost forgotten about. It came from Iceland now
> back to Europe, and what it is, it's a fermented milk.

According to the Icelanders, skyr was introduced by the Vikings and is an
intrinsic part of the island's history, which made a local Icelandic producer
accuse Arla of making 'unauthentic' skyr. Nonetheless, Arla has been able to
turn skyr into an industrialized product by using and further innovating their
nanofiltration technologies, as a related continuous change. However, the epi-

sodic continuity reaching into the distant past advanced both the innovation of the product itself and the related branding of skyr as a different type of yogurt product. As summarized by the head of innovation: 'We could have invented a skyr type product without the historic example, only then, most likely, we would have called it differently, because skyr is what it was called, and then the story wouldn't be so nice to tell.' Thus, episodic continuity influenced both the specific substance of the product, the narrative about it, and its potential perceived authenticity among consumers.

Scholars have also shown how episodic continuity is related to continuous change in organizational identity. One example is a study by Basque and Langley (2018) of the Desjardin Group, a cooperative financial services organization. The authors discuss how the founder, Alphonse, has been invoked in the continuous change of identity across a long duration of time. The study discovers five different types of invocations of the past in the ongoing identity work, which we take to be examples of episodic continuity enabling continuous changes of the organizational identity. The five types of invocations are existential, imperative, justificatory, conservatory, and progressive invocations (Basque & Langley, 2018, p. 1694). As suggested by the labelling of the types of invocations, they refer to the various ways in which episodic continuity has influenced the changes in identity, such as by articulating (existential), preserving (conservative), or refreshing (progressive) central, distinctive, and enduring elements of organizational identity (referring to the definition by Albert and Whetten (1985) of organizational identity mentioned above). Another example is found in the study of 'Track Town' by Howard-Grenville et al. (2013), the city where the Nike company was founded in Oregon. They show how actors continuously strived to connect to the identity of a forgotten past of the Nike heritage through what they label as 'recursive processes of identity reproduction and resurrection' (Howard-Grenville et al., 2013, p. 113. Similar to the discussion of authenticity in the case of Arla Foods (Hernes, Feddersen, & Schultz, 2021), the authors conceive the processes of continuous identity change as a process of 'authentication', whereby episodic continuity enhances the experienced authenticity of 'Track Town' for each round of resurrection.

Episodic and ongoing continuity

Episodic continuity signifies the creation of continuity between events and periods in an organization's past and future. Imagine Apple's journey from the iconic Macintosh computer in 1984 to the contemporary Apple MacBooks. The journey has included a number of products, most notably the iPad and the iPhone. Imagine first the changes along the journey. They are significant, to say the least, in terms of computing power, versatility, and design. But then again, there is also a high level of continuity running through many of the products. We discern the countless, ongoing improvements towards more intuitive use, minimalist design, and vertical integration of product ranges as ongoing continuity. However, such continuity does not come easily and is interrelated with instances of episodic continuity through time. For example, Steve Jobs disapproved of the 'Home' button, the only mechanical button on the iPhone when it was first launched, which led to dramatic events in trying to change the design. Another example is the touchscreen introduced on the iPhone, which is both minimalist and versatile. The story of the Gorilla˙ Glass (Isaacson, 2021) is exemplary. Extremely robust glass was necessary for the iPhone, and Jobs found a manufacturer in the USA who had previously manu-factured a glass that could be used. After long negotiations, it was finally agreed to produce the glass to the quality and in the volume needed to launch the iPhone. The glass represented a change, because it had never been used before, but it also represented a hard-won episodic continuity by giving a sleek design to the iPhone similar to that of other Apple products in the past. As Isaacson (2021, p. 472) writes:

> The new design ended up with just a thin stainless steel bezel that allowed the Gorilla˙ Glass display to go right to the edge. Every part of the device seemed to defer to the screen. The new look was austere, yet also friendly. You could fondle it. It meant they had to redo the circuit boards, antenna, and processor placement inside, but Jobs ordered the change.

Episodic continuity, thus, is not created out of thin air. Any form of change or continuity is enacted at various events where people meet to talk or make deci-sions. At such events, they may not refer explicitly to change or continuity, but to new product development, budget revisions, modification of routines, per-formance measurement issues, sustainability issues, or many other topics. Yet, most topics refer implicitly or explicitly to some form of change or continuity or, as we have seen, both change and continuity, sometimes even represented by the same processes. The interaction at such events, such as at regular meet-ings on design and innovation in Apple, forms what we call ongoing continu-ity. Although meetings may be organized according to sequential agendas to coordinate the discussion, the experienced process of the meeting is more like interwoven and sometimes indistinguishable flows. But ongoing interaction is mostly oriented towards events that have taken place in the near past or that are expected to take place in the immediate future. However, in those ongoing improvements, significant events stand out across time, enabling actors to forge connections between events from a more distant past (e.g., the simple intuitiveness of the first Macintosh) to aspirations for the future (e.g., phones and tablets without a Home button). Such strings of events underpin episodic continuity in a company such as Apple.

The organizational change diamond

Conceiving episodic continuity as a form of organizational change implies that organizational change comprises four basic conceptions of the relationship between change and continuity. Although they give different emphasis to change, such as episodic and continuous change; and to continuity, such as episodic and indivisible continuity, they all share the assumption that organizational change and continuity are complementary and mutually constitutive in a world on the move. Taken together they constitute what we label the organizational change diamond (Figure 2.2).

The organizational change diamond points at several opportunities for future research in the further conceptualization and management of organizational change.

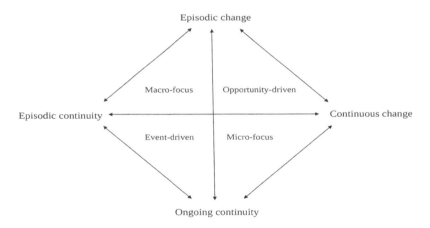

Figure 2.2   Organizational change diamond

Interrelated organizational change

The organizational change diamond suggests that the four forms of organizational change are *interrelated*. Although they may each be further developed, we offer a first attempt at characterizing the interrelations of the four forms.

Episodic change and episodic continuity are particularly interrelated through their 'macro-focus'. However, they hold different assumptions about what constitutes 'macro'. Whereas 'macro' in episodic change relates to the strategic, organization-wide macro-level in the organization, 'macro' in episodic continuity refers to past and future 'macro-events', that is, events of significance to the situation in which they are brought to bear. Several of the above examples suggest how a mutual reinforcement between episodic change and continuity increases the likelihood of large-scale, transformative change. Likewise, continuous change and ongoing continuity share a focus on 'micro'. Their focus also differs between micro-processes among actors located at the operational and horizontal levels in the organization (continuous change), and microscopic past and future events (ongoing continuity) constituting dynamic patterns of interactions. The shared micro-focus paves the way for studies of how continuous change is sustained through strands of microscopic continuity.

The mutual relations between episodic and continuous change are the most elaborated on in previous research. Orlikowski and Hofmann (1997) particularly stress the opportunity-driven shift from continuous to episodic change. However, we argue that emerging opportunities may also drive shifts from episodic change to continuous change. Such opportunity-driven shifts may occur, for example, as episodic change becomes embedded in changing practices; or as top management's attention to episodic change declines and the change processes are dispersed and transformed into continuous change among middle managers. Therefore, we label these interrelations 'opportunity-driven'.

Finally, both episodic and ongoing continuity share a conceptual origin in 'events' as the fundamental constitution of time, whether they refer to significant events, such as the founding of a company, or micro events, such as the previous meeting. In both forms of organizational change, continuity is created as actors weave together events that have unfolded in the past with events that may happen in the future.

Expanding organizational change

The four forms of organizational change and their interrelations have broadened the scope for managing and navigating organizational change. Our development of episodic continuity suggests an expansion of the opportunities for framing and influencing organizational change that may be further explored in future research. Episodic continuity points at how managers deliberately may invoke sources from both the near and the distant past, which are used to weave together strands of continuity reaching into a near or a distant future. Insights from previous research suggest that episodic continuity enables large-scale and/or transformative change because actors are more inclined to commit to change that is part of a larger and meaningful trajectory than to commit to change that seems more disconnected (see Hernes & Bévort, 2018; Malhotra & Hinings, 2015). In addition, episodic continuity may sustain the continuous change that is intrinsic to implementing large-scale change. This connection between episodic and continuous change may be particularly forceful if episodic continuity is enhanced by pockets of ongoing continuity, implying that local teams or units – central to transformative change – are continuously able to (re)create a sense of coherence among themselves, as they engage in the numerous activities taking place amidst episodic change. Thus, combining the four forms of organizational change opens a pathway for how to generate commitment and innovativeness in large-scale transformative change.

We expect that all kinds of organizations, companies as well as governmental institutions, increasingly will be confronted with a need for transformative change. The push for the green transition of societies will have significant implications for all parts of organizations' value chains, just as stakeholders increasingly expect companies to be proactive and innovative in addressing climate change. As demonstrated, for example, in the Science-Based Target Initiative (see https://sciencebasedtargets.org/), companies make pledges that require significant changes in the way they operate. In many cases, each roadmap pointing towards a more zero-carbon future entails a series of episodic changes, where managers are confronted with challenges of creating commitment to and connections with continuous changes (e.g., Hernes & Schultz, 2020). Although such episodic changes clearly point at future events, the above examples suggest that organizations also previously have been able to transform themselves in ways that can generate inspiration and motivation for the future. Here, the deliberate use of episodic continuity may help managers in keeping the momentum in the numerous connected episodic and continuous changes.

Finally, organizational change, whether large-scale transformative change or small-scale continuous change, unfolds on a backdrop of ongoing continuity in the numerous events that constitute life in organizations. All kinds of change processes unfold through patterns of social interaction, such as meetings, projects, seminars, workshops, workstreams, sprints, and so on. In all these situations, deliberate combinations of episodic and ongoing continuity may provide a sense of directionality that otherwise may easily get lost in the experienced time pressure that often characterizes transformative change.

The contribution of episodic continuity

The enactment of episodic continuity in relation to the various forms of organizational change suggests that episodic continuity may contribute to organizational change in multiple ways. Although none of these are fully developed, they suggest pathways for future research.

First, episodic continuity may add meaning to a trajectory of change in the sense that future changes are seen as extensions, revisions, elaborations, or deliberate deviations from past trajectories. In each case, episodic continuity enables the development of a more coherent narrative of what the organization has been and what it is becoming (Schultz & Hernes, 2013; Kaplan & Orlikowski, 2014). Companies increasingly articulate such trajectories as a corporate purpose, which, for example, raises questions about how episodic continuity connects the long-term development of purpose with the more short-term episodic changes in strategy (Schultz & Hernes, 2020).

Second, episodic continuity may facilitate innovation, because it opens a rich reservoir of past ideas, artefacts, and experiences, all of which actors may leverage in their creation of novelty. By the same token, the search for future solutions can sensitize actors to forgotten products and production methods, as found in many food-and-beverage-related industries. This can include both the reinvention of past materiality (e.g., Hernes, Feddersen, & Schultz, 2021) and the combination of different types of narratives, such as past-oriented structured narratives and future-oriented provisional narratives (Bartel & Garud, 2013). Also, as in the case of Apple, episodic continuity may enhance persistent aspirations for future innovations that are reinforced by events that become significant as actors move through time.

Third, episodic continuity may work as a source of authenticity. Such referencing of the past may occur particularly when actors refer to the origin of an innovation, such as the skyr case (Hernes, Feddersen, & Schultz, 2021), or to the authenticity associated with the founder of the organization. This was the case in the invoking of Alphonse, the founder of the Canadian cooperative financial services organization (Basque & Langley, 2018), the reinterpretation of the will of the founder of the Carlsberg Group (Schultz & Hernes, 2020; see also Hatch & Schultz, 2017), and the authentication of a future as 'Track Town' by tapping into the early running days of the Nike founders (Howard-Grenville et al., 2013).

Last but not least, episodic continuity may reduce the experience of loss and anxiety among actors directly engaged in change processes. For example, the acknowledgement by managers that the past holds insights and experiences relevant to the future in the making may reassure actors that their experiences and competencies are not (completely) redundant in the future. This has particularly been the case in the hype concerning 'disruptive change', where actors at times were led to believe that absolutely nothing of what they had learned in the past had any relevance for the future.

The organizational change diamond expands how we may conceive and navigate organizational change through interrelations between the four forms of organizational change. In developing the organizational change diamond, we have further elaborated the notion of ongoing continuity and have suggested a novel form of organizational change, defined as episodic continuity. The organizational change diamond is developed from a temporal view that frames the numerous mutual relations between change and continuity as actors move through time. We argue that such a view suggests how change and continuity are interwoven, because episodic and/or continuous changes across time may also provide a sense of continuity to actors, whether such continuity emerges from connections between past and future events (episodic continuity) or between micro-processes within localized settings (ongoing continuity). The organizational change diamond is a way to further develop and connect change and continuity which paves the way for a rethinking of organizational change and the opportunities to influence change processes at all levels of the organization – let alone the need to engage with an increasing number of stakeholders in the transformative changes needed in the next decade.

References

Albert, S., & Whetten, D. A. (1985). Organizational identity, in L. L. Cummings & M. M. Staw (eds), *Research in Organizational Behavior* (Vol. 7, pp. 263–75), Bingley: JAI Press.

Anteby, M., & Molnár, V. (2012). Collective memory meets organizational identity: remembering to forget in a firm's rhetorical history, *Academy of Management Journal*, 55, 515–40.

Bartel, C. A., & Garud, R. (2013). The role of narratives in sustaining organizational innovation, *Organization Science*, 20(1), 107–17.

Basque, J., & Langley, A. (2018). Invoking Alphonse: the founder figure as a historical resource for organizational identity work, *Organization Studies*, 39(12), 1685–708.

Bluedorn, A. C., & Standifer, R. L. (2006). Time and the temporal imagination, *Academy of Management Learning & Education*, 5, 196–206.

Brunninge, O. (2009). Using history in organizations: how managers make purposeful reference to history in strategy processes, *Journal of Organizational Change Management*, 22, 8–26.

Chia, R., & Tsoukas, H. (2004). Everything flows and nothing abides: towards a 'rhizomic' model of organizational change, transformation and action, Process Studies, 32, 196–224.

Cloutier, C., & Ravasi, D. (2020). Identity trajectories: explaining long-term patterns of continuity and change in organizational identities, *Academy of Management Journal*, 63(4), 1196–235.

Farjoun, M. (2010). Beyond dualism: stability and change as duality, *Academy of Management Review*, 35(2), 202–25.

Feuls, M., Hernes, T., & Schultz, M. (2021). Transcending time horizons: how actors project innovative solutions toward distant climate goals, *Academy of Management Annual Meeting Proceedings*, https://doi.org/10.5465/AMBPP.2021.13188abstract.

Hatch, M. J., & Schultz, M. (2017). Toward a theory of using history authentically: historicizing in the Carlsberg Group, *Administrative Science Quarterly*, 62(4), 657–97.

Hatch, M. J., Schultz, M., & Skov, A. M. (2015). Organizational identity and culture in the context of managed change: transformation in the Carlsberg Group 2009–2013, *Academy of Management Discoveries*, 1(1), 56–88.

Hernes, T. (2022). *Organization and Time*, Oxford: Oxford University Press.

Hernes, T. (2014). *A Process Theory of Organization*, Oxford: Oxford University Press.

Hernes, T., & Bévort, F. (2018). *Organisering i en verden i bevægelse*. Samfundslitteratur.

Hernes, T., Feddersen, J., & Schultz, M. (2021). Material temporality: how materiality does time in food organising, *Organization Studies*, 42(2), 351–71.

Hernes, T., Hussenot, A., & Pulk, K. (2021). Time and temporality of change processes: applying an event-based view to integrate episodic and continuous change, in M. Poole & A. Van de Van (eds), *Oxford Handbook of Organizational Change And Innovation* (chapter 27), Oxford: Oxford University Press.

Hernes, T., & Schultz, M. (2020). Translating the distant into the present: how actors address distant past and future events through situated activity, *Organization Theory*, 1(1), 1–20, https://doi.org/10.1177/2631787719900999.

Howard-Grenville, J., Metzger, M., & Meyer, A. D. (2013). Rekindling the flame: processes of identity resurrection, *Academy of Management Journal*, 56(1), 113–36.

Isaacson, W. (2021). *Steve Jobs*, New York: Simon & Schuster.

Kaplan, S., & Orlikowski, W. (2013). Temporal work in strategy making, *Organization Science*, 24, 965–95.

Kaplan, S., & Orlikowski, W. (2014). Beyond forecasting: creating new strategic narratives, *Sloan Management Review*, 56(1), 23–8.

Lewin, K. (1947). Frontiers in group dynamics: concept, method and reality in social science, social equilibria and social change, *Human Relations*, 1, 5–41.

Malhotra, C. R., & Hinings, B. (2015). Unpacking continuity and change as a process of organizational transformation, *Long Range Planning*, 48, 1–22.

Mintzberg, H. (1987). The strategy concept I: five Ps for strategy, *California Management Review*, 30(1), 11–24.

Orlikowski, W. J. (1996). Improvising organizational transformation over time: a situated change perspective, *Information Systems Research*, 7, 63–92.

Orlikowski, W. J., & Hoffman, J. D. (1997). An improvisational model for change man-agement: the case of Groupware Technologies, *Sloan Management Review*, Winter, 11–21.

Poole, M., & Van de Van, A. (eds) (2021). *Oxford Handbook of Organizational Change and Innovation*, 2nd edition, Oxford: Oxford University Press.

Poole, M. S., & Van de Ven, A. H. (eds) (2004). *Handbook of Organizational Change and Innovation*, 1st edition, Oxford: Oxford University Press.

Ravasi, D., & Schultz, M. (2006). Responding to identity threats: exploring the role of organizational culture, *Academy of Management Journal*, 49(3), 1–30.

Romanelli, E., & Tushman, M. (1994). Organizational transformation as punctuated equilibrium: an empirical test, *Academy of Management Journal*, 37(5), 1141–66.

Schultz, M., & Hernes, T. (2013). A temporal perspective on organizational identity, *Organization Science*, 24(1), 1–21.

Schultz, M., & Hernes, T. (2020). Temporal interplay between strategy and identity: punctuated, subsumed and sustained modes, *Strategic Organization*, 18(1), 106–35.

Stouten, J., Rousseau, D. M., & De Cremer, D. (2018). Successful organizational change: integrating the management practice and scholarly literature, *Academy of Management Annals*, 12(2), 752–88.

Suddaby, R., Foster, W. & Quinn Trank, C. (2010). Rhetorical history as a source of competitive advantage, in J. A. C. Baum & J. Lempel (eds), *Advances in Strategic Management: The Globalization of Strategy Research* (pp. 147–73), Bingley: Emerald.

Tsoukas, H., & Chia, R. (2002). On organizational becoming: rethinking organizational change, *Organization Science*, 13, 567–82.

Weick, K. E., & Quinn, R. (1999). Organizational change and development, *Annual Review of Psychology*, 50, 361–86.

Whitehead, A. N. (1929). *Process and Reality*, New York: The Free Press.

3 Complex and dynamic complementarities of continuity and change revealed in outsourcing and backsourcing

Kätlin Pulk

Introduction

Resuming the continuity of once discontinued activities and connecting them across longer timespans is a serious effort, and not every organization is able to do that. Renewing continuity requires rebuilding internal competencies and skills lost due to outsourcing and reintegrating once outsourced activities back into the ongoing organizational activities. Renewing the continuity of activities and reintegrating them back could be so challenging that organizations may find themselves locked into the outsourcing deal's continuous continuity (Bary and Westner, 2018; Law, 2018).

In global competition, organizations face constant pressure to improve their economic outcomes. One possibility to improve economic outcomes is to enhance labor productivity by focusing on so-called core activities (Freytag, Clarke, and Evald, 2012; Sako, 2010; Veltri, Saunders, and Kavan, 2008). Increased focus on core activities and improving cost efficiency may lead to the strategic decision to stop making things in-house but buy from the market at a cheaper price (Sako, 2010; Veltri et al., 2008). The decision of whether to make or buy could be extended to continuing performing some activities in-house or buying services from an external vendor. Deciding to buy instead of continuing to make or perform something in-house is called outsourcing. Outsourcing is defined as "a conscious abdication of selected value chain activities to external service providers" (Contractor, Kumar, Kundu, and Pedersen, 2010: 1417). Therefore, outsourcing is the decision to discontinue carrying out some activities in-house.

However, like with every strategy, organizations may reconsider their strategic decisions to outsource and bring outsourced activities back in-house (Nagpal, 2015). Therefore, backsourcing is the strategy to reverse outsourcing and bring once outsourced activities back in-house to restore full ownership and control (e.g. Bhagwatwar, Hackney, and Desouza, 2011; Hirschheim, 1998; Veltri et al., 2008; Wong, 2008). An organization may decide to backsource either because the outsourcing contract expires and there is no intention to extend the contract with the current partner, search for new sourcing partners, or opt for premature termination (Lacity, Willcocks, and Rottman, 2008; Nagpal, 2015). The latter case is usually motivated by the clients' dissatisfaction with service costs and quality and a desire to regain control (Bary and Westner, 2018; Lacity et al., 2008; Veltri et al., 2008). By definition, backsourcing can always happen only after the initial outsourcing (Bary and Westner, 2018) and requires resuming continuity by uniting activities across timespans.

While outsourcing has received much attention from practitioners and academics alike as a widespread business practice (e.g. Contractor, Kumar, Kundu, and Pedersen, 2011; Hirschheim, Heinzl, and Dibbern, 2006; Oshri, Sidhu, and Kotlarsky, 2019; Peck, 2017), backsourcing is a less investigated phenomenon (e.g. Bary and Westner, 2018; Oshri et al., 2019). However, there is a general agreement that both outsourcing and backsourcing are challenging endeavors. In both cases, most of the research has focused on the motivational factors of these strategies. At the same time, less is said about the relationship between (dis)continuity of activities and organizational change and (dis)continuity these strategies create. This chapter explores organizational change, continuity, and discontinuity in business process outsourcing and backsourcing.

Continuity and change in outsourcing/backsourcing business processes

Continuity and change

According to Smith (1982: 135), "Dealing with continuity is not a simple or easy task." Smith (1982) stresses that continuity is a process that simultaneously manifests both persistence and change, and, for example, Pettigrew (1985: 1) points out, "The more we look at present-day events, the easier it is to identify change; the longer we stay with an emergent process and the further back we go to disentangle its origins, the more likely we are to identify continuities." However, the length of an observed period is not the only aspect that affects our perceptions about something as changing or continuing. Our perceptions and understandings about something as changing or continuing could differ based on whether an emic or etic view (Martin, 2009) is applied; that is, whether change/continuity is observed from a researcher's external position or an internal position of organizational actors (Hernes, Hussenot, and Pulk, 2021).

Also, what is changing or what is not, and what is continuing and what is not, depends on the level of observation. For example, episodic change as an exogenous planned intervention at the organizational level (Weick and Quinn, 1999) may not directly impact continuity at the level of particular activities (Hernes et al., 2021). In other words, redesigning organizational structures or replacing one technological solution with another does not necessarily affect the continuity of activities or cause any perceived changes in ongoing practices. At the same time, as a result of a continuous change (Hernes et al., 2021) as an endogenous adaption to slight variation in everyday coping (Dreyfus, 1991), activities could change significantly while still maintaining their persistence (Hernes, 2014). Therefore, it is hard to make a clear-cut distinction between continuity and change.

While recognizing, on the one hand, the reciprocal relationship between organizational change and (dis)continuity and, on the other hand, the challenges to making a clear distinction between the two stemming from the level of observation, Hernes, Hussenot, and Pulk (2021) propose to analyze change and (dis)continuity from the perspective of actors. To signify ongoing change and continuity from the actors' perspective, they use the term "an immanent temporal trajectory that actors constantly redefine as a way to define the continuity of their activity" (Hernes et al., 2021: 745). According to Hernes et al. (2021), a trajectory expresses persistent or ongoing continuity maintained by the continuous change and ongoing temporality of activities that connects practices from an immediate past to the immediate future (see also Hernes, 2014, 2018). Therefore, the continuous or "on-going continuity has foreseeable, habitual and taken-for-granted qualities" (Hernes, 2018); it enables the accumulation of situational knowledge and requires situational knowledge to keep carrying on. In other words, by preserving existing patterns while adding new elements, continuous continuity requires situational knowledge (Smith, 1982), and it helps to sustain an immanent temporal trajectory. However, situational procedural knowledge is quick to vanish without a continuous performance of activities (Hernes, 2014; Orlikowski, 2002). The reciprocal relationship between the performance of activities and practice-based knowledge implies that discontinuity in the performance of activities affects the knowledge and competence base and leads to organizational forgetting (Argote, 2013).

However, besides the persistent or continuous continuity that operates within a limited temporal span of immediate past and immediate future, continuity may work across longer timespans by uniting more distant past and future events and activities (Hernes, 2018; Smith, 1982). In other words, resuming continuity could be needed across longer timespans instead of relying on "continuous" or ongoing continuity. Resuming continuity cannot be taken for granted because of the organizational forgetting associated with the discontinued performance of activities (Argote, 2013; Hernes, 2014; Orlikowski, 2002). Joining together more distant past and future events and activities entails risk and uncertainty while offering possibilities for novelty and innovation (Smith, 1982). Therefore, in addition to an exogenous and endogenous change discussed earlier, both continuous continuity and resuming continuity also have important implications in the case of business process outsourcing and backsourcing.

Outsourcing

Business process outsourcing (BPO) is a strategic decision to unbundle (Sako, 2010) and move some of an organization's internal activities to an external service provider (Saxena and Bharadwaj, 2009). Similar to outsourcing, the primary motivation of BPO is cost efficiency (Handley, 2012; Kotlarsky and Bognar, 2012). However, BPO is never a single standalone decision. Instead, it could be viewed as part of an organizational redesign aiming to increase corporate functions' efficiency through enhanced labor productivity (Oshri et al., 2011; Sako, 2010). The latter is expected to be achieved by combining "the standardization and consolidation of business processes, greater specialization, and moving into higher-value-added segments" (Sako, 2010: 504). BPO means discontinuity in the performance of selected activities or some of their sub-parts that usually go together with or presuppose some planned organizational change in the form of restructuring or redesign to enable that kind of rearrangement. At the same time, while viewing activities as commodities (Oshri et al., 2011), BPO tends to ignore continuous endogenous change as a characteristic of evolving ongoing processes (Hernes et al., 2021; Hernes, 2014), including activities (Schütz, 1967). Put differently, BPO does not count with the evolving nature of activities and their tendency to become otherwise. The latter could create severe challenges in maintaining control over outsourced activities.

The scale and complexity of outsourcing may differ, ranging from a single function to an entire department. Based on the contract, only particular activities are transferred to the service provider, specific activities with employees, or particular activities with employees and equipment (Bhagwatwar et al.,

2011). For example, the outsourcing/backsourcing literature widely refers to JP Morgan Chase and IBM BPO contract from 2003. Besides the data centers, help desks, data and voice networks services, some resources and systems, and 4000 IT employees and contractors were transferred. Similarly, the outsourcing contract between Sainsbury and Accenture from 2000 included the transfer of 470 IT employees and IT assets with a total value of around £60 million from Sainsbury to Accenture (Bhagwatwar et al., 2011). Therefore, BPO tends to be a more complex process than just ceasing to perform some activities in-house.

Alternatively, if the outsourcing decision does not include the transfer of employees from a client to a vendor, it usually includes layoffs. As a rule, offshore outsourcing, which transfers activities to overseas countries like China, India, the Philippines, Ireland, and Poland, aims to benefit from labor arbitrage (Solli-Sæther and Gottschalk, 2015). Therefore, offshore outsourcing usually does not include the transfer of employees but layoffs. However, as a downside of more affordable labor costs comes different cultural backgrounds and possible language barriers, which may make maintaining control over offshored activities and managing offshore outsourcing partnerships more difficult and expensive (Peck, 2017). As a result of the closure of entire departments and layoffs or transfer of employees, organizational forgetting – a loss of organizational knowledge and competencies – is a serious challenge to tackle (Argote, 2013). Instead of gradually diminishing knowledge and competencies occurring over time, organizational forgetting may happen quickly and abruptly.

Organizations, aware of the risk of forgetting, are trying to compensate for the potential loss of knowledge and competencies via detailed guidelines, manuals, process descriptions and maps, and technological artifacts, like software (Pentland and Feldman, 2008). However, those static artifacts could capture only explicit aspects of knowledge (Pulk, 2016) while falling short in capturing implicit knowledge embedded in the contextual background (Shotter, 2006) and the dynamic and evolving nature of activities (Hernes, 2014; Schütz, 1967). Continuous endogenous change characterizes distinctive processes, a broader contextual and organizational background, and the relationship between activities and background (Pulk, 2016). Neither the knowledge about nor the outsourced activities remain as they were at the moment of outsourcing; instead, they are triggered by the continuous change of activities (Hernes, 2014; Hernes et al., 2021).

At the same time, the deeper meaning is grounded in the organizational meaning structures partly available and maintained through implicit knowledge and tacit articulation of organizational meaning structures (Hernes, 2014). Therefore, "Any act can but disclose a limited section of a meaning structure, leaving many connections in the dark" (Hernes, 2014: 126). However, the connections *left in the dark* are not insignificant; far from that, they just stay invisible or unobservable while still being present and playing their role in constituting the whole.

However, it is important to highlight that "It appears that most companies have difficulty in distinguishing between 'core' processes that they must control, 'critical' processes that they must buy from expert vendors, and 'commodity' processes that they can outsource" (Oshri et al., 2011: 22). Moreover, like transaction cost calculations may become obsolete, the distinction between core and non-core activities may require reconsideration. This reconsideration could happen in light of new organizational strategies or available new technological solutions and motivate organizations to backsource.

Backsourcing

Backsourcing is the strategy to reverse outsourcing and bring the outsourced activities back in-house (Ejodame and Oshri, 2018; Wong, 2008). Somehow surprisingly, the literature points out that the decision to backsource is often motivated by the same factors as the decision to outsource – to reduce costs and enhance service quality (e.g. Ejodame and Oshri, 2018; Veltri et al., 2008), indicating that possibly the initial expectations related to outsourcing are unmet. Additional motivators for backsourcing could be a desire to regain control over outsourced activities or management politics (Oshri et al., 2019). Like motives, so tend also the assumptions behind backsourcing to be mostly the same as in the case of outsourcing – it is possible to transfer activities as commodities and perform them with higher quality and lower costs in-house.

Continuity and change in outsourcing/backsourcing business processes

Some scholars view outsourcing and backsourcing as two sides of the same coin (i.e. Oshri et al., 2019). Therefore, with the expected increase in the BPO market (Grand View Research, 2021), we can expect to see a rise, although maybe not necessarily symmetrical, in backsourcing cases. However, there is an essential difference in assumed continuity between outsourcing and backsourcing. On the one hand, outsourcing with associated discontinuity of activities introduces a shift in or even discontinuity of a particular temporal trajectory. On the other hand, it assumes a continuous continuity or preserved continuance of outsourced activities and knowledge about and control over them.

In contrast, backsourcing implies resumed continuity, uniting or joining discontinued activities across longer timespans and re-establishing the trajectory once disrupted. The discontinuity combined with assumed continuous continuity of knowledge about and control over activities and ignored endogenous change could lead to lock-ins, explaining the expected or observed asymmetry in the number of out- and backsourcing cases (Law, 2018). Law (2018) sees possible lock-ins as serious outsourcing-related threats that could turn outsourcing into a path-dependent strategy. An organization may find itself in involuntary continuous continuity (Hernes, 2018) and find it hard to break free. Put differently, an organization may find itself moving along a temporal trajectory it is unable to change. It could be risky and costly to change the current trajectory by breaking the path of continuous continuity as the preserved continuance and switching it to a resumed continuity by connecting activities across longer timespans. Therefore, while outsourcing is referred to as a path-dependent strategy, backsourcing is referred to as a path-breaking strategy (Law, 2018), and path-breaking is not necessarily an easy task. However, the path-breaking is only half of the challenge associated with backsourcing. The other half of the challenge stems from the required ability to reunite the longer timespans and reintegrate activities into the broader organizational context.

Continuity and change in the implementation of F&A offshore outsourcing

In this section, I analyze continuity and change in organizational activities in the case of BPO. My experience with offshore outsourcing in finance and accounting dates from 2005/06 when I worked as a chief accountant in the local subsidiary of MultiNational (pseudonym). MultiNational is a privately held company with a global presence in component production and technical solutions. Although Europe is its primary market, MultiNational has a global reach with factories or sales offices in the U.S.A., South America, Asia, Middle-East, South Africa, Australia, and India. Since 1996 MultiNational has been organizing its operations according to divisional design, and its production and sales were split into three business divisions.

Starting from 2001, the pressure on business divisions to improve their efficiency and profitability intensified. One step to support business divisions to meet these targets was to move all the supportive back-office activities previously part of the business divisions into the European Interservice, which operated as a separate cost center, and simultaneously replace a divisional structure with a matrix structure. The European Interservice, covering Europe, Middle-East, and South Africa (EMA), was followed by the Business Services Americas and Asia and Pacific Countries Interservice. In May 2004, the European Interservice was combined with Business Services Americas and Asia and Pacific Countries Interservice into one global function called Global Business Services. Global Business Services (GBS) operated as an integrated back-office serving three business segments by providing on-site services in finance and accounting (F&A), human resources, facility management, and general administration.

BPO allowed a new objective to be set – to reduce costs by 50 percent from €6.6 million to €3.3 million annually. The primary source of the cost cut was an expected decrease in headcount from 220 to 110–120 full-time employees in combination with a labor arbitrage (Pulk, 2010).

The timeline of the offshore BPO in MultiNational is presented in Figure 3.1. Although the implementation of BPO in GBS-EMA officially lasted one and a half years, considering the internal restructuring and SAP (enterprise resource planning software) implementation as a necessary preparation for BPO allows for drafting a much longer timeline (Figure 3.1). As SAP is a common platform used by BPO vendors, it could be considered a prerequisite for F&A offshore outsourcing. Therefore, as mentioned before and indicated by the figure, BPO is never a standalone decision/project. Instead, the precondition to discontinue performing some activities or parts of some activities may require significant changes in the existing organizational design and technical solutions.

While F&A BPO targeted only a small part of the entire company, it was a strong movement for MultiNational going beyond the bottom-line improvement into changing the whole business model. Being the first down-sizing program affecting white-collar employees only, BPO shook the culture and values rooted in the organizational history dating back to 1933 when MultiNational was founded. Therefore, it is essential to recognize that BPO did not mean drastic changes for GBS-EMA only but also for production and sales employees in three business divisions. For example, the sales/production and finance departments were previously accustomed to working side by side with intensive daily communication between the two functions. Resulting of the BPO, some tasks once carried out by the local F&A were assigned to the local sales and marketing people. At the same time, in F&A-related questions,

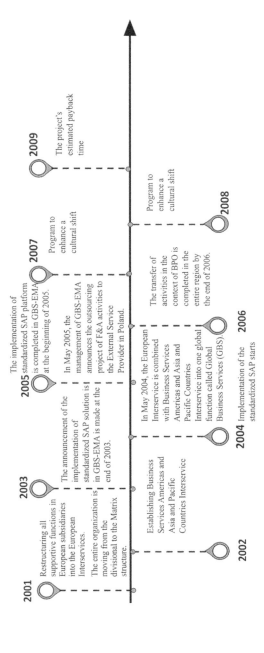

Figure 3.1   The timeline of changes

local sales/production organizations should approach the accounting clerk in Poland.

> Invoices are often paid too late. An invoice cannot be divided between different cost centers in Krakow – you have to do it yourself + divide the amounts. Filling out the different cost centers, accounts, and manager numbers takes a lot of time, and it has created a lot of extra work for us who are not professionals in bookkeeping [a marketing person with regular contacts with the External Service Provider]. (Pulk, 2010: 77)

As the case description shows, BPO is a demanding endeavor, incorporating strategic preparation in the form of a series of changes, including organizational restructuring and redesign, knowledge and task transfer, layoffs, and cultural change. It may require significant investments in systems, like SAP implementation in the described case.

Continuity and change in the implementation of F&A backsourcing

The following section is about continuity and change in the backsourcing process. My involvement in F&A backsourcing took place in ModernGroup (a pseudonym), where I held a senior professional position.

The background of the backsourcing case

Like MultiNational, ModernGroup is a European multinational company with a global divisional structure. More precisely, its operations were divided into six different business divisions. Unlike family (foundation)-owned MultiNational, the ModernGroup is a publicly traded company listed on two Nordic stock markets. At the beginning of 2007, ModernGroup decided to outsource its Western and Central European subsidiaries' high-volume, low-value-adding accounting routines to the External Service Provider in Poland. The External Service Provider, in turn, used the services of its Asian subsidiaries. The F&A BPO was finalized in 2009.

Considering ModernGroup is a listed company, the six business divisions were under constant pressure to increase profit margins. However, each division was granted relative independence in its strategic decisions to meet financial targets. One of the divisions, Rebel (a pseudonym), saw the cost-saving possibility of backsourcing F&A activities. Instead of bringing accounting back into each company, Rebel set up a shared service team in Estonia. Despite the

ModernGroup top management's high skepticism towards the backsourcing idea, permission was granted. However, the permission was given on the condition that the shared service team would follow an already established global process model (GPM), including all the internal controls, and internal and external reporting deadlines, without any deflection. The requirement to follow one-to-one all internal controls and keep reporting deadlines was understandable, considering that as a listed company, ModernGroup was obligated to provide accurate and timely financial information to the stock market. However, that requirement also assumed that it is possible and reasonable to transfer activities precisely as performed by the External Service Provider. As it turned out later, that was too strong an assumption.

The Rebel division established a pilot project to backsource the accounting services of its 14 smaller entities. Those 14 smaller entities included three companies from the Czech Republic, two from Austria, two from Estonia, two from Latvia, two from Lithuania, and three newly acquired companies from Finland. However, it turned out that to integrate three newly acquired Finnish companies into the general setup, we needed to call back to duty a lately retired employee who was serving as a chief account in one of the group's companies before the BPO. As all other chief accountants of Finnish companies were hired after the BPO, they did not know how the outsourced activities should be performed or reintegrated into the existing setup. Also, an external SAP consultant was hired to support the technical side of the transfer. However, due to a high number of country and business-specific customization in SAP, she could not provide any significant support in the process, underscoring, once again, the inability of artifacts to serve as reliable reservoirs of knowledge.

Resumed continuity of activities versus the expected ongoing continuity of internal controls

To make sense of the activities target of transfer, the backsourcing team went through the official knowledge transfer sessions and had several informal conversations with the External Service Provider team members. Some tensions occurred in debates over the copyrights of the detailed guidelines of customized SAP solutions created and used by the External Service Provider. The ModernGroup top management agreed with the External Service Provider that although the External Service Provider created these descriptions, the ModernGroup has the moral right to see them, and the External Service Provider is obliged to share these files when asked. The reasoning was that how the External Service Provider runs the outsourced activities cannot be confidential to the client company. Considering that it was generally a "friendly" backsourcing, meaning that the contract's total monetary value and duration remained intact, and just a limited number of companies stepped out, the relative ease in reaching the agreement may not represent a general rule. Additionally, several formal and informal conversions were held with the in-house chief accountants of country accounting services and business controllers. While analyzing the expectations and needs of business controllers and in-house accountants and comparing these to the process descriptions provided by the External Service Provider teams, we identified several transformations in the meaning of outsourced activities.

The backsourcing project lasted nine months and was finalized in June 2013. Against all odds, the backsourcing team met all the reporting deadlines. Once again, the reporting discipline is crucial for the listed company. However, it became clear that it was unreasonable to transfer all the activities precisely according to the GPM and follow all the internal controls.

For example, in the initial takeover phase, the colleague responsible for accounts payables complained that following the standard setup of internal controls, she must check her work four times. It turned out that the high task fragmentation had led to the loss of understanding of the entire process, and the internal control of outgoing payments ignored the specific nature of accounts payable, resulting in triple or even quadruple checks instead of the intended double checks. The formal process ignored that most of the invoices were intercompany invoices, that is, invoices issued by one ModernGroup subsidiary to another ModernGroup subsidiary. Intercompany invoices imply that the money stays in the group in case of outgoing payments. All intercompany payables/receivables were checked twice a month and reconciled at the end of each month.

Moreover, up to one-fifth of the intercompany invoices were uploaded to SAP in automated batches from integrated production/sales programs and checked by local sales managers and business controllers (Figure 3.2). When we analyzed my colleagues' complaints, we discovered that the External Service Provider teams in Asia and Poland handled different sub-tasks, each with an additional internal control setup. They never analyzed the entire process.

Therefore, instead of double checks, quadruple checks were performed in the case of intercompany accounts payable, but that only became visible when one person took control of the entire process and analyzed the process in detail in its entirety. Notably, although the External Service Provider teams performed these tasks, they alone cannot be blamed for the inefficiencies resulting from the setup. The internal control in force that demanded a 100 percent check of all outgoing payments, irrespective of their distinctive nature, was approved

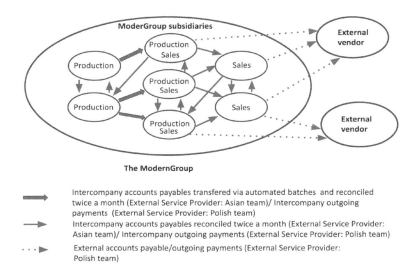

Figure 3.2   Intercompany accounts payable, outgoing intercompany payments, and outgoing payment

by ModernGroup, indicating the lost overview and control of the activities. Despite the initial demand to follow GPM without any alterations, this specific case was approved later by ModernGroup's internal auditors as one of the exceptions.

The follow-up conversation with the operating director occurred late in 2017, approximately 4.5 years after the backsourcing project, revealing two interesting aspects. First, he confirmed that despite the initial skepticism from the top management side, the in-house solution justified itself as being reliable and cost-efficient:

> This special in-house service contract still covers these 14 subsidiaries, and there are no intentions to change that. The in-house solution is working smoothly compared to the outsourcing contract, and the service is eight times cheaper.

However, besides significant cost efficiency, the in-house solution had another important impact on outsourced activities. Namely, it started to serve as a laboratory for the accounting at ModernGroup by providing an understanding of their activities and enabling them to develop these further without relying blindly on the external service provider:

> We have learned a lot from this in-house setup. We are better equipped to implement full automation to a part of our outsourced routines. I wouldn't say that without this internal cell, we wouldn't have moved on with automatization, but I can see how painful that could have been.

Therefore, additional merit of the in-house solution was the regained knowledge about their activities. The latter was necessary to develop services further and explain accounting processes to external auditors. The latter is vital for any listed company whose financial reports are under heightened scrutiny.

Implications for management practice in organizations

The described cases reveal several aspects of change and (dis)continuity that directly affect organizational management practices. There are two main learnings from the cases. First, outsourcing as discontinuing activities may require substantial changes in organizational structures, systems, and culture. Second, as with most strategies, outsourcing decisions could be a target of reconsideration and reversal. Therefore, it is advisable to consider the back-sourcing possibility as early as drafting the outsourcing contract. The need to reflect on a possible reversal stems from the fact that change and continuity at the organizational and activities level could have unexpected and unintentional outcomes that are hard to manage afterward. As a rule, an organization considering backsourcing is forced to deal with information asymmetries favoring the service provider (Ejodame and Oshri, 2018). Therefore, successful backsourcing requires collaboration with the outsourcing partner.

However, the outsourcing partner may lack any interest in collaborating when the client organization decides either not to extend the contract or terminate the contract prematurely. Resuming the continuity of activities in-house through backsourcing could become a highly challenging, if not impossible, project without support from the service provider. Therefore, it is advisable to include references to parties' expected behavior in the initial contract, including the copyright of documentation created during the outsourcing contract and principles of information sharing in the case of contract termination. The inability to resume the continuity of outsourced activities means that organization is unable to change its strategy and is forced to accept the path dependence as an ongoing continuity of lock-ins.

The fragmentation of activities introduced with outsourcing could cause inefficiency in processes. Unbundling interdependent activities, cutting them into fragmented subtasks, and selectively discontinuing performing some of them could cause the loss of the overview of the whole process. A lost overview of the process interconnections and interrelatedness leads to inefficiency (i.e. unnecessary internal controls). As the empirical examples indicate, the meaning and performance of the outsourced activities tend to change because of the detachment from their previous performance and the organizational background. Detaching the performance of activities from its "own 'parts' at some earlier point in time" (Shotter 2006: 591) cuts off activities' internal temporality, their extension or continuity in time. At the same time, the attentive performance of activities is dependent on their interplay with background knowledge (e.g. Ejodame and Oshri, 2018; Hernes, 2014; Schütz, 1967; Shotter, 2006) which is also dynamic and evolving, embedded in the continuously ongoing temporality of the organization. Because background knowledge is the ultimate source of intelligence and because of its continuously evolving nature, it is unreasonable to expect one-to-one transferability of activities in the case of backsourcing. Instead, resuming the continuity of once discontinued activities and reintegrating them back into the continuously evolving organizational setup requires paying close attention to the activities' nature and interdependences.

It is important to recognize that with outsourcing, the organization voluntarily gives away a part of its practice-based knowledge and procedural memory (Argote, 2013; Hernes, 2014; Orlikowski, 2002). In other words, by ceasing to perform outsourced activities, a company can hardly maintain its practice-based knowledge of these activities. Discontinuing performing outsourced activities implies that organizational meaning structures associated with these activities will change and likely disappear (Hernes, 2014). Therefore, discontinuity in performing outsourced activities may lead to forgetting (Argote, 2013) and cause an unintended change in the organization's temporal trajectory.

As a result of unbundling and outsourcing some of the activities, organizations may find themselves locked, either voluntarily or involuntarily, into the outsourcing partnership (Law, 2018). On the one hand, there could be significant costs related to outsourcing implementation, which makes it psychologically hard to reverse outsourcing. On the other hand, organizations have a narrower scope of actions, which translates to fewer competencies. According to Law (2018: 342), "Organizations are said to follow a path-dependent pattern whenever they are constrained to an increasingly narrow scope of actions and have no other alternative. This lock-in results from self-reinforcing mechanisms that foster the adoption of initially and potentially inefficient paths." In other words, the discontinuity of activities caused by outsourcing could lead to involuntary continuous continuity.

The backsourcing case highlights the interdependence of organizational activities and reveals that the endogenous change in performing activities influences the performance of other activities. Unbundling some activities and transferring them to another organization implies that their meaning changes according to the new organizational context and background knowledge. While guidelines and scripts could be valuable tools in presenting explicit knowledge and describing a current situation, they are insufficient for maintaining the ability to perform and sustain control over activities. From the control perspective, the outsourced activities, shaped by a new context, will create new temporal patterns, altering their performance and meaning. Scripted rules are neither able to restrict nor grasp this transformation. At the same time, the performance of activities loses its sensitivity toward the organizational whole. Therefore, the possibilities of finding innovative solutions tend to diminish when the performance of activities or subpart of activities is cut off from its context.

A theoretical contribution to organizational continuity and change

Change and continuity are not contradictory but complementary concepts, meaning maintaining continuity requires change, and change is both a prerequisite for and outcome of continuity. However, the complementarity between the two could lead to different forms of change and continuity. Not every change nor all continuity is necessarily planned or desired. On the one hand, continuous actions can unintentionally induce the emergence of new organizational paths without providing the ability to control those paths (Law, 2018). On the other hand, contingencies of the planned change could lead to an undesired path of ongoing continuity, allowing an organization to operate only within the scope of the imminent past and future, unable to break this pattern and shift its trajectory. As a result, ongoing continuity could lead to lock-ins. That kind of lock-in could happen as an unintended consequence of outsourcing.

On the one hand, outsourcing could require so expensive planned organizational change that turning it around may be perceived as a direct failure. On the other hand, the transfer of organizational competencies and knowledge base caused by outsourcing and accompanying organizational change in structures and personnel could be so deep that restoring activities in-house is challenging. It follows that while ongoing continuity is required to accumulate situational knowledge and understanding that enable organizational existence and persistence over time, it contains a risk of degrading into limited coping characterized by habitual, envisaged, and predictable performance lacking novelty.

To break involuntary ongoing continuity resulting from outsourcing requires breaking the short-term and closed orientation of activities with a narrow focus on the immediate past and future (Pulk, 2022) and recreating or resuming disrupted continuity (Ejodame and Oshri, 2018) of activities from a more distant past. Therefore, rather than discussing incorporating, using, or connecting the elements from past experiences (e.g. Schultz and Hernes 2013), the challenge is to resume or recreate the continuity of the activities we lack past experience with practical performance. Bringing outsourced activities back in-house requires competencies and knowledge to handle these activities, which are often lost in the initial outsourcing (Ejodame and Oshri, 2018). Attempting to recreate or resume continuity by connecting activities from a more distant past and future could be risky and entail uncertainty. While thinking about resuming the continuity of once-disrupted activities, we can imagine recreating the continuity of the once-disrupted temporal trajectory (Hernes et al., 2021). Recreating the continuity of a once-disrupted temporal trajectory allows us to view backsourcing as a path-breaking strategy (Law, 2018).

Besides a well-documented risk of outsourcing related knowledge and competence loss, the is also a need to "re-bundle" once "unbundled" activities with other ongoing activities and reintegrate them back to organizational meaning structures. It is unlikely that the operational context and organizational background to remain the same when some activities are unbundled and outsourced. The organizational background as a collection and combination of experiences, memories, knowledge, ideas, and beliefs evolves and becomes different. The remaining activities and their interdependencies are developing in their own way over time, meaning that reintegrating once outsourced activities require some change in their setup and performance. Therefore, resuming the continuity of specific activities is only a part of the challenge, while reintegrating the resumed continuity of activities into the evolved context is another (Ejodame and Oshri, 2018).

However, "re-bundling" will not likely happen without conscious effort, and it entails both a risk of failure and involves the possibility of novelty and innovation. The novelty and innovation could stem from external developments in the context, technology, or surrounding activities or from joining different timespans and connecting activities with the distant past to create a novel future.

Conclusion

While maintaining continuity requires change, change is both a prerequisite for and outcome of continuity. However, it is not necessarily self-evident what is changing and how or what continues. Instead, tracking both change and continuity requires close attention. Planned changes in organizational structures or used technologies could disrupt the continuity of activities or leave them unaffected. At the same time, an unplanned endogenous change could cause a significant change in performing activities without breaking activities' ongoing continuity. Continuity, in turn, could be either ongoing or resumed, desirable or undesirable, and could fuel change with various qualities like expected, favorable, unintentional, and disadvantageous. Notably, the dynamic and reciprocal relationship between change and continuity makes controlling and managing intra-organizational change and continuity challenging tasks.

References

Argote, L. (2013). *Organizational Learning: Creating, Retaining and Transferring Knowledge*, New York: Springer Science Business Media.

Bary, B. v., & Westner, M. (2018). Information systems backsourcing: a literature review, *Journal of Information Technology Management*, 29, 62–78.

Bhagwatwar, A., Hackney, R., & Desouza, K. C. (2011). Considerations for information systems "backsourcing": a framework for knowledge reintegration, *Information Systems Management*, 28(2), 165–73.

Contractor, F. J., Kumar, V., Kundu, S. K., & Pedersen, T. (2010). Reconceptualizing the firm in a world of outsourcing and offshoring: the organizational and geographical relocation of high-value company functions, *Journal of Management Studies*, 47(8), 1417–33, https://doi.org/10.1111/j.1467-6486.2010.00945.x.

Contractor, F. J., Kumar, V., Kundu, S. K., & Pedersen, T. (eds) (2011). *Outsourcing and Offshoring: An Integrated Approach to Theory and Corporate Strategy*, Cambridge: Cambridge University Press.

Dreyfus, H. L. (1991). *Being-in-the-World: A Commentary on Heidegger's Being and Time, Division I*, Cambridge, MA: The MIT Press.

Ejodame, K., & Oshri, I. (2018). Understanding knowledge re-integration in backsourcing, *Journal of Information Technology*, 33(2), 136–50, https://doi.org/10.1057/s41265-016-0007-5.

Freytag, P. V., Clarke, A. H., & Evald, M. R. (2012). Reconsidering outsourcing solutions, European Management Journal, 30(2), 99–110, https://doi.org/10.1016/j.emj.2011.11.002.

Grand View Research (2021). Business process outsourcing market size, share & trends analysis 2021–2028, https://www.grandviewresearch.com/industry-analysis/business-process-outsourcing-bpo-market (accessed 15 November 2021).

Handley, S. M. (2012). The perilous effects of capability loss on outsourcing management and performance, Journal of Operations Management, 30, 152–65.

Hernes, T. (2014). A Process Theory of Organization, Oxford: Oxford University Press.

Hernes, T. (2018). The surprising lack of change in continuity, the 34th EGOS Colloquium keynote speech, 4 July 2018, Tallinn, Estonia.

Hernes, T., Hussenot, A., & Pulk, K. (2021). Time and temporality of change processes: applying an event-based view to integrate episodic and continuous change, in M. S. Poole & A. Van de Ven (eds), The Oxford Handbook of Organizational Change and Innovation, 2nd edition (pp. 731–50), Oxford: Oxford University Press.

Hirschheim, R. (1998). Backsourcing: an emerging trend? Outsourcing Journal, September.

Hirschheim, R., Heinzl, A., & Dibbern, J. (eds) (2006). Enduring Themes, New Perspectives and Global Changes, 2nd edition, Berlin/Heidelberg: Springer-Verlag.

Kotlarsky, J., & Bognar, L. (2012). Understanding the process of backsourcing: two cases of process and product backsourcing in Europe, Journal of Information Technology Teaching Cases, 2, 79–86.

Lacity, M. C., Willcocks, L. P., & Rottman, J. W. (2008). Global outsourcing of back office services: lessons, trends and enduring challenges, Strategic Outsourcing: An International Journal, 1(1), 13–34.

Law, F. (2018). Breaking the outsourcing path: backsourcing process and outsourcing lock-in, European Management Journal, 36(3), 341–52, https://doi.org/10.1016/j.emj.2017.05.004.

Martin, J. (2009). Meta-theoretical controversies in studying organizational culture, in Christian Knudsen and Haridimos Tsoukas (eds), The Oxford Handbook of Organization Theory (pp. 392–420), Oxford: Oxford University Press.

Nagpal, P. (2015). Backsourcing: a review and theoretically motivated view, Academy of Information & Management Sciences Journal, 18(1), 53–8.

Orlikowski, W. (2002). Knowing in practice: enacting a collective capability in distributed organizing, Organization Science, 13(3), 249–73.

Oshri, I., Kotlarsky, J., & Willcocks, L. P. (2011). The Handbook of Global Outsourcing and Offshoring, 2nd edition, London: Macmillan.

Oshri, I., Sidhu, J. S., & Kotlarsky, J. (2019). East, west, would home really be best? On dissatisfaction with offshore-outsourcing and firms' inclination to backsource, Journal of Business Research, 103, 644–53, https://doi.org/10.1016/j.jbusres.2017.11.008.

Peck, J. (2017). Offshore: Exploring the Worlds of Global Outsourcing, Oxford: Oxford University Press.

Pentland, B., & Feldman, M. S. (2008). Reconceptualizing organizational routines as a source of flexibility and change, Administrative Science Quarterly, 48, 94–118.

Pettigrew, A. M. (1985). The Awakening Giant: Continuity and Change in Imperial Chemical Industries, Oxford: Basil Blackwell.

Pulk, K. (2010). Organisational Change Evaluated in Cultural Context: Business Process Outsourcing in Danfoss, Saarbrücken: LAMBERT Academic Publishing.

Pulk, K. (2016). Making time while being in time: a study of the temporality of organizational processes, PhD series, no. 43.2016, Copenhagen Business School, Frederiksberg.

Pulk, K. (2022). *Time and Temporality in Organizations: Theory and Development*, Cham: Palgrave Macmillan/Springer Nature.

Sako, M. (2010). Technology strategy and management outsourcing versus shared services, *Communications of the ACM*, 53(7), 27–9.

Saxena, K. B. C., & Bharadwaj, S. S. (2009). Managing business processes through outsourcing: a strategic partnership perspective, *Business Process Management*, 15(5), 687–715.

Schultz, M., & Hernes, T. (2013). A temporal perspective on organizational identity, *Organization Science*, 24(1), 1–21.

Schütz, A. (1967). *The Phenomenology of the Social World*, London: Heinemann Educational Books.

Shotter, J. (2006). Understanding process from within: an argument for 'withness'-thinking, *Organization Studies*, 27(4), 585–604.

Smith, M. E. (1982). The process of sociocultural continuity, *Current Antropology*, 23(2), 127–42.

Solli-Sæther, H., & Gottschalk, P. (2015). Stages of growth in outsourcing, offshoring and backsourcing: back to the future? *Journal of Computer Information Systems*, 55(2), 88–94.

Veltri, N. F., Saunders, C. S., & Kavan, C. B. (2008). Information systems backsourcing: correcting problems and responding to opportunities, *California Management Review*, 51(1), 50–76.

Weick, K. E., & Quinn, R. (1999). Organizational change and development, *Annual Review of Psychology*, 50, 361–86.

Wong, S. F. (2008). Drivers of IT backsourcing decision, *Communications of the IBIMA*, 2, 102–8.

4 Notes on continuity and change during innovation

Raghu Garud and Jacob A. Klopp

Introduction

Scholars across disciplines approach continuity and change in different ways. Within economic history, some use continuity and discontinuity as adverbs qualifying change, as in continuous or discontinuous change (Gerschenkron, 1962). Within technology studies, some view change as an evolutionary process with discontinuities punctuating continuous change (e.g. Tushman & Anderson, 1986). Within psychology, scholars have found that actors perceive changes when there are "just noticeable differences" in phenomena (e.g. Schiffman et al., 2014).[1] And, within sociology, some view change as shifts in ongoing taken-for-granted practices, mores, and norms (Powell & DiMaggio, 2012).

We approach continuity and change from the perspective of innovation studies wherein these concepts are central (e.g. Garud, Tuertscher, & Van de Ven, 2013). Innovation, the quest to create something novel with utility, is a distinguishing characteristic of human efforts. Consequently, the study of continuity and change through innovation has broad relevance to all domains of human activities, including those unfolding within organizations.

The core thesis that we develop in this chapter is that the meanings of continuity and change depend on the perspective with which one views innovation – *innovations as outcomes* or *the process of innovation*. Innovation as outcomes refers to an accomplished state, whereas the process of innovation refers to the steps leading to the outcome. To better understand the meanings of continuity and change for the actors involved from these perspectives, we examine episodes during the emergence of Post-it Notes at 3M. Thereafter, we summarize what we learned through second-order reflections where we also entertain thoughts on continuity and change from a third perspective: *innovation as process* (Garud, Gehman, Kumaraswamy, & Tuertscher, 2016). Innovation as process refers to ongoing meaning making around innovation as actors incorporate the past, present, and future through narratives. Then, we offer further abstractions through third-order reflections on the three different perspectives and their implications for gaining an understanding of continuity and change. In conclusion, we suggest that our theorization sets the stage for further exploration of these concepts in multiple settings.

Innovations as outcomes and the process of innovation

To understand innovations as outcomes, we begin with a working definition: innovation is novelty that can generate value in use. Viewed this way, innovations are novel objects[2] experienced as change by one or more sets of users. For instance, some users may find that Apple's latest operating system iOS 16 offers useful functionalities different from those offered by previous versions. For these users, the latest version will represent a change punctuating an earlier period of continuity. However, other users of iOS 16 may not call the latest version an innovation, finding no salient differences from previous versions. For these users, the earlier period of continuity persists.

In addition to innovations as outcomes are the processes underlying their emergence. A convenient way to understand the process of innovation is to consider innovations progressing through three periods: *ideation, implementation*, and *institutionalization* (3I) (Garud et al., 1997). Ideation refers to the emergence of novel ideas (inventions) around which some seek intellectual property protection. Implementation refers to all the activities that actors undertake to convert an idea into something of value to users. Institutionalization refers to the widespread diffusion of the innovation across multiple contexts of use. This model is based on an ordering of events across a linear progression of time; however, Garud et al. have considered the process of innovation as unfolding in complex ways, "characterized by multiple temporal rhythms and experiences rather than by a single linear conception of time" (2013: 793).

This 3I model is partially informed by literature on the social construction of technological systems (SCOT) (Bijker, Hughes, & Pinch, 1987). Scholars in this tradition draw attention to the roles that multiple actors play in shaping innovation based on their "frames of reference." The concept of frames of reference refers to the vantage points from which actors view innovations-in-the-making based on their prior experiences and future imaginaries. Relatedly, the SCOT literature offers the concept of "levels of inclusion," referring to the extent to which actors become entangled with phenomena as "insiders" and "outsiders" (Garud & Ahlstrom, 1997). A difference between the experiences of insiders from the experiences of outsiders is that moments of episodic discontinuities are triggered endogenously for the former and exogenously for the latter. Although some insiders may not perceive any change unfolding during their day-to-day activities (Garud & Ahlstrom, 1997), other insiders see their ongoing activities as giving rise to moments of episodic change (Garud & Turunen, 2021; Hernes, Hussenot, & Pulk, 2021; Van de Ven, 2021).

Drawing on the above insights, we use the 3I model to structure our inquiry on continuity and change during the emergence of a particular innovation considered a novel product when introduced – Post-it Notes. We use this model as a convenient way to describe what happened based on a linear view of time wherein Post-it Notes progressed from invention to implementation to institutionalization. We could have employed other views on time to describe what happened, such as event time, or narrative time experienced by the various actors. Our choice of the 3I model is deliberate; it provides a linear structure as a backdrop against which we can draw attention to other notions of time (and therefore notions of change and continuity) with which we engage in our second- and third-order abstractions.

Our analysis of the episodes underlying the emergence of Post-it Notes yields several insights. First, regarding *innovations as outcomes* punctuating moments of continuity, we unpack the ways that different actors saw or did not see novelty and value around Post-it Notes once completed as a product. Second, regarding *the process of innovation* progressing through three periods, we show proponents framing the innovation in-the-making in strategic ways to others in order to emphasize either continuity or change and the others expressing reactions ranging from indifference to active resistance. Third, in contrast to *innovations as outcomes* and *the process of innovation* views, we explicate another view of innovation to explain the case of Post-it Notes: *innovation as process*. With respect to the latter, actors are likely to "explore" new possibilities in the very act of "exploiting" old certainties (March, 1991) to the extent they can endogenize time through the cultivation of Kairotic (i.e. opportune) moments within an arch of time spanning the past, present and future, which we label as Aionic time (Garud & Turunen, 2021). For such actors, change is immanent in continuity, and vice versa.

The continuity and change dance during innovation

Based on multiple documented sources (e.g. Lindhal, 1988; Nayak & Ketteringham, 1986), the episodes we cover during the emergence of Post-it

Notes include: (1a) 3M's Spence Silver stumbling on a material with properties and functionalities antithetical to those he was looking for, (1b) successful efforts by 3M at gaining IP protection for Silver's invention, (2) 3M's efforts at prototyping and capability development, and (3) successful efforts by 3M to gain widespread acceptance for Post-it Notes.[3]

Episode 1a: ideation through serendipity

The origins of Post-it Notes can be traced to an experiment Spence Silver was conducting at 3M. In an interview with Lindahl, Silver noted:

> Well, I was doing some experiments with a new polymer system and I made this material and said, 'This is interesting.' When I looked at it under the microscope, it was beautiful! Little crystalline-like spheres. Clear polymer spheres that kind of sparkled in the light. The first time I saw it, I said, 'This has got to be something.'

According to Nayak and Ketteringham (1986), most at 3M would have disregarded the material that Silver had stumbled upon, with some even considering his experiment a failure. This was Silver's experience as well, who recounted:

> Then I started telling people about it. Anyone who would listen. Technical directors, other scientists, the tech group I was part of. For the most part, I didn't succeed at getting people excited about the adhesive. These people are busy. They're not just sitting around waiting for the wild-eyed scientists from Corporate Research to come in and say, 'Hey, I've got something really nifty. You should try it out.' I managed to get it into the labs, but it became a dead issue rather quickly. (In Lindhal, 1988)

This episode highlights actors experiencing the same phenomenon (the strange glue) in different ways. The substance that Silver had discovered was not salient to those who were immersed in their continuous flow of activities, and so was met with indifference (i.e. experienced as lack of change). However, for Silver, the discovery of the substance was a serendipitous moment with the potential to bring about unplanned change (see also Rauch & Ansari, 2021; Van de Ven, 2021 for notions of unplanned change).

Building on Merton and Barber (2011), by serendipity we mean actors finding something of value other than what they were looking for. Silver's discovery certainly qualifies as serendipitous (Garud, Gehman, & Giuliani, 2018). He was looking for a permanent adhesive, but instead discovered a substance that was impermanent, that is, a "glue that did not glue." When asked by Lindahl as to whether he considered his experiment a failure (given that he was trying to invent an adhesive that would bond permanently), Silver replied "No. Not at all. I have had arguments with people about this: They want to call it 'a mistake that worked.' I like to think of it as a solution that was looking for a problem to solve." In other words, by thinking of the substance he had stumbled on as a "solution looking for a problem," Silver kept open the possibility that the new substance could be useful even though he did not know which problem the substance he had stumbled upon could solve in the future. Bakken et al. (2013) associate such openness with "Series A" thinking where actors can play around with the past, present and future, which opens possibilities for imagination (see also Ellwood & Horner, 2020; McTaggart, 1908 for discussions on "Series A" and "Series B" events, the latter referring to the ordering of events in time).

Why did Silver see potential for change in the material that others barely noticed even when Silver brought it to their attention? We offer two explanations. First, Silver was a trained chemist. For instance, in Nayak and Ketteringham's (1986) *Breakthroughs!* (a book that featured 3M's Post-it Notes) Silver remarked:

> In the course of the exploration I tried an experiment with one of the monomers in which I wanted to see what would happen if I put a lot of it into the reaction mixture. Before we had used amounts that would correspond to conventional wisdom. The key to the Post-it adhesive was doing this experiment. If I had really seriously cracked the books and gone through the literature, I would have stopped. The literature was full of examples that said you can't do this.

Thus, this was in part a case of "chance favoring the prepared mind" (à la Louis Pasteur).

A second explanation is Silver's curiosity and his being open to surprises that led to "the prepared mind favoring chance" (Dunbar, 1999). Silver observed:

> People like myself get excited about looking for new properties in materials. I find that very satisfying, to perturb the structure slightly and just see what happens. I have a hard time talking people into doing that – people who are more highly trained. It's been my experience that people are reluctant just to try, to experiment – just to see what will happen! (From Nayak & Ketteringham, 1986: 57–8)

According to Schön (1983), being open to surprise is an important attribute of individuals who "reflect-in-action." Such individuals can engage in "acts of insight," which are based on novelty and change even as they engage in iterative "acts of skill" that actors may experience as continuity (Usher, 1954). Consequently, individuals who are open to surprise are more likely than the others to experience change within a stream of continuous activities. For such individuals, change is endogenous to ongoing practices.

To encourage such mindful engagement with work, the narratives of innovation that circulate throughout the company showcase a temporal structuring mechanism that allows 3M employees the use of 15 percent of their time to explore novel ideas (Bartel & Garud, 2008). One can view this mechanism as affording employees 15 percent of their worktime measured chronologically to explore. But our engagement with 3M suggests a different notion of time and events that we label as Kairotic moments: occasions when individuals serendipitously stumble upon ideas within a flow of ongoing activities (Garud, Gehman, & Kumaraswamy, 2011). Because of the institutionalization of this temporal structuring mechanism, individuals have the autonomy to experience change while carrying out their daily chores.[4]

Besides highlighting this temporal structuring mechanism that legitimizes productive deviations at 3M, narratives also serve as a way for actors to entertain broader arches of time involving the past, present, and future. Through these broader arches of time, narratives generate meaning for actors with the potential to disturb a sense of continuity (Ricœur, 1984). Specifically, it is through narrative time that memories, expectations, and attention are activated to create meanings. Such a view goes beyond operating "in time" to "time in us" (Sherover, 1986), wherein narration imbricates the past the present and the future into one totalizing meaningful whole. Although deeply meaningful, such temporal work is always a difficult and tenuous accomplishment, especially given intertextuality across narratives of multiple actors who also narrativize phenomena in interconnected, shifting, and sometimes contradictory ways.

Episode 1b: ideation and gaining IP protection

In the second episode, we recount what happened when 3M's attorney sought a patent for this strange glue. Patents not only protect the inventor from others who want to replicate the idea without permission, but also serve as markers of a person's creativity. As Silver noted, "That's a very singular event in a person's career, to get a patent."

But obtaining a patent is not an easy task. The applicants must convince the patent examiners that their inventions are novel, non-obvious, and have utility. Novelty implies change given continuity (the latter referred to as prior art, which is established in the form of citations to other patents from the past). Moreover, the invention should not be obvious to those who are similarly trained in the domain (i.e. the category) within which the patent is being sought. Finally, utility refers to the value that the invention may have in use, which in the case of the strange glue, was difficult to fathom when discovered.

We don't have all the details of the negotiations that must have unfolded between the patent lawyers at 3M and the patent examiners, and therefore rely on what Silver had this to say – "It was really tough getting a patent for the microsphere adhesive. We had trouble convincing the examiner that what we had was novel. He rejected our application twice. The second one came back stamped: 'THIS REJECTION IS FINAL,' in capital letters."

Again, we can see that the same phenomenon was experienced differently by various actors. Some, such as Silver, saw change, while others, such as patent examiners, continuity. However, this episode goes beyond reconfirming our first view on continuity and change (i.e. the heterogeneity of responses to continuity and change). The additional insight is that actors such as Silver may frame a phenomenon in terms of change, whereas others such as the patent examiners will challenge such claims by framing them as continuity. In this regard, we see that continuity and change are negotiated outcomes (see also Sonenshein, 2010). As Silver recounted:

> I told our attorney, Walt Kern, 'I know this is new. I've never seen anything like this before. We're just not convincing this examiner about what's going on.' So Walt picked up the phone and said, 'We're gonna call the examiner, Spence. Be ready to answer any questions he might have.' I was really nervous.

Eventually, Silver prevailed, and he was able to convince the examiner that the substance was indeed novel and ought to be considered as change: "When we talked about the invention – with plenty of questions and answers – we were able to make our position much clearer. He agreed we had a patentable invention and allowed the case."

This episode shows that the proponents and the claimants of change must work hard to accomplish their goals, especially when they encounter resistance and challenges. The work involved is evident when it comes to seeking patent rights. To claim novelty given prior art requires actors to frame a phenomenon in such a way that it lies within evaluators' consideration set and yet is considered distinctive by the latter. If the phenomenon is completely within a knowledge structure of the categories that already exist, then it will not be considered novel by the examiner. Paradoxically, if it lies completely outside, it may not be recognizable. It is in the straddling of the known and the unknown (i.e. an optimal positioning strategy) that novelty claims may be made. Presenting a phenomenon to audiences in a way that it straddles what they know and what they do not requires considerable work, as was the case with the glue that did not glue.

Episode 2: implementation

Inventions, by their very nature, are "hopeful monstrosities" (Goldschmidt, 1940; Mokyr, 1990). They are monstrosities because they have yet to be developed and are not easily recognizable by audiences. They are hopeful because they may be valuable in the future for their utility to users because of their functionality and their aesthetic qualities.

Silver's glue that did not glue was one such hopeful monstrosity. It was a glue with functions antithetical to the ones 3M employees were accustomed. Yet, Silver was hopeful that it could serve as a solution to some unknown problem. Indeed, this glue captures what Bacon said many years ago:

> As the births of living creatures at first are ill-shapen, so are all innovations, which are the births of time … . It were good therefore, that men in their innovations would follow the example of time itself; which indeed innovateth greatly, but quietly, by degrees scarce to be perceived. (1765: 479)

To transform Silver's "caterpillar into a butterfly," several experiments unfolded within 3M, of which one involved the application of the strange glue on boards onto which paper could be stuck. This effort was not successful. Our speculation is that, besides paper, other materials would have stuck to the glue on the board. Furthermore, the stickiness of the glue would have worn out over time, thereby depreciating the value of the product. In any case, this "gluey board" idea was not scaled up.

The experimentation with the board falls within a process dynamic labeled as prototyping (Thomke, 2003). Prototyping is a flow of activities wherein artifacts and identities are materialized even if temporarily. With respect to the gluey board, we can well imagine the excitement of the actors at the prospect of identifying a use for the glue when applied on boards. We can also imagine the potential disappointment of those involved when they realized that their gluey board would not generate the revenue stream 3M required for its businesses. In any case, by abandoning the idea of the gluey board, the additional value of the board in the service of such a product did not materialize.

Irrespective of whether a prototype is successful, prototyping is an activity that makes it possible for multiple actors to collaborate with one another, and in the process reflect-in-action, experiencing both continuity (working with earlier ideas and artifacts) and change (trying out new ideas and artifacts). It is through such collective reflection in action that the actors can identify some possibilities while foreclosing others (Boland & Collopy, 2004; Buchheit, 2009; Usher, 1954). Even if some success criterion is used to evaluate prototypes, as in a stage-gate model (Cooper, 2008), the lack of success of a particular proto-type (as was the case with the gluey board) or even an outcome that is consid-ered a failure could still be considered valuable by the actors to the extent that innovation is viewed in processual terms.

Appreciating the possibility that many ideas will not make it immediately, 3M allows its employees to keep potentially valuable ideas alive, as was the case with the Post-it Notes. Driven by Silver's tenacity, and in combination with colleagues' heedfulness, another moment of serendipity occurred five years after the discovery of the strange glue. Rather than the discovery of the glue, this time, however, a use for the strange glue was identified. At church choir practice, upon losing his paper marker in his hymn book, Fry suddenly remembered his colleague's glue and wondered about its utility as a place marker.

Fry's identification of a use for this glue highlights the links between atten-tion, memory, and anticipation inherent in the continuity-change dynamics of innovation as process. Specifically, Fry was able to remember relevant facets of his past (i.e. Silver's impermanent glue) to imagine a future solution (a place marker) to address a problem that he was confronting in the present (loose scraps of paper used as place markers). Elsewhere, we have discussed how narratives interrelate the past, present, and future (Garud et al., 2018). Here, we note that this view of time speaks to how continuity and change are interconnected. Continuity here aligns with the term's origins in the Latin word "continuāre" (Chambers, 1988), and means the joining together of prior phenomena with future possibilities in the service of innovation.[5]

We have labeled Fry's act as Type 2 serendipity, that is, one that involves finding a use for a substance through "exaptation" (that is, finding function-alities for existing phenomena) (Gould & Vrba, 1982) in contrast to Type 1 serendipity, which has to do with the discovery of materials (Garud et al., 2018). To go back to Silver's original discovery, Fry had identified a problem for which the glue would serve as a solution. Acknowledging Fry's role, Silver noted: "The discovery sort of starts the ball rolling. There are so many hoops that a product idea has to jump through. It really takes a bunch of individuals to carry it through the process. It's not just a Spence Silver or an Art Fry. It's a whole host of people."

The "ball" in this case (i.e. the glue that did not glue) serves as a "boundary object" (Star & Griesemer, 1989). A boundary object is stable enough to make it possible for different social groups to engage in a project, yet plastic enough for them to apply their specific ways of knowing (for example, maps and Excel spreadsheets can serve as boundary objects). Consequently, this boundary-spanning work implicates both continuity and change simultaneously.

Nicolini, Mengis, and Swan (2012) noted that boundary objects motivate collaboration, allow participants to work across different types of boundaries (Carlile, 2002), and constitute the fundamental infrastructure for the activities that unfold. The glue that did not glue certainly served these purposes. The substance was coherent enough to pique the interests of a variety of social groups, yet plastic enough to afford interpretive flexibility (Pinch & Bijker, 1987) (e.g. its application on bulletin boards and eventually on paper).

However, unlike traditional boundary objects such as maps or Excel spreadsheets, the ball (i.e. the innovation) itself continued changing. As it progressed from its early manifestation (a hopeful monstrosity) to its later incarnations (hopeful debutants), the challenges encountered by its proponents required additional innovations. For instance, besides Silver and Fry, 3M's Courtney and Miller invented a way to ensure that the glue would remain on the Post-it Note surface and not peel off onto the surface on which the Post-it Note was used as a marker. Additionally, there were others who modified 3M's manufacturing capabilities to facilitate the mass production of paper with glue applied on one side.[6] Art Fry offered this observation as to how the whole of 3M served as an experimental playground:

> At 3M we've got so many different types of technology operating and so many experts and so much equipment scattered here and there, that we can piece things together when we're starting off. We can go to this place and do "Step A" on a product, and we can make the adhesive and some of the raw materials here, and do one part over here, and another part over there, and convert a space there and make a few things that aren't available. (From Nayak & Ketteringham, 1986: 66–7)

Before proceeding on to the next episode, we first summarize what we can learn about continuity and change. First, as in the earlier episodes, this episode too confirms the presence of multiple actors, each experiencing continuity and change in different ways. Second, we see that the implementation of innovation involves considerable trial-and-error through prototyping. Prototyping is one way to benefit from the generative dance between "knowledge as possession" and "knowing in practice," each shaping the other as the process unfolds (Cook & Brown, 1999). Both continuity and change are involved in these processes.

Episode 3: institutionalizing the innovation

Now that the product had been designed, and manufacturing capabilities were in place, one would have thought that Post-it Notes would have taken off. But this was not the case. Despite considerable progress with the design of the product and with manufacturing capabilities, users did not readily embrace the product.

Whereas the challenge during ideation is for individuals to perceive change and then convince others that such "change" is worth pursuing, the challenge during institutionalization is to bring about stability and closure. To accomplish the latter, the promoters of innovations (as outcomes) may frame them as if they were continuations of earlier practices. As an example, Edison introduced his electric lighting system as if it was a continuation of earlier gas lighting practices (see Hargadon & Douglas, 2001). He did so to overcome the lack of legitimacy that innovations suffer with users.

Although the practice of writing notes preceded the Post-it Note, the situation with Post-it Notes was different from the one that Edison confronted. The use of Post-it Notes was not replacing a deeply entrenched practice (such as the use of gas lighting). Instead, the use of Post-it Notes would initiate a new practice (i.e. posting notes onto a page or a surface) to the extent that users became habituated to the product. In academic parlance, such goods are known as "experience goods" (Nelson, 1974), where preferences emerge or are revealed in and through use. Trying to promote such products as commodities for which preferences have already formed (i.e. search goods) is problematic.

Those promoting Post-it Notes first encountered this problem within 3M. Unable to gain the attention of those in the marketing department, advocates of Post-it Notes decided to leave behind samples with top management secretaries with instructions on how to use the product. As 3M executives became "addicted" to Post-it Notes, they began asking for more samples from their secretaries. However, when the secretaries requested more samples, the promoters of the product asked them to redirect their request to the marketing department, thereby catching their attention. In sum, those who wanted to make Post-it Notes a reality familiarized others within 3M who were unfamiliar with the product through demonstration and by facilitating their experiential use of the product.

Eventually, those in the marketing department began promoting the product. But how does one communicate the utility of a new-to-the-world product to potential users who have never used it before? Today, Post-it Notes' functionalities are well known, and users can search for the product to suit their purposes. However, this was not the case at that time.

3M's Nicholson, now a supporter of the Post-it Notes, was able to entice his boss, Ramey, to visit Richmond with him. There, they left behind samples with potential users with instructions as to how the products could be used. At the same time, 3M's CEO sent out samples to the CEOs of other corporations along with instructions on how they were to be used. Once again, the product became a part of users' daily practices, leading them to request more samples. In this way, the use of Post-it Notes became widespread across the corporate world.

How does this episode inform us about continuity and change? Post-it Notes falls within a class of products that neither disrupts nor sustains existing practices of users (see Christensen 1997 for these distinctions). As a need for Post-it Notes did not pre-exist, the product did not trigger users' attention when first introduced. In such instances, not only must users form new cognitive schemas around the innovation to become familiarized, but also understand its utility through use. Consequently, those promoting such products must establish both cognitive and pragmatic legitimacy (Aldrich & Fiol, 1994; Suchman, 1995). That is, change for users happens gradually as they become habituated to a new set of practices.

Second-order ruminations

What can we learn about continuity and change from these episodes? To address this question, we revisit the distinction we offered in the introduction of this chapter between *innovations as outcomes* and *the process of innovation*. After investigating continuity and change from these perspectives, we then turn to the third perspective evident in the episodes: *innovation as process*. By *innovation as process*, we mean that innovation is inherent in any process, especially to the extent that actors entertain a temporal perspective that is open to serendipitous discoveries within a larger arch of time with which to endow these discoveries with meaning.

Innovations as outcomes

One way to view Post-it Notes is as an innovative outcome once it had gained wide-spread acceptance by users after its introduction in the marketplace. Typically, scholars tend to categorize innovations as outcomes based on the type of change, the degree of change, and their impacts. With respect to the type of change, Post-it Notes was a product innovation as opposed to a process, service, or business model innovation. With respect to the degree of change, one could categorize the product as a radical innovation, because nothing like it had existed before. With respect to its impact, many may consider it a "mundane" innovation delighting users.

Irrespective of how we classify innovations as outcomes, these efforts tend to assume a fundamental stability against which innovation brings about change that is foregrounded in clear and recognizable ways. This way of thinking is consistent with an "entitative" view (Rescher, 1996), in which artifacts have certain features and actors have enduring identities. From an entitative way of thinking, innovation implies a change in the features of artifacts and in the identities of the people involved. Engendering such change is difficult, as actors encounter inertia and resistance that arise from a given backdrop of continuity upon which innovation unfolds.

Research taking such an entitative perspective on innovation tends to produce synoptic accounts of change wherein phenomena exist in different states at different points in time (Tsoukas & Chia, 2002: 570; see also Romanelli & Tushman, 1994 for punctuated equilibrium change and Weick & Quinn, 1999 for episodic change). Even from a synoptic view, however, there can be product extensions as in the case of Post-it Notes. 3M has continued making changes to Post-it Notes over the decades. Some new products are based on resizing the Post-it Notes. Others are based on digitalization (e.g. digital Post-it Notes). Those who ask if these products are "true" innovations, and whether these products have any connections with the first Post-it Notes only reinforce the point we have been trying to make and which we address in detail in the next section: changes to and continuity of phenomena are framed by some actors, and these efforts are accepted, ignored, or challenged by others.

The process of innovation

The view of innovations as outcomes tends to obscure the process of innovation. The process of innovation, based on Series B (Bakken, Holt & Zundel, 2013; Ellwood & Horner, 2020) (such as ideation, implementation, and institutionalization), is a messy one with ups and downs, false starts, and dead ends (Coyne, 1999; Van de Ven et al., 1999). The episodes of ideation, implementation, and institutionalization during the emergence of Post-it Notes highlight different people becoming involved with the process at different stages of its journey, each experiencing continuity and change in different ways, with some framing the phenomenon for strategic purposes. The episodes we recounted here in conjunction with the insights derived from other cases suggests a pattern that we summarize below.

During ideation, insiders (i.e. those who engage with the phenomenon in the making) who are "prepared" and "open to surprise" are likely to experience change inherent in continuity. Others who are outsiders, unprepared, or not open to surprise, may not experience such change inherent in continuity. As in the Post-it Notes case, there is a possibility that the latter group of people may completely ignore phenomena considered novel by the insiders. Alternatively, the outsiders may be threatened by novel phenomena if they have the potential to disrupt their practices. Furthermore, there are those such as patent examiners who will challenge novelty claims, as the successful defense of patent claims has economic consequences.

During implementation, actors' attention shifts to prototyping and capability development in areas such as manufacturing and marketing. Each practice (i.e. prototyping, manufacturing, marketing) is a bundle of routines interconnected with others. Consequently, changes in one set of practices hold implications for the others. Furthermore, these interconnections continue to bring multiple parties into contact, each bringing their experiences of change and continuity to bear on the phenomenon.

During institutionalization, we move from ideation and implementation to largescale use. Post-it Notes, when introduced, was an example of an innovation that did not replace users' earlier practices. For such "hopeful debutants," users must use the product to experience its utility. In other words, users' preferences emerge in and through use, and as they become habituated to the product.[7]

Innovation as process

Perspectives on *innovations as outcomes* and *the process of innovation* are unable to capture the "ongoingness" of innovation in everyday life. A view of innovation ongoing in everyday practices is consistent with "process metaphysics" (Rescher, 1996) where everything is in flux, and experiences of "novelty" are materialized along the way as phenomena become entangled (Barad, 2003). The challenge here is different from the one associated with entitative thinking. Specifically, given the ongoing flow of process, some stabilization of phenomena must be accomplished, even if provisional.

Research taking a processual view tends to produce performative accounts of change. This means that change is viewed as an ongoing performance and is revealed through insight into its actual emergence and accomplishment (Tsoukas & Chia, 2002). Such models deal with change by engaging with the complex networks of material and temporal relations among actors and, therefore, highlight the instability associated with change.

Along these lines, our efforts to gain an understanding of the relationship between continuity and change generated a third finding – that change is ongoing within a stream of continuous ongoing activities (the iterational element of temporal agency in Emirbayer & Mische, 1998). Supporting this position are the numerous incidents recounted in the narratives of innovation circulating within 3M when acts of insight (exploration) emerged even as actors engaged in acts of skill (exploitation) (Bartel & Garud, 2008).

In certain organizations, exploration unfolds within parts of the organization separated from mainstream operations designed around exploitation (Smith & Alexander, 1988). However, in organizations such as 3M, employees generate novel ideas all over the organization even as they go about their daily work (see also March, 1982 where he highlights that change happens as people go about their business). This is partly because of 3M's 15 percent temporal structuring mechanism. For instance, Silver and Fry reported how they initially took advantage of this facility to ideate, incubate, and cultivate the strange glue even as they went about their daily activities. Additionally, over the Post-it Notes' 12-year journey, Silver and Fry were also able to draw on the 15 percent discretionary time of other 3M employees who were willing to explore possibilities with the strange glue. In other words, 3M's temporal structuring mechanism (along with a dictum at 3M that "technology belongs to the organization") makes it possible for novel ideas from one stream of activities within the company to interconnect with ideas from other streams thereby embodying continuity and change.

It is important to note that the whole process, from the discovery of the strange glue to its commercialization, took over 12 years. Reminiscing about the process, Silver noted "It was more like a slow crescendo of things, which is typical of the discovery process. Things build up and you begin to see the options that this discovery creates." Understanding the value of real options, the whole company is organized as a "real-options" generator, where ideas and activities with potential are neither abandoned nor scaled up prematurely, but instead kept alive for future activation and reconfiguration.

In such a view, there will be ups and downs, false starts, and dead ends, which are all a part of "becoming." As a result, there will be ideas that will not make it in real time (such as the gluey board) but may influence other ideas over time

(Post-it Boards today). Usher's (1954: 70) observations are of relevance here. He noted:

> Failures are thus of explicit historical importance. They are not solutions, but they are not without relation to a solution. They reveal explicit consciousness of the potentialities of some new mode of action, or of some new contrivance. They are evidence of the emergence of tensions and strivings that are likely to result in a positive achievement, even if it be long postponed and realized only a generation or more after the earliest recognizable emergence of the new objective.

In other words, innovation as an integral part of process reminds us to go beyond a linear view of time and therefore beyond a view of continuity and change as contradictions. Instead, change is continuous. Even a non-success in real time can become a blockbuster later. Echoing these sentiments, Steve Jobs noted "You can only connect the dots looking backwards."[8] Here, change being continuous means that the "dots" are connected and reconnected by actors in an ongoing manner as they make meaning of their experience. This is how it is possible for a "useless discovery" (e.g. a glue that does not glue) to become an "impactful innovation" (e.g. a Post-it Note).

But how can one connect the dots looking backwards? Is there not a "retrospective fallacy" which leads to the imposition of stages and phases? If we take a representational view, then the answer to the latter question is perhaps yes. However, if we take a performative view, then "looking backwards to go forwards" falls into the realm of meaning making through temporal agency (Garud, Kumaraswamy & Karnøe, 2010; Saylors, Lahiri, Warnick, & Baid, 2021; Schultz & Hernes, 2014). Accordingly, the dots that we connect are based not only on memory, but also anticipation, and recognition.

Third-order abstractions

Table 4.1 is an attempt on our part to offer thoughts at a higher level of abstraction. We have taken the liberty to build in additional ideas from the literature on innovation. We offer this quilt work of ideas on continuity and change not to settle any debate, but instead to foster one.

Table 4.1   Continuity and change based on innovations as outcomes, the process of innovation, and innovation as process

	Innovations as outcomes	The process of innovation	Innovation as process
Metatheoretical orientations	Events as entitative shifts	Processual understanding of events as sequences	Processual experiencing of events as constitutive of phenomena
Orienting concepts	Different kinds of innovations as outcomes of a process, e.g. radical or incremental innovations	Innovation in stages such as ideation, implementation, and institutionalization	Innovation as ongoing, meaning making, performativity
Relationality	Context is given, generating resistance to change	Context is emergent through the sayings and doings of actors as an innovation journey unfolds	Actors contextualize through narratives
Temporality	Largely based on Chronos	Chronos and Kairos	Chronos, Kairos, and Aion
Continuity & change	Moments of change punctuating continuity	Continuity and change experienced and framed differently by multiple actors	Continuity and change entangled with one another

Across the columns in the table are the three perspectives that we examined: *innovations as outcomes*, *the process of innovation*, and *innovation as process*. The orienting concepts within the *innovations as outcomes* perspective are "typologies of innovations" such as radical or incremental innovations. Given an entitative orientation, existing structures present themselves as exogenous contexts generating forces impeding change to further continuity. Based largely on chronological notions of time, continuity is punctuated by moments of change.

The *process of innovation* perspective considers novel phenomena unfolding across phases and stages such as ideation, implementation, and institutionalization. Context is emergent and in-the-making through the sayings and doings of multiple actors who experience, frame, and manage continuity and change in heterogeneous ways across these three temporally bracketed periods.

Besides chronological notions of time, Kairos also plays a role. Kairotic moments are events experienced by those who are "fortunate" because they have a "prepared mind."

Innovation as process is based on a perspective where continuity and change are entangled (Garud & Turunen, 2021; Hernes, 2014; Tsoukas & Chia, 2002). In other words, change occurs continually through the performativity of iterational practices, and continuities are changed through narrative meaning making as actors continue "connecting the dots," both old and new ones. This implies that continuity and change can always be seen inside one another, and the degree to which one is salient over the other depends on actors' frames of reference, levels of inclusion, and temporal orientations. Temporal orientation is of special importance here. To generate meaning, actors operate in time by melding the past, present, and future through narratives (Ricœur, 1984). Narratives transcend linear chronological (Chronos-based) notions of time or liminal Kairotic (Kairos-based) notions of time by including Aionic time, which references Aion, a third Greek God of time. Aionic time orients actors toward a temporal trajectory involving anticipation (present-future), memory (present-past), and attention (present-present) (Ricœur, 1984) with which to make meaning around Kairotic moments of serendipity that can arise even within chronologically entrained processes (Garud & Turunen, 2021). Here, "the prepared mind favors chance" (Dunbar, 1999). Like Silver, these are "playful" individuals (Gadamer, 2013; Schrage, 1999) who actively cultivate the "technology of foolishness" (March, 1982) by purposely going beyond reason, and in doing so suspend clock time to generate Kairotic moments.

Conclusion

By identifying different conceptions of continuity and change when approached from innovation, our ruminations have opened Pandora's box. How continuity and change are experienced, framed, and managed depend not only on the scholarly disciplines from which we view these constructs, but also on actors' metatheoretical assumptions – whether entitative or processual, and with respect to the latter, whether actors follow the process of innovation or innovation as process. After all the evils have emerged from Pandora's box, hope remains. Our hope is that readers will see continuity and change as idiographic concepts rendered meaningful through the ongoing and innovative performances of day-to-day activities.[9]

Notes

1. We use the term phenomena because: (a) the term innovation is applied broadly (e.g. products services, business models) and (b) it conceptualizes innovations as sociomaterial entanglements.

2. We use the term "objects" broadly to refer to phenomena in general including products, artifacts, software, etc.

3. Actors navigating their worlds-in-the-making may not explicitly think in terms of continuity and change. Yet, whether actors experience continuity and/or change can be inferred contextually.

4. See also Hernes (2014) and Orlikowski and Yates (2002) for additional insights on temporal structuring in organizations.

5. We thank Tor Hernes and Miriam Feuls for suggesting this connection between continuity and change in their call for book chapters.

6. The cumulative synthesis of the small changes made it possible to experience the innovation as ongoing and continuous from the inside but as change from the outside.

7. This process stands in contrast to the Edison case that we offered previously. In the latter, the new electric lighting system could have been considered disruptive by users as they were accustomed to an alternative gas lighting system. A challenge for innovators in such cases is to frame the innovation in such a way that that it is perceived by users to fall partially within their existing schemas, while being persuaded to try out the new functionalities offered by the innovation (see Hargadon & Douglas, 2001).

8. Jobs offered this observation during a convocation address at Stanford based on his own temporal experiences with process as innovation. Paraphrasing him, Jobs engaged in multiple activities including cursive writing, the benefits from which became abundantly clear later when he and his colleagues were designing the Mac. Moreover, Jobs noted that the non-successes that he experienced in real time played a role in the successes over time.

9. We are grateful to Miriam Feuls and Tor Hernes for their inputs on earlier versions of this chapter. We thank Joel Gehman, Arun Kumaraswamy, Philipp Tuertscher, Marja Turunen and Andy Van de Ven for the many conversations we have had with them on topics that are relevant to this chapter. We dedicate this chapter to Andy who passed in 2022. Though he is no more, his ideas continue informing scholars of continuity and change.

References

Aldrich, H. E., & Fiol, C. M. (1994). Fools rush in? The institutional context of industry creation, *Academy of Management Review*, 19(4), 645–70.

Bakken, T., Holt, R., & Zundel, M. (2013). Time and play in management practice: an investigation through the philosophies of McTaggart and Heidegger, *Scandinavian Journal of Management*, 29(1), 13–22.

Bacon, F. (1765). Of innovation, in *The Works of Francis Bacon, Baron of Verulam, Viscount St. Alban, and Lord High Chancellor of England* (5 vols), vol. 1, London: A. Millar in the Strand.

Barad, K. (2003). Posthumanist performativity: toward an understanding of how matter comes to matter, *Signs*, 28, 801–31, http://dx.doi.org/10.1086/345321.

Bartel, C., & Garud, R. (2008). The role of narratives in sustaining organizational innovation, *Organization Science*, 20(1), 107–17.

Bijker, W. E., Hughes, T. P., & Pinch, T. (1987). *The Social Construction of Technological Systems*, Cambridge, MA: MIT Press.

Boland, R., & Collopy, F. (eds) (2004). *Managing as Designing*, Stanford, CA: Stanford Business Books.

Buchheit, P. (2009). Communicating with code, available at http:// paulbuchheit .blogspot.com/2009/01/communicating-with-code.html (accessed 10 January 2010).

Carlile, P. R. (2002). A pragmatic view of knowledge and boundaries: boundary objects in new product development, *Organization Science*, 13(4), 442–55.

Chambers (1988). Continuously, in C. Schwarz et al. (eds), *Chambers English Dictionary*, Cambridge: Chambers.

Christensen, C. M. (1997). *The Innovator's Dilemma: When New Technologies Cause Great Firms to Fail*, Boston, MA: Harvard Business Review Press.

Cook, S. D., & Brown, J. S. (1999). Bridging epistemologies: the generative dance between organizational knowledge and organizational knowing, *Organization Science*, 10(4), 381–400.

Cooper, R. G. (2008). Perspective: the stage-gate® idea-to-launch process—update, what's new, and nexgen systems, *Journal of Product Innovation Management*, 25(3), 213–32.

Coyne, W. E. (1999). Foreword, in A. H. Van de Ven, D. E. Polley, R. Garud, & S. Venkataraman (eds), *The Innovation Journey* (pp. vii–viii), New York: Oxford University Press.

Dunbar, K. (1999). How scientists build models in vivo science as a window on the scientific mind, in *Model-based Reasoning in Scientific Discovery* (pp. 85–99), Boston, MA: Springer.

Ellwood, P., & Horner, S. (2020). In search of lost time: the temporal construction of innovation management, *R&D Management*, 50(3), 364–79.

Emirbayer, M., & Mische, A. (1998). What is agency? *American Journal of Sociology*, 103(4), 962–1023.

Gadamer, H. G. (2013). *Truth and Method*, London: Bloomsbury.

Garud, R., & Ahlstrom, D. (1997). Technology assessment: a socio-cognitive perspective, *Journal of Engineering and Technology Management*, 14, 25–48.

Garud, R., Gehman, J., & Giuliani, A. (2018). Serendipity arrangements for exapting science-based innovations, *Academy of Management Perspectives*, 32(1), 125–40.

Garud, R., Gehman, J., & Kumaraswamy, A. (2011). Complexity arrangements for sustaining innovation: lessons from 3M Corporation, *Organization Studies*, 32(6), 737–67.

Garud, R., Gehman, J., Kumaraswamy, A., & Tuertscher, P. (2016). From the process of innovation to innovation as process, in A. Langley & H. Tsoukas (eds), *The SAGE Handbook of Process Organization Studies* (pp. 451–66), Thousand Oaks, CA: Sage.

Garud, R., Kumaraswamy, A., & Karnøe, P. (2010). Path dependence or path creation? *Journal of Management Studies*, 47(4), 760–74.

Garud, R., Nayyar, P., & Shapira, Z. (1997). Technological choices and the inevitability of errors, in R. Garud, P. Nayyar & Z. Shapira (eds), *Technological Innovation: Oversights and Foresights* (pp. 345–54), Cambridge: Cambridge University Press.

Garud, R., Tuertscher, P., & Van de Ven, A. H. (2013). Perspectives on innovation processes, *Academy of Management Annals*, 7(1), 773–817.

Garud, R., & Turunen, M. (2021). Microfoundation of innovation as process: Usher's cumulative synthesis model, in M. S. Poole & A. Van de Ven (eds), *The Oxford Handbook of Organizational Change and Innovation* (pp. 583–610), Oxford: Oxford University Press.

Gerschenkron, A. (1962). Economic backwardness in historical perspective, in N. Barma & S. K. Vogel (eds), *The Political Economy Reader: Markets as Institutions* (pp. 211–28), London: Routledge.

Goldschmidt, R. (1940). *The Material Basis of Evolution*, New Haven, CT: Yale University Press.

Gould, S. J., & Vrba, E. S. (1982). Exaptation: a missing term in the science of form, *Paleobiology*, 8, 4–15.

Hargadon, A. B., & Douglas, Y. (2001). When innovations meet institutions: Edison and the design of the electric light, *Administrative Science Quarterly*, 46(3), 476–501.

Hernes, T. (2014). *A Process Theory of Organization*, Oxford: Oxford University Press.

Hernes, T., Hussenot, A., & Pulk, K. (2021). Time and temporality of change processes: applying an event-based view to integrate episodic and continuous change, in M. S. Poole & A. Van de Ven (eds), *The Oxford Handbook of Organizational Change and Innovation* (pp. 731–50), Oxford: Oxford University Press.

Lindhal, L. (1988). Spence Silver: a scholar and a gentleman, *3M Today*, January, 15(1), 12–17.

March, J. G. (1981). Footnotes to organizational change, *Administrative Science Quarterly*, 26(4), 563–77.

March, J. G. (1982). The technology of foolishness, in J. G. March & J. P. Olsen (eds), *Ambiguity and Choice in Organizations* (pp. 69–81), Bergen: Universitetsforlaget.

March, J. G. (1991). Exploration and exploitation in organizational learning, *Organization Science*, 2(1), 71–87.

McTaggart, J. E. (1908). The unreality of time, *Mind*, 17(68), 457–74.

Merton, R. K., & Barber, E. (2011). *The Travels and Adventures of Serendipity*, Princeton, NJ: Princeton University Press.

Mokyr, J. (1990). Punctuated equilibria and technological progress, *American Economic Review*, 80(2), 350–54.

Nayak, P. R., & Ketteringham, J. M. (1986). *Breakthroughs!* New York: Rawson Associates.

Nelson, P. (1974). Advertising as information, *Journal of Political Economy*, 82(4), 729–54.

Nicolini, D., Mengis, J., & Swan, J. (2012). Understanding the role of objects in cross-disciplinary collaboration, *Organization Science*, 23(3), 612–29.

Orlikowski, W. J., & Yates, J. (2002). It's about time: temporal structuring in organizations, *Organization Science*, 13(6), 684–700.

Pinch, T. J., & Bijker, W. E. (1987). The social construction of facts and artifacts: or how the sociology of science and the sociology of technology might benefit each other, in W. E. Bijker, T. P. Hughes, & T. J. Pinch (eds), *Social Construction of Technological Systems* (pp. 17–50), Cambridge, MA: MIT Press.

Powell, W. W., & DiMaggio, P. J. (eds) (2012). *The New Institutionalism in Organizational Analysis* Chicago, IL: University of Chicago Press.

Rauch, M., & Ansari, S. (2021). From 'publish or perish' to societal impact: organisational repurposing towards responsible innovation through creating a medical platform, *Journal of Management Studies*, 59(1), https:// onlinelibrary .wiley .com/ doi/epdf/10.1111/joms.12737.

Rescher, N. (1996). *Process Metaphysics: An Introduction to Process Philosophy*, New York: SUNY Press.

Ricœur, P. (1984). *Time and Narrative*, Chicago, IL: University of Chicago Press.

Romanelli, E., & Tushman, M. L. (1994). Organizational transformation as punctuated equilibrium: an empirical test, *Academy of Management Journal*, 37(5), 1141–66.

Saylors, R., Lahiri, A., Warnick, B., & Baid, C. (2021). Looking back to venture forward: exploring idea and identity work in public failure narratives, *Entrepreneurship Theory and Practice*, https://doi.org/10422587211057027.

Schiffman, L, O'Cass, A., Paladino, A., & Carlson, J. (2014). *Consumer Behaviour*, 6th edition, Melbourne: Pearson.

Schön, D. A. (1983). *The Reflective Practitioner: How Professionals Think in Action*, Cambridge, MA: Basic Books.

Schrage, M. (1999). *Serious Play: How the World's Best Companies Simulate to Innovate*, Boston, MA: Harvard Business Press.

Schultz, M., & Hernes, T. (2013). A temporal perspective on organizational identity, *Organization Science*, 24(1), 1–21.

Sherover, C. M. (1986). Are we in time? *International Philosophical Quarterly*, 26(1), 33–46.

Smith, D., & Alexander, R. (1988). *Fumbling the Future: How Xerox Invented, Then Ignored, the First Personal Computer*, New York: William Morrow & Co.

Sonenshein, S. (2010). We're changing—or are we? Untangling the role of progressive, regressive, and stability narratives during strategic change implementation, *Academy of Management Journal*, 53(3), 477–512.

Star, S. L., & Griesemer, J. R. (1989). Institutional ecology, translations and boundary objects: amateurs and professionals in Berkeley's Museum of Vertebrate Zoology, 1907–39, *Social Studies of Science*, 19(3), 387–420.

Suchman, M. C. (1995). Managing legitimacy: strategic and institutional approaches, *Academy of Management Review*, 20(3), 571–610.

Thomke, S. H. (2003). *Experimentation Matters: Unlocking the Potential of New Technologies for Innovation*, Cambridge, MA: Harvard Business Press.

Tsoukas, H., & Chia, R. (2002). On organizational becoming: rethinking organizational change, *Organization Science*, 13(5), 567–82.

Tushman, M. L., & Anderson, P. (1986). Technological discontinuities and organizational environments, *Administrative Science Quarterly*, 31(3), 439–65.

Usher, A. P. (1954). *A History of Mechanical Inventions*, Cambridge, MA: Harvard University Press.

Van de Ven, A. H. (2021). Projecting backward and forward on processes of organizational change and innovation, *The Journal of Applied Behavioral Science*, 57(4), 436–46.

Van de Ven, A. H., Polley, D., Garud, R., & Venkataraman, S. (1999). *The Innovation Journey*, Oxford: Oxford University Press.

Weick, K. E., & Quinn, R. E. (1999). Organizational change and development, *Annual Review of Psychology*, 50(1), 361–86.

5 New ways of working or not? Transcending the continuity versus change conundrum through boundary events

Anthony Hussenot and Jeremy Aroles

Introduction

While change concerns novelty and difference, continuity is often understood as a form of stability or repetition of the same. Through this dualism between change and continuity, academics (but also journalists, intellectuals and society at large) can either emphasize the novelty of a given organizational phenomenon or highlight its historical inscription in older, existing practices. This ambivalence is particularly noticeable with the debate on new ways of working. The recent surge in teleworking in the context of the (ongoing) Covid-19 crisis is a case in point, with some stating that working from home brings a radical change to how people work, while others have aptly reminded us that telework has existed for a long time in a way or another and, as such, does not constitute a new practice. Mindful of these two opposite and contradictory stances, some others have analysed remote working as a first step towards a radical change in the world of work based on flexible workspace and new managerial methods. Finally, others have seen in the rise of teleworking just another sign of the ineluctable casualization of labour that began a long time ago. As such, a same phenomenon can be perceived as either a change that can lead to even more radical changes in the future or simply as a continuation of what has been occurring for quite some time.

Attempting to overcome this long-standing dualism, scholars have developed different views to integrate both continuity and change into a same framework. Orlikowski (1996) has suggested understanding change as endemic to situated practices. For her, change is continuous as it occurs through improvisation, innovation and adjustment of routines. Following this perspective, Weick and Quinn (1999) have advocated operating a shift from the notion 'change' to that of 'changing' to pay more attention to the ongoing and embedded nature

89

of change. In the same vein, Chia (1999), Feldman (2000) and then Tsoukas and Chia (2002) have suggested rejecting the idea of episodic change and focusing instead on the continuity of change. From this standpoint, change is understood as an ongoing process. Other scholars have endeavoured to further problematize the intricate relation between continuity and change, stating, for example, that 'stability can be both an outcome and a medium of change' (Farjoun, 2010, p. 202).

Finally, others have sought to build up a new understanding of the continuity and change dualism by relying on process philosophy. In such a view, there is no such thing as stability or change but only a 'becoming of continuity' (Whitehead, 1929/1978). Stability and change can be seen as the materialization of dynamic relations between complex processes of repetition and difference *sensu* Gilles Deleuze (see Aroles & McLean, 2016). This metaphysical view of reality means that stability and novelty are only situated experiences and reifications made of the flow of continuous change(s). Following Henri Bergson's philosophy (1896/2010, 1889/2013, 1907/2009, 1911/2011) and more generally a process philosophy perspective (Rescher, 1996; Langley & Tsoukas, 2010, 2017), we can posit that we live in a flow of continuous change. Yet, to make our reality tangible and practical, we need to create 'things' that essentially cut and divide the flow of continuous change. These 'things' (called images in Henri Bergson's philosophy) enable us to experience the reality as being tangible and intelligible.

However, this tangibility and intelligibility only occur through the enactment of temporalities. Enactment here means that when people act, they produce material, spatial, symbolic and temporal 'elements' (Weick, 1988). Enactment is thus a social process in which the flow of experiences is made more or less tangible by actors to serve their action (as material, temporal, spatial and symbolic structures both constrain and enable actors). A temporality is thus a structure of past, present and future events produced through action; a temporality endows the current moment with its sense of continuity defining both the meaning and 'concreteness' of the lived moment (Hussenot & Missonier, 2016; Hernes, 2020; Hussenot, Hernes, & Bouty, 2020). Following this view, the experience of stability or change is a situated and temporary outcome resulting from the way actors enact past, present and anticipated events in their current moment.

In this chapter, our aim is to show the individuals' assessment of organizational phenomena (such as the development of teleworking) as either a form of continuity/stability or a new practice is essentially contingent on how they mobilize, negotiate and translate past, present and future miscellaneous events, thus forming and assembling different temporalities. By leveraging a temporal view on the matter of new ways of working, our aim is to delve into how various actors perceive a same phenomenon as a new (or not) work practice. More precisely, we argue that 'new' ways of working are neither never completely new nor a simple repetition of the same, but only part of 'immanent temporal trajectories' mobilizing different interpretations (Hernes, Hussenot, & Pulk, 2021). This has, we contend, important implications for how we understand the future of work; the future of work is never a radical shift, disconnected from the current ways of working but is rather a projection based on the enactment of past, present and future events.

The main contribution of this chapter lies in the articulation of a perspective that both encapsulates a process view that sees reality as a becoming of continuity (in which the stability and change dualism needs to be overcome) and captures the situated experience of actors through which stability and continuity/stability are tangible ways to materialize and qualify lived moments. We argue that scholars often conflate the two views, leading to a confusion between a metaphysical development emphasizing the indivisible flux of continuous change on one hand, and the way actors define their intelligible and tangible reality by materializing this indivisible flux in terms of stability and novelty on the other (Hernes, Feddersen & Schultz, 2021). However, this materialization of reality is not unique; various temporalities are enacted by actors leading to qualify a same phenomenon differently as either a mere continuation or a change.

As such, we propose the concept of *boundary event* to account for how a same event can lead to different temporalities for various people. A boundary event is essentially a common event that is experienced differently. Consequently, these *boundary events* participate in the shaping of various temporalities, leading to different continuities. Ultimately, this partly explains why actors do not always experience the same reality despite enacting the same events.

Transcending the continuity and change conundrum

What we call continuity is the way we make the indivisible movement of life intelligible. Considering Bergson's philosophy, life is an indivisible movement in which there are no predefined 'things' (see Hussenot, 2022). We sometimes experience this indivisible movement of life in some moments of meditations, trances, creations or even reading, as suggested by one of the editors of this book. However, to make the world intelligible and tangible, people have to experience it as a set of *images*. In Bergson's work (1896/2010, 1889/2013, 1907/2009), images are the only way to create a tangible reality. In other words, life is an indivisible movement, but to make sense and act in the current moment, we create rather stable images, thus defining what we call reality. Images can be anything that makes the world tangible. Words, objects, people, events (etc.) may be seen as images. Importantly, Henri Bergson does not posit that reality does not exist, rather that the very existence of reality lies in images. It does not mean either that reality is merely subjective. Images become endowed with objectivity as we experience them as exterior to us. Moreover, these images are shared among people; when people reach a common view about those images, they participate in the building of a shared reality.

From this perspective, continuity is the ability to relate our current moment with some past, present and/or future events. Continuity is what makes sense about the current moment. The expression 'make sense' is here close to the notion of sensemaking found in organization studies (Weick, 1995 ; Maitlis & Christianson, 2004), that is, 'a process of meaning-making in which people attempt to comprehend ambiguous, unexpected, and/or confusing events' (Rheinhardt & Gioia, 2021, p. 77). In other words, we have a sense of why and how the current moment is happening thanks to our ability to relate this moment to a past, a present and a future. More precisely, continuity emerges from the retention of past events and the protention of possible future events (Husserl, 1927/1964). Let's say you are watching a yacht entering the port. As explained by Blattner (2020), to experience the gliding of a yacht from point A (the entrance of the yacht into the port) to point B (the mooring at the dock), we experience the yacht as moving in motion: 'In other words, when you see the yacht at point B, you see it at point B-as-having-earlier-been-at-point-A' (p. 16). To make sense of this current moment, we have to enact simultaneously some past events (the yacht outside the port), present event (the yacht entering the port) and future event (the yacht being moored at the dock). Retention of past events and protention of future events make the experience of a movement intelligible. This is why we can make sense of what's going on with this yacht gliding into the port. Consequently, a current moment can never be isolated from the past, the present and the future, and is always intricately related to them.

In other words, our reality becomes tangible through the enactment of temporalities that are based on the retention of past events and the protention of expected future events. Retention and protention of events form a plausible and useful account enabling us to answer the 'what', 'why' and 'how' questions of the current moment. As such, temporality enables us to make sense of the current moment (me watching a yacht gliding in a port) because we can relate this current moment to some past and future events. Importantly, people do not need to live all the past events to enact them (and of course, the same goes for future events). To extend Blattner's (2020) example, one can say that if I'm watching a yacht gliding to the dock, I can easily make sense of this current moment by enacting (among others) the past event about the boat entering into the port even if I was not there when it happened. The same can be said about a future event. Even if I cannot wait till the yacht is moored at the dock, I can easily anticipate this event, and this is why this current moment (a yacht gliding in the port) can make sense to me. Even if past and future events are not directly lived by actors, they are plausible enough to make sense of the current moment.

Conversely, novelties, surprises, astonishments or even shocks happen when past and/or future events do not match the expected temporality from which we are supposed to experience the current moment. Most of the time, it just requires a bit of adjustment in the way we enact our temporality to make sense of the current moment. For instance, one can be very surprised if the yacht we were watching going into the port suddenly turns around and leaves the port, instead of gliding through the port to be moored. Consequently, this current moment would not make any sense. Why does the yacht suddenly turn around? What's wrong? To answer these questions, we would need either to find some explanations or articulate some hypotheses: 'Does it have a technical problem? Is it the wrong port? Etc.'. This unexpected event would change our sense of continuity related to this current moment and we would have to reconsider the events enacted, to define a new temporality, even if it would be partly made of some hypotheses about what happened and what will happen for this yacht.

The current moment can sometimes be such a radical shift that it can take a lot of time and effort to (re)create a sense of continuity, especially when what is happening seems to be impossible, at first glance, to relate to any past and future events. This is essentially what happens when we witness an event that has no precedent in our mind, such as a terrorist attack. We unfortunately lived this moment on 11 September 2001 (called 9/11), when we witnessed commercial airliners crashing into the New York World Trade Center twin towers, the Pentagon, and in a Pennsylvania field. For most of us, while we were horrified, it also took a while to make sense of what was happening (i.e. to relate this current moment to past historical events such as the American tensions with al-Qaida and Taliban in Afghanistan and future ones), as we could guess that the (western) world was entering into a new era, made of wars against terrorism. As such, whatever happens (even the most disruptive and shocking events) in our life, we always seek to establish some form of continuity. This continuity emerges from the temporality we enact, that is the way we relate the current moment to past, present and future events. Even the most radical change is always temporally positioned in such a way that continuity is re-performed. It is our only way to make sense of the current moment. From this perspective, the past, the present and the future continually change through their constant (re)enactment by people. The past, the present and the future are thus always situated to make sense of the current moment (Hussenot, 2019; Hernes & Schultz, 2020).

For example, a wedding day is an important event that can be often re-enacted to make sense of other moments in our personal life, happy or not (birth, wedding anniversary, divorce, death, etc.). As such, the way we enact this wedding day evolves through time. It is essentially 'adapted' to the current moment. Consequently, the way we depict a wedding day, the meaning we give to this event, the way we interpret people's behaviour and speeches during this day (and so on) are slightly (or more radically) different each time we enact this event. By doing that, we make sense of changes happening in our life. Whatever the reason, the way we enact an event is always situated; it is always enacted in a way that resonates with the current moment, a way that contributes to making the current moment intelligible and tangible. From this perspective, changes – inasmuch as they are enacted events – are always in a state of becoming (i.e. they are never given once and for all but are constantly redefined and revisited). Moreover, past, present and future events enacted by people to make sense about these changes are not defined once and for all either, but are redefined and revisited as well. Those past, present and future events form structures of events that are enacted again and again along the activity, leading to (re)definitions, deletions, or integrations of new events into the global structure of events (Hernes, 2014a, 2014b; Hussenot & Missonier, 2016; Hernes, Hussenot, & Pulk, 2020). However, a shared event (such as a wedding day, for instance) is not always part of the same temporalities (i.e. a shared narrative made of past, present and future events). Individuals can experience a same event very differently and/or re-enact this event very differently over time. A same wedding day can be part of a happy story for some and a sad one for others. Moreover, a wedding day can be interpreted as a happy day at first but be re-interpreted as a sad one later on, as people can re-interpret what happened during this event and/or enact other events altering their interpretation.

Introducing the concept of boundary event

A same shared event can thus be interpreted differently, and consequently, be part of very different narratives. This can explain partly why a same event – such as the quick adoption of teleworking in March 2020 in the context of the Covid-19 – can be experienced as a continuation for some people or a change for others. To understand how a same event can be interpreted very differently by people and be part of very different temporalities, we here propose the concept of boundary event.

The concept of boundary event is partly derived from the concept of boundary object developed by Star and Griesemer (1989) (see Levina & Vaast, 2005 and Spee & Jarzabkowski, 2009 – among others – for some developments in organization studies). A boundary object has a common identity and a shared symbolic structure; it 'is common enough to more than one world to make them recognizable' (Star and Griesemer, 1989, p. 393). As such, boundary objects are 'flexible epistemic artifacts that inhabit several intersecting social worlds and satisfy the information requirements of each of them' (Star and Griesemer, 1989, p. 393).

Following this definition, boundary events are common enough to be recognizable by different people or social groups but are enacted differently. In other words, it means that a boundary event is partly shared by a large group of people, but, at the same time, is interpreted and related to other past, present and future events differently. Paraphrasing Star and Griesemer (1989), boundary events inhabit several intersecting temporalities of different people and groups of people. Hernes and Schultz (2020, p. 8) have recently suggested the notion of singular event to deal with unique and vivid past or future events: 'they are easily evoked, communicated and visualized because they have essential features that are readily recognizable'. The concept of boundary event, as developed in this chapter, can be understood as a sort of past, future or even present singular event that has 'features' that are shared by most actors, but still does not necessarily build a common understanding about a phenomenon. A boundary event is common enough among people, but still enacted to different structure of events, either complementary or opposite, leading to very different stories about a same phenomenon. As such, the notion of boundary event can help us to understand how some events can create both a shared understanding as well as differences and oppositions.

To understand how a same event can be interpreted as a mere continuation or as a radical shift, we now turn our attention to the development of telework in

France in the context of the Covid-19 pandemic in 2020–22. We focus on the quick adoption of teleworking in France in March 2020 (i.e. during the first lockdown) and show that if the adoption of teleworking was largely enacted by people as the start event of a new story (the collective story of the pandemic), it led to very different stories that have been disputed and translated. Consequently, the quick adoption of teleworking in France in March 2020 is here seen as a boundary event enacted at the same time by numerous workers but still participating in the definition of various temporalities leading to different 'stories' about the evolution of work.

Empirical illustration: change and continuity in the development of telework in France

On 12 March 2020, the French President announced the first nation-wide lockdown. The spread of the virus COVID-19 and the increasing mortality rate forced the French government (and many others across the globe) to make a radical decision. People were asked to stay at home and only some categories of workers – named 'essential workers' – were allowed to go to work. For others, they either had to stop working or were urged to work from home. Consequently, 24 per cent of French workers worked from home during the first lockdown[1] (according to the survey published by Odoxa) while only 3 per cent of workers in France had worked remotely in 2017 (according to INSEE[2]). For some of these new teleworkers, it was an unexpected and radical change. As they had never experienced telework before, working from home full-time appeared as a novelty. Far from their colleagues and office, 'forced' to use collaborative and videoconference software and having to reconfigure their home into an office space (Estagnasié, Bonneau, Vasquez, & Vayre, 2021), telework was lived and experienced, for many, as a radical shift. In a way, experiencing telework as a radical change is easily understandable, as this work practice essentially questioned common principles about the world of work. As a consequence, 25 per cent of managers still considered this way of working as inappropriate in December 2020 (according to the Malakoff Humanis annual teleworking barometer 2021).

Conversely, for a large part of new teleworkers, the same event – the adoption of teleworking in March 2020 – was experienced as an expected evolution. For instance, the average satisfaction score about teleworking was 7.2/10 in December 2020 in France (Malakoff Humanis annual teleworking barometer 2021). In fact, teleworking was not really new for most of those 'new' teleworkers. As Estagnasié, Bonneau, Vasquez, and Vayre (2021) remind us, the notion of 'telework' appeared for the first time in 1972 in a *Washington Post* article written by the journalist Jack Schiff. Since the 1970s, numerous ways of working remotely have been developed. Digital nomadism, as a practice emerged in the late 1980s and has been conceptualized in the academic literature since the 1990s, notably by Makimoto and Manners (1997) (see Aroles, Granter, & de Vaujany, 2020). In addition, the idea of running an entire company or administration remotely was imagined in the early 1990s, notably by Mowshowitz (1994) and Handy (1995) with the notion of virtual organization. It means that working remotely – even in its most radical way (i.e. by giving up any physical facility and location) – is not new at all and has been part and parcel of managerial debates for almost 40 years. More recently, numerous companies have been known for adopting such remote ways of working these last two decades (Automattic, Buffer, GitHub, etc.). Adding to this, numerous blogs, accounts on social media, YouTube channels and press articles have been promoting this way of working over the last decade.

In the end, is working-from-home really new for new teleworkers? Is a work practice actually new when we are aware of it? Of course, there is no definite answer to this question but only situated ones. For some people, it will be new, for others, it will only be about adopting an existing practice. So, why don't practitioners have the same interpretation about what is new and what is not?

This question is probably even more relevant for academics. In the field of management and organization studies, the notion of new ways of working – often labelled 'NWW' in the literature – is loosely defined (see Aroles, Mitev, & de Vaujany, 2019), which is particularly visible in discussions on time and place, independent work, self-management, flexible employment relations and new media technologies supporting remote working (see Jemine, 2021 for an extensive critical literature review). In fact, the label NWW seems to refer more to a management ideology than a proper well-defined set of theories and methods. Actually, the notion of new ways of working has been crafted mainly by consultants (Jemine, 2021) such as Veldhoen (2005), Bijl (2011), and Broere (2016) in order to promote their vision about work. This leads to an important limit for scholars as this way of researching new ways of working seems to be more about imposing an ideology and some work practices (such as coworking, nomadism, DIY, etc.) rather than studying evolutions at work as they are experienced by workers.

In other words, are scholars legitimate to qualify a way of working as 'new' or 'old' (see Liang, Aroles, & Brandl, 2022)? For instance, the uberization of the economy could be seen, according to Acquier (2017), as an updated version of the domestic system which played an important role in the economy between the seventeenth and nineteenth centuries. This historical work is helpful as it allows us to monitor the evolution of work and create a sense of continuity. However, it is not always what it is experienced by workers. For instance, workers experiencing teleworking for the first time in 2020 did not necessarily know the history of teleworking and its beginning in the 1970s. Even still, knowing this history does not make this work practice less new for some workers experiencing it for the first time. If you have never swum in your life, you would probably experience your first swimming experience as something radically new, even if you know that it has always been an ability of human beings. At the same time, knowing that a work practice is new for yourself but not in general can help to find meaning in its adoption. Adopting telework could be a radical new experience but at the same time, most of the new adopters knew that it was not an entirely new practice as they could even relate their own experience with a broader trend. As such, comprehending the adoption of teleworking in March 2020 as a boundary event enables us to capture how a same shared event can be experienced as a mere continuation or a radical change and above all, to surpass the continuation and change conundrum and understand them as situated, sometimes coexisting and embedded into various temporalities. We discuss these theoretical contributions of the concept of boundary event in our understanding of continuity and change in the next section.

Theoretical contribution: the role of boundary events in change and continuity

To summarize, the challenge is here to understand why a same work practice – such as teleworking – can be experienced as a change by some actors or as a continuation by others. As was underlined previously, it is very much contingent upon the way past, present and future are enacted by actors. If this way of working has already been experienced in one way or another, it might be experienced as a continuation of what has existed before (as this current moment would be related to some past events without being experienced as a temporal rupture for actors). However, if this way of working has never been experienced before, it might be perceived as a change as actors cannot relate this way of working with past events.

In that sense, change and continuity concern the way people relate this way of working to their past, current and future expected experiences. These temporalities emerging from past, present and future events bring coherence and integrity in human experience. However, temporalities continually evolve to constantly re-create coherence and integrity along activities (Blattner, 2020). Consequently, the co-definition and the pairing of past, present and future is thus constantly adapted to make sense of what individuals are living. A same event can thus be enacted and interpreted differently by a same person or by different groups of people. We proposed the concept of boundary event to deal with these events shared by enough individuals to form a common event that most people can refer to, but lead to very different temporalities. In that sense, boundary events can be a shared turning point for all, but they do not belong to the same narrative.

From this perspective, continuity and change are about the way one or even several boundary events are integrated in a structure of past, present and future events. A boundary event is experienced as part of a continuity when it is enacted as a smooth evolution of some past events and a gentle transition toward expected future events. Conversely, a boundary event is experienced as part of a change when enacted as a temporal cut, leading to some radical shifts. However, it is not always that simple, as people can experience continuity and change simultaneously. In the context of the evolution at work, this can be observed when a way of working is known as an 'old' one by actors but experienced for the first time. Experiencing teleworking for the first time in March 2020 was probably very new for a lot of workers, but most of them already heard about teleworking before. They probably already read press articles, watched news about teleworking and/or met teleworkers before. This means that to experience change and continuity simultaneously, individuals have to enact at least two different temporalities folded within a same boundary event. It can be a very local(ized) one, such as experimenting telework for the first time and a more global one, such as the general evolution of work practices. These two temporalities are not necessary opposite but can be complementary. This has been observed and conceptualized many times in organization studies, either by early neo-institutionalist scholars (Meyer & Rowan, 1977) or in the theory of diffusion of innovation (Rogers, 1995), both insisting on the role of social pressure in the adoption of work practices and/or technologies. In other words, one can trigger some change so as to join a trend. Change and continuity can thus display complementarity through the enactment of boundary events.

However, saying that change and continuity can be simultaneously triggered by the enactment of boundary events does not mean that a boundary event is necessarily past or present. It can also be future. It is the case when a change is expected to happen, like a future marketing campaign or the anticipated launch of a new product. These can be seen as boundary events too as they are shared by people but also can partly shape different temporalities. More precisely, these future boundary events can be depicted as either a radical rupture from the present or not. There are numerous anticipated events that are envisioned by some groups of people as radically different from the present. The potential rising level of the sea due to climate change or even a potential third world war due to the war in Ukraine are some of the current future boundary events enacted by most people in the West (at least in May 2022 when we were writing this chapter).

Nevertheless, these future boundary events always rely on some past and current evolutions, such as scientific knowledge, innovations, global stakes and artistic work. As any other event, future boundary events are always co-defined with other past, present and future events. In other words, the future is always a projection made from past and/or current weak signals, that is, emergent issues, technologies, scientific knowledge, social trends (etc.) that could become significant in the future. In such an events-based view, future can sometimes be a form of memory actualized through current moments. Tsoukas and Shepherd (2004) have drawn on the notion of memories future to highlight the importance of the previously imagined future. It means that the future is not defined in the current moment from scratch but rather it is a 'past projection about the future' actualized in time. This has been illustrated notably by Schultz and Hernes (2013) in their study of the Lego company or by Hernes, Feddersen and Schultz (2021) in their study of the Carlsberg and Arla companies. These empirical studies have shown how the future of those companies has been envisaged through a new understanding and redefinition of their past. In these empirical studies, actors rely on their past to define a desirable shared future (boundary future events). By doing this, actors enact different past and future boundary events that can then lead to different temporalities according to their activities. The designer can translate these past and boundary future events into the designing of new products, the marketer into a new logo, slogan, and so on. Each worker can define their own temporalities to act accordingly, while still sharing the same past and future boundary events that make their collective activities possible.

Conclusion

The question of novelty is one that never ceases to generate interest, both in academic spheres and in the general press. This is particularly noticeable in debates pertaining to the presumed transformation of the world of work and the acceleration of those transformations through digital technologies. As shown through our example of telework in the context of the on-going pandemic, drawing conclusions as to where novelty lies is a rather difficult endeavour as practices are embedded in long and complex history on one hand and experienced very differently by various actors on the other. Here, we sought to go beyond the individual, subjective understanding of novelty to grasp how, collectively, some phenomena are constructed as new or not and how narratives involving past, present and future events partake in this process. Our argument is that matters of continuity and change can occur simultaneously as a same event can be shared but still enacted very differently, a phenomenon which we refer to as boundary event. Boundary events connect different temporalities that are constantly re-assembled in such a way that what is new is simultaneously an extension and a departure from what happened.

Our focus on temporalities and boundary events might be a way of circumventing the classical continuity/change conundrum that, in our opinion, may take us away from the exploration of work practices and more generally speaking, organizational phenomena. We contend that too much attention might have been given to finding out where novelty exactly lies at the detriment of attempting to understand what those practices might mean to those who experiment with them on a daily basis. Paradoxically then, these discussions might have contributed to obfuscating research on work practices by setting up a 'false' dichotomy between old and new work practices. In addition, if it is true that a certain ideology underlies NWW, then this surely rings true for the portrayal of a given practice as new or not. Finally, there might also be an element of cyclicality that frames the development of work practices. Is novelty that which hasn't been found yet or that which has been forgotten about and is later rediscovered? Would it be too far-fetched to imagine that future generations may at some point rediscover on-site work?

Notes

1. This rate has since remained rather stable. In June 2021, teleworkers represented 26 per cent of the population of workers in France (according to DARES).
2. INSEE, L'économie et la société à l'ère du numérique, Édition 2019.

References

Acquier, A. (2017). Retour vers le futur? Le capitalisme de plate-forme ou le etour du 'domestic system', *Le Libellio*, 13(1), 87–100.

Aroles, J., Granter, E., & de Vaujany, F.X. (2020). 'Becoming mainstream': the professionalization and corporatization of digital nomadism, *New Technology, Work and Employment*, 35(1), 114–29.

Aroles, J., Mitev, N., & de Vaujany, F. X. (2019). Mapping themes in the study of new work practices, *New Technology, Work and Employment*, 34(3), 285–99.

Aroles, J., & McLean, C. (2016). Rethinking stability and change in the study of organizational routines: difference and repetition in a newspaper-printing factory, *Organization Science*, 27(3), 535–50.

Bergson, H. (1889 [2013]). *Essai sur les données immédiates de la conscience*, Paris: Presses Universitaires de France.

Bergson, H. (1896 [1939]). *Matière et mémoire*, Paris: Presses Universitaires de France.

Bergson, H. (1907 [2009]). *L'évolution créative*, Paris: Presses Universitaires de France.

Bergson, H. (1911 [2011]). *La perception du changement*, Paris: Presses Universitaire de France.

Bijl, D. W. (2011). Journey towards the New Way of Working: Creating Sustainable Performance and Joy at Work, Zeewolde, NL: Par CC.

Blattner W. (2020). Temporality, aspect and narrative: a Heideggerian approach, in J. Reinecke, R. Suddaby, A. Langley & H. Tsoukas (eds), *Time, Temporality, and History in Process Organization Studies* (pp. 15–28), Oxford: Oxford University Press.

Broere, A. (2016). *Het Nieuwe Werken. Hoe Werk je Effectiever en Productiever*, Houten/Antwerp: Spectrum.

Chia, R. (1999). A "rhizomic" model of organizational change and transformation: perspective from a metaphysics of change, *British Journal of Management*, 10(3), 209–27.

Estagnasié, C., Bonneau, C., Vasquez, C., & Vayre, E. (2021). Créer l'espace habité de travail: pratiques de rematérialisation du travail à distance, in E. Vayre (ed.), *La digitalisation du travail: nouveaux espaces et nouvelles temporalités de travail*, London: ISTE Groupe.

Farjoun, M. (2010). Beyond dualism: stability and change as a duality, *Academy of Management Review*, 35(2), 202–25.

Feldman, M. (2000). Organizational routines as a source of continuous change, *Organization Science*, 11(6), 611–29.

Handy, C. (1995). Trust and the virtual organization, *Harvard Business Review*, May–June, https://hbr.org/1995/05/trust-and-the-virtual-organization.

Hernes, T. (2014a). *A Process Theory of Organization*, Oxford: Oxford University Press.

Hernes, T. (2014b). Alfred North Whitehead, in J. Helin, T. Hernes, D. Hjort & R. Holt (eds), *Oxford Handbook of Process Philosophy and Organization Studies* (pp. 255–71), Oxford: Oxford University Press.

Hernes, T. (2020). Events and the becoming of organizational temporality, in J. Reinecke, R. Suddaby, A. Langley & H. Tsoukas (eds), *Time, Temporality, and History in Process Organization Studies* (pp. 29–43), Oxford: Oxford University Press.

Hernes, T., Feddersen, J., & Schulte, M. (2021). Material temporality: how materiality 'does' time in food organizing, *Organization Studies*, 42(2), 351–71.

Hernes, T., Hussenot, A., & Pulk, K. (2021). Time and temporality of change processes: applying an event-based view to integrate episodic and continuous change, in M. S. Poole & A. H. Van de Ven (eds), *The Oxford Handbook of Organizational Change and Innovation* (pp 731–50), Oxford: Oxford University Press.

Hernes, T., & Schultz, M. (2020). Translating the distant into the present: how actors address distant past and future events through situated activity, *Organization Theory*, 1(1), 1–20.

Hussenot, A. (2019). *L'organisation à l'épreuve des makers. Propositions pour une approche par les événements*. Presses Universitaires de Laval.

Hussenot, A. (2022). A modus vivendi between movement and materiality: Henri Bergson and the matter of organization, *M@n@gement*, 25(1), 79–84.

Hussenot, A., Hernes, T., & Bouty, I. (2020). Studying organization from the perspective of the ontology of temporality: introducing the event-based approach, in J. Reinecke, R. Suddaby, A. Langley & H. Tsoukas (eds), *About Time: Temporality and History in Organization Studies* (pp. 50–68), Oxford: Oxford University Press.

Hussenot, A., & Missonier, S. (2016). Encompassing novelty and stability: a process event-based approach, *Organization Studies*, 37(4), 523–46.

Husserl, E. (1927 [1964]). *Leçons pour une phénoménologie de la conscience intime du temps*, Paris: Presses Universitaires de France.

Jemine, G. (2021). Deconstructing new ways of working: a five-dimensional conceptualization proposal, in N. Mitev, J. Aroles, K. A. Stephenson & J. Malaurent (eds), *New Ways of Working, Technology, Work and Globalization* (pp. 453–80), Cham: Springer.

Langley, A., & Tsoukas, H. (2017). Introduction: process thinking, process theorizing and process researching, in A. Langley & H. Tsoukas (eds), *The SAGE Handbook of Process Organization Studies* (pp. 1–25), Thousand Oaks, CA: Sage.

Langley, A., & Tsoukas, H. (2010). Introduction: perspectives on process organization studies, in T. Hernes & S. Maitlis (eds), *Process, Sensemaking and Organizing* (pp. 1–26), Oxford: Oxford University Press.

Levina, N., & Vaast, E. (2005). The emergence of boundary spanning competence in practice: implications for implementation and use of information systems, *MIS Quarterly*, 29(2), 335–63.

Liang, Y., Aroles, J., & Brandl, B. (2022). Charting platform capitalism: definitions, concepts and ideologies, *New Technology, Work and Employment*, 37(2), 308–27.

Maitlis, S., & Christianson, M. (2014). Sensemaking in organizations: taking stock and moving forward, *Academy of Management Annals*, 8(1), 57–125.

Makimoto, T., & Manners, D. (1997). *Digital Nomad*, Chichester: Wiley.

Meyer, J. W., & Rowan, B. (1977). Institutionalized organizations: formal structure as myth and ceremony, *American Journal of Sociology*, 83(2), 340–63.

Mowshowitz, A. (1994). Virtual organization: a vision of management in the information age, *The Information Society*, 10(4), 267–88.

Orlikowski, W. J. (1996). Improvising organizational transformation over time: a situated change perspective, *Information Systems Research*, 7(1), 63–92.

Rescher, N. (1996). *Process Metaphysics: An Introduction to Process Philosophy*, Albany: State University of New York Press.

Rheinhardt, A., & Gioia, D. (2021). Upside-down organizational change: sensemaking, sensegiving, and the new generation, in M. S. Poole & A. H. Van de Ven (eds), *The Oxford Handbook of Organizational Change and Innovation* (pp. 77–105), Oxford: Oxford University Press.

Rogers, E. (1995). *Diffusion of Innovation*, 4th edition, New York: Free Press.

Schultz, M., & Hernes, T. (2013). A temporal perspective on organizational identity, *Organization Science*, 24(1), 1–21.

Spee, A. P., & Jarzabkowski, P. (2009). Strategy tools as boundary objects, *Strategic Organization*, 7(2), 223–32.

Star, S. L., & Griesemer, J. R. (1989). Institutional ecology, "translations" and boundary objects: amateurs and professionals in Berkeley's Museum of Vertebrate Zoology, 1907–39, *Social Studies of Science*, 19(3), 387–420.

Tsoukas, H., & Chia, R. (2002). On organizational becoming: rethinking organizational change, *Organization Science*, 13(5), 567–82.

Tsoukas, H., & Shepherd, J. (2004). Coping with the future: developing organizational foresightfulness, *Futures*, 36, 137–44.

Veldhoen, E. (2005). *The Art of Working*, The Hague: Academic Service.

Weick, K. E. (1988). Enacted sensemaking in crisis situations, *Journal of Management Studies*, 25(4), 305–17.

Weick, K. E. (1995). *Sensemaking in Organizations*, Thousand Oaks, CA: Sage.

Weick, K. E., & Quinn, R. (1999). Organizational change and development, *Annual Review of Psychology*, 50, 361–86.

Whitehead, A. N. (1929 [1978]). *Process and Reality*, New York: The Free Press.

6 The communicative constitution of organizational continuity and change in, through and over time

Mie Plotnikof and Nicolas Bencherki

Introduction

In this chapter, we explore the relations between continuity and change, and more specifically the temporal underpinning of these relations, based on the assumption that they are communicatively constituted. To do so, we focus on the way continuity and change have been addressed within the interdisciplinary field of organizational discourse studies (ODS) and communicative constitution of organization (CCO) perspective. While these studies are varied, they share the premise that organizational phenomena – such as organizational continuity or change – emerge through discourse and communication. Figuring out how continuity or change take place, then, is a question of understanding everyday communicative practices across, for example, meetings, e-mails, policy and strategy documents, symbolic artifacts, and so on (Phillips & Oswick, 2012; Schoeneborn et al., 2019). This claim rests on the assumption that:

> [A] constitutive perspective, informed by the linguistic and practice turns, shows how discourse and communication are not simply activities that occur within organizations or the surface-level manifestations, or conduits, of more putatively 'real' factors and containers. They are symbiotic, interdependent, and mutually constitutive in constituting organization. (Kuhn & Putnam, 2014: 437)

In recognizing that discourse and communication are *constitutive* of organizational phenomena, ODS and CCO offer critical approaches to studying continuity and change (Grant et al., 2005). They steer us away from functionalist assumptions, that is, from viewing organizations as existing a priori and from reducing continuity and change to intentionally planned efforts. Instead, ODS and CCO rethink continuity and change by leaving behind the conventional view that communication accompanies change and is transmissive, arguing that communication and discourse are fundamentally constitutive and per-formative of organizing change and continuity, whether they are intended or not (Grant & Marshak, 2011; Hardy & Thomas, 2014; Plotnikof & Pedersen, 2019). Rather than viewing continuity and change as fixed end states or neces-sarily opposite, these are better understood as communication and discursive tensions emerging in dynamic relation to each other in, over and through time.

This chapter introduces how this constitutive perspective offers a relational understanding of both intended and unintended organizational continuity and change as *emerging and entangling* in communicative practices and discursive constructions in, through and over time. Such a perspective enables us to concretely observe how continuity and change are interactively relating and performed in everyday activities. Studying those activities reveals how the two phenomena are entangled, as they are discursively produced, communicatively enacted and thereby materialize across actors, spaces and times. However, while ODS and CCO perspectives are saturated by underlying assumptions of time – such as communicative practices emerging *in time*, text-conversation dialectics moving *through time*, and discursive power relations reproducing *over time* – temporality often remains implicit (Plotnikof & Mumby, 2023). This means that the role of time and the temporal underpinning of commu-nicative practices are blind spots, limiting a more fine-grained, temporally sensitive theorizing of continuity and change within CCO and ODS. We argue that greater sensitivity to temporality allows to move beyond static views on communication in continuity and change, and to further a more fundamental consideration of the communicatively and discursively constructed pace of continuity and change relations in organizing processes.

As shown below, communication has often been limited to function at spe-cific moments in change efforts, either to collect information or to transmit it to specific audiences. Thinking that communication is merely a vehicle for preexisting pieces of information is problematic (Axley, 1984), as that reduces change to a rational, disembodied *decision* to change that can then be "commu-nicated." Such transmission views on communication miss how that decision is performed and negotiated through concrete, often precarious interactions and, furthermore, they fail to understand how intended change only emerges and propagates insofar it is enacted communicatively through equally tangible situations. In contrast, ODS and CCO perspectives enables detailed attention to how particular communicative interactions and discursive constructions of change unfold and scale up to changing organizational reality (Basque et al., 2022; Thomas et al., 2011). However, they assume – rather than explicate – what it means that these interactions unfold *in, through and over time*. To further contribute to what a fundamentally constitutive understanding of communication and discourse means to continuity and change, then, ODS and CCO must also make their view of time more explicit.

To do so, this chapter unpacks how continuity and change are approached in ODS and CCO, examining three specific conceptualizations of continuity and change relations in this literature, namely (1) strategic versus resisting communication and discourses, (2) text-conversation dialectics, and (3) micro-interactional analysis. Works within these conceptualizations, each in its own way, present continuity and change as emergent and "fleeting" processes, in which time plays a central part (see also Cooren et al., 2015). After reviewing these studies, we identify key relations between change, continuity and temporality constituted through discourse and communication, thereby contributing to elucidate the performative role that temporality plays in ODS and CCO perspectives. Altogether, this offers timely concepts to understand the fundamentally communicative, discursive constitution of organizational continuity and change.

Discourse and communication views on continuity and change

Research on communication in relation to organizational change has traditionally considered it as a means to a goal, in one of two ways. First, it is said that communication prepares for change, for instance as organizations are implementing strategic changes and want to ensure that staff and other actors support it (e.g. Schulz-Knappe et al., 2019), or when organizations share information about possible external threats, such as environmental crises, and communicate about strategic changes in response (e.g. Lewis, 1999). Discourse and communication also allow sharing meaning and sensemaking, which is key to enabling both long-term changes and more agile decisions in the early stages of change (Balogun & Johnson, 2004; Brown et al., 2015). Second, communication is considered as a vehicle to propagate a strategy once it is decided, helping manage later stages of change by sharing a sense of purpose (e.g. Köhler & Zerfass, 2019). These views mostly consider change as a rare occurrence, and communication as a tool to collect information and disseminate decisions with respect to it (see Axley, 1984; Weick & Quinn, 1999).

Continuity, for its part, is often discussed in the guise of resilience towards external factors and changes, for example when a business restores continuity following a crisis (Doerfel & Harris, 2017). In that sense, continuity is the ability to conserve some features despite change, such an organizational culture (in agreement with the "unfreeze, change and refreeze" model by Lewin, 1947; e.g. LeCouvie & Pendergast, 2014). Communicating continuity, in such understandings, is again considered chiefly according to a transmission metaphor; it is described as an effort to strategically legitimize a certain course of action as coherent with existing organizational identities and goals, and to reassure actors (employees, clients, stakeholders) that the change in fact keeps the organization on track (DePamphilis, 2015).

Both understandings limit the role of communication and discourse to managerial tools used at specific stages of change or continuity efforts: either they help decide about change prior to it, or they inform and implement it afterwards, or they manage stakeholders' expectations regarding the organization's continuity. Discourse and communication, then, function as effective management tools for change or continuity-fulfilling normative tasks, intended to work before, during or after decisions of change or continuity. However, in challenging this more *conventional view* on change or continuity as stages in a dichotomic relation, and communication and discourse as managerial tools or medium, a stream of process studies have advanced out conceptualization of change and continuity (see, for instance, chapters 5 and 12 of this volume), suggesting that we view these as emerging relations integral to all organizing processes becoming in flux (Chia & Tsoukas, 2003; Langley et al., 2013). Such a novel process approach to change and continuity, however, requires an equally novel theorizing of the role of discourse and communication in this regard (Grant et al., 2005; Thomas et al., 2011), one that moves past its reduction to managerial tools acting as a medium between change managers and their audiences.

Indeed, a closer reading of literature taking a *constitutive view* on communication and discourse shows that this also completely recasts the relationship between continuity and change (Grant et al., 2005; Grant & Marshak, 2011). Discourse and communication turn out to play a more crucial role in enabling both continuity and change than the transmission view reserved for them, as they also suppose different ways of conceptualizing time. A key aspect of these novel conceptualizations consists in a relational approach to continuity and change, where communication and discourse enact and materialize shifting relations, whose reconfiguration constitute change or continuity (Cooren, 2018). Acknowledging the variety of these studies, many follow a broad definition of communication as interplays of texts and conversations, in which conversations are observable interactions, and texts are symbolic materialization, through which organizing is becoming in, through and over time (Koschmann et al., 2012; Taylor & van Every, 2000). Further, text/conversation interplays enact discourses, understood as sets of interrelated texts and associated practices of production, distribution and consumption that bring an idea or object into being (Grant & Marshak, 2011; Plotnikof & Pedersen, 2019). Methodologically speaking, this also defines the object of study: the researcher examines the way interactions, talk and texts interrelate and perform change and continuity. This allows such studies to follow change and continuity as they unfold in everyday practices of more or less strategic concern.

To further unpack how this view advances our understanding of organizational continuity and change, we discuss three main analytical conceptualizations taking a constitutive view of communication and discourse. We order them according to how intentional they consider continuity and change to be located in (1) strategic versus resisting communication and discourse; (2) text/conversation dynamics; and (3) interactional approaches. As we will see, however, each of them challenges the conventional view of intentional or planned change, but also our very understanding of continuity and change, and brings into the picture new understandings of time and temporality.

Continuity and change in strategic versus resisting communication and discourse

Strategic efforts to manage and organize change or continuity have been studied widely, including in ODS and CCO perspectives (Hardy & Thomas, 2014; Plotnikof, 2015; Vásquez et al., 2018). Without suggesting that either change or continuity are necessarily questions of strategy, such work scrutinizes how various concerns may become powerful and gain authority, thereby becoming strategic in specific, consequential ways through communication and discourse. Such studies have, for example, looked at narratives, whether they are written in annual reports or told during meetings (Robichaud, 2003; Vaara et al., 2016). They have found that other temporal foci, especially towards the past, press on the present and the future through their mobilization in narratives and other communicative practices (Basque & Langley, 2018; Hjorth & Dawson, 2016). In that sense, strategy discourses and communication, including narratives, have performative effects and function powerfully in the way that they may relate and legitimize continuity and change in constituting organization reality (Hardy & Thomas, 2014). Without being explicitly mentioned, temporality is central in such studies, as strategic efforts may span several years, and documents such as meeting minutes, reports, grant applications, emails, and so on, play a key part in creating change or continuity across singular events (Vásquez et al., 2018). Such dynamics also exist across much shorter timespans, as concerns gain strategic status even within the same conversation and are commutatively made present and crystalized into a course of action for the future (Bencherki et al., 2021). These studies show that, rather than well-articulated intention, it is complex discursive dynamics and networks of communication, in precarious, tensional relation to each other, *that make any change or continuity become reality.*

Relatedly, others look at resistance to change, and suggest that change and resistance are inherent to each other, and some even see resistance as co-constructive of change and continuity efforts (Thomas & Hardy, 2011; Frandsen et al., 2018). Such research elucidates how power-resistance dynamics challenge the distinction between change and continuity. For example, studies show that organizing and legitimizing change emerge through ongoing discursive negotiations and communicative resistance, for example, during meetings, or through emails, and documents (Thomas et al., 2011; Plotnikof & Pedersen, 2019). Such perspectives make resistance integral to change and hence relate change to continuity, by arguing that ongoing power-resistance dynamics shape negotiations of what change may mean and how it come to matter to the situated work practices and actors. These studies unpack fine-grained analysis of change discourses, meaning negotiations and counter-narratives situated in specific moments, seeking to change the future of organizational plans. Further, examining such moments in detail across events and meetings reveal how these communicatively interrelate or contrast change and continuity through power-resistance dynamics. Others unpack resistance to politically decided changes, accentuating the precarity of both change and continuity as depending on power-resistance dynamics that are enacted through multimodality and multivocality across actors over time (Buchanan & Dawson, 2007; Mumby & Plotnikof, 2019; Thomas & Davies, 2005).

This literature highlights how discourse and communication interweave and negotiate meanings of change and continuity through power-resistance dynamics that constitute organizational reality in and across time. In that sense, change and continuity is not constituted despite each other, but in ongoing relation to one another. This body of knowledge highlights the multi-directional and multivocality of discourse and communication constitutive to rethinking both change and continuity. In so doing, they show how change or continuity may be demarcated in a strategy, but also reveal how they are implied by one another and entangle in messy ways through the communication emerging amongst actors and spaces embodying them in, over and through time.

Viewing strategic and resisting efforts of continuity and change as relations constituted through discourse and communication, including narratives and counter-narratives, is underpinned by temporal assumptions of such constructions occurring in, through and over time. Yet, they are freed from the temporal assumption of planning. First, as we hinted, information collection, strategy formulation, dissemination and resistance turn out to be multidirectional and simultaneous, rather than steps in a well-disciplined procedure. They involve communicative practices taking place across years, a few meetings or within the same conversation, as new information may appear, suggesting other courses of action, causing negotiations or rejections of ideas (e.g. Cooren et al., 2015). Second, the fact that communication and discourse materialize in multimodal, fragmented ways in the situation, allows multiple voices and concerns to co-emerge in time, but also through time and over time. This is because they can re-emerge across events, interactions and ideas, which by their relation may appear as strategic, resisting and conflictual, yet which may reconfigure across different past-present-future constructions; for example through anecdotes from participants' past, stakeholder concerns expressed earlier or predicted future horizons or outcomes (Bencherki et al., 2019; Plotnikof & Pedersen, 2019; Wenzel et al., 2020).

Continuity and change in text/conversation dynamics

A key notion in studies adopting a constitutive perspective is the text/conversation interplay, which directly addresses continuity and change. Early scholarship on communication's constitutive role was centrally concerned with the way principles, values and ways of doing things are negotiated in conversations that may sediment and stabilize into texts, which again may be renegotiated in further conversations (Taylor et al., 1996; Taylor & Van Every, 2000). Text and conversations may be woven together into "metaconversations" that, in their turn, sediment into authoritative texts that define what the organization is about (Kuhn, 2008; Robichaud et al., 2004), as well as what changes may be discursively reproduced or resisted (Grant & Marshak, 2011; Mumby & Plotnikof, 2019). This iterative or recursive dynamic is how organizing unfolds, as the continuity that texts provide is put in productive tension with the change that conversations afford.

The notion of text, though, should be understood broadly: a text is any description of the organization, irrespective of the empirical form it takes. It may be a document, a piece of technology, a story that is told again and again, and so on. What distinguishes texts and conversations, then, is not their material form, as they may in fact both be oral (as when someone quotes a rule) or textual (as when discussing on an online forum). Instead, conversations are distinguished in that they *reflexively* re-examine texts and allow them to make a difference in the ongoing situation, as when people invoke a rule to account for their action (Taylor & Van Every, 2000). The iterative nature of text-conversation dynamics entails that continuity and change are shaped as people refer to what others have said and written previously, that is, as they "ventriloquize" texts in a citational chain that maintains continuity across situations over time, while also altering the original texts and giving them new meaning, thus performing change (Cooren, 2010, 2012).

The relationship between text and conversation has led authors to recognize that continuity and change, or order and disorder, are not two different states, but rather simultaneous occurrences (Vásquez et al., 2016; Vásquez & Kuhn, 2019). Any effort to order and organize things, whether in everyday conversations or over longer timespans, thus inevitably also creates disorder and disorganization. However, rather than regret this fact, it should be recognized that it is crucial for organizations to be living, adaptive creatures (Bencherki & Iliadis, 2021; Vásquez et al., 2022).

For continuity and change, acknowledging the text/conversation interplay also entails recognizing that continuity necessarily involves change, as any identity, routine, history, procedure, rule, or other text must also be enacted to make a difference in the ongoing situation. Continuity is moot if it does not affect the conversations where it could potentially change – and where, potentially, a different decision could be made (Grothe-Hammer, 2022). On the other hand, change also supposes continuity, to the extent that conversations are about something (i.e. they reflexively refer to texts), if only to the linguistic norms that substantiate communication, or risk being nothing but unintelligible and disorganized babble (Cooren, 2010).

The text/conversation interplay has two important consequences for the way we understand temporality and time. First, it highlights that continuity and change are simultaneously present in any given situation. Indeed, conversations and texts coexist in meetings and other decision-making arenas, as people talk about the documents they show each other, jolt the ideas they talk about on a flipchart or comment on PowerPoint slides (e.g. Bourgoin & Muniesa, 2016; Cooren, 2007). The apparent continuity of texts is therefore subject to change through talk where the inscriptions of the past are made present and can act through the bodies and voices of those who interpret them (Vásquez & Kuhn, 2019). For instance, notes from a meeting are written to create continuity until the next one, but at that time, people must read them and voice them, with the risk of betrayed what their past selves intended (Vásquez et al., 2018). Continuity and change are therefore not stages, as conventional models may have suggested, but different rhythms and paces afforded by different communicative modalities. Second, the fact that conversations reflexively concern texts, which are themselves stabilizations of prior conversations, means that any utterance or writing already folds into itself other temporalities, in a polyphonic manner (Benoit-Barné & Martine, 2022). Organizational time, then, does not flow from the past to the future, but rather takes a multitude of twists depending on the layering of text and conversation.

Continuity and change in interactional approaches

Studies interested in the text/conversation interplay often – but not always – analyze it in naturally occurring interactions. In that sense, researchers on communication's constitutive power, but also some discourse scholars, rely on interactional analysis to make sense of communicative data (Cooren, 2007). They are often inspired by ethnomethodology (EM) and conversation analysis (e.g. Llewellyn & Hindmarsh, 2010). Such an approach views the construction of social order (i.e. of the organization) as sequentially emerging in each situation where it is practically dealt with (Garfinkel, 1967). This is why these scholars are reluctant to explain what takes place within a given situation by drawing from outside "context," as if societal or organizational forces overlaid empirical reality (Pomerantz et al., 2018). Instead, they consider the reflexivity of interacting participants as a key analytical resource.

Ascribing reflexivity to participants supposes that, when interacting, people are concerned with maintaining a viable social order and adapting it to emerging needs: in other words, it is through interaction that people deal with continuity and change. This view of how social order is interactionally and reflexively constituted rests on the notion of accountability (Samra-Fredericks, 2010). This term refers to the fact that, when they interact, people expect each other to produce their behavior in a way that is recognizably relevant to the situation at hand, or else to provide an account – or initiate a "repair" – to restore their behavior's meaning (Heaphy, 2013). For instance, talking about a new issue when looking at the sheet on which the meeting's agenda is printed makes clear that the speaker is not merely drifting off topic (with respect to the previous issue), but transitioning to a next item (Cooren et al., 2015), and therefore also highlighting that there is, in fact, continuity. Thus, an action is meaningful in the context of other actions that provide its "meaning-context," as well as reactions that display others' recognition of its contribution in the ongoing activity (Schutz, 1967). Producing a behavior that is not recognized as relevant may, at best, appear as a misunderstanding of the shared activity – for instance, saying "goodbye" because you thought the meeting was over – or lead to anger and other strong emotions if they are viewed as a disregard for shared expectations – as when someone leaves an interaction abruptly (Llewellyn & Butler, 2011).

The expectation that people will produce behavior that is *accountable* ensures that some degree of continuity is collaboratively enforced by participants in an interaction, and that any change contributes positively to the ongoing activity. Even highly institutionalized situations designed to maintain continuity, such as a judge having to adjudicate a legal case to ensure social order is maintained, are fact interactional accomplishment: they can be seen as conversations between lawyers and judges comparing framings of the situation, and as reflexive dialogue between different situational expectations (Cooren, 2015). Similarly, a classic case of producing change is that of creativity; however, constitutive perspectives of communication have shown that a "creative" idea is interactionally assessed on the basis of its ability to maintain a link to legitimate forms of creativity, thus maintaining a degree of continuity with established ways of doing things (Martine et al., 2017). Likewise, interactional studies have shown how continuity in (Western) medical standards may be upheld despite the different expectations of emergency humanitarian work, and how unwanted change is averted (Matte & Bencherki, 2019). At times, the very expectations that are held in common must be reflexively inspected, as when an organization adopts a new identity that questions its very substance (Chaput et al., 2011).

In the same way as we noted that the strategic and resisting studies highlighted the sequence of communicative practices through which continuity and change were accomplished, or that documents and texts were renegotiated through conversation, interactional studies point to the micro-temporalities of talk (Rawls, 2005). Such "micro" time is crucial to study as it is through such situatedness that multiple temporalities interweave in constituting various organizational times (Clark & Pinch, 2010; Plotnikof & Mumby, 2023). In keeping with the EM roots of interactional perspectives to the constitutive role of communication, the latter must be understood as implying a reflexive reconstruction of the history of practical action (Kim, 1999). Indeed, jointly figuring out what social order is being constructed also supposes jointly characterizing what has been happening so far, whether in the immediate past of the conversation or in the broader history of the interacting parties. Importantly, this characterization occurs in the interaction's present time, acknowledging it as a key relevant temporality (Basque et al., 2019). The past and the future exist to the extent that they are made relevant in the unfolding of the current interaction: they are here-and-now accomplishment, thus pointing to their situatedness.

In sum, the three analytical strategies are not only specific kinds of continuity and change – for instance, "communicative change" – but rather ways of looking at any organizational change, turning our attention to the key role communication plays in it. Aligned with process theorizing, constitutive views of discourse and communication consider that, while dealing with continuity and change, people link together the past, the present and the future – for instance, through interpreting the past, envisioning the future, all the while debating in the present (Kaplan & Orlikowski, 2013). They do so simultaneously, meaning that different time horizons are involved at once in any (communicative) action (Schultz & Hernes, 2020). This is the case because, in fact, the past and future are enacted through the present in a process of becoming, which implies that the present cannot be talked about as such before it has reached a closure, thus already being in the past (Hernes et al., 2021).

More specifically, across these perspectives we argue that viewing communication and discourse as constitutive, challenges three commonly held assumptions about time: that it flows in a linear, unidirectional manner; that temporalities (i.e. the past, the present and the future) are stable, distinct entities; and that time is objective. When taken together, these challenges reveal a conception of time as a multidirectional, fragmented, and relationally constructed phenomenon (Plotnikof & Mumby, 2023). In turn, this view of time has important implications for the way continuity and change are conceived which we will unfold below.

To illustrate this point, we turn to an example based on an important, urgent tension between these two notions as they co-emerge and are negotiated in a case of climate change and related politics. Indeed, while scientists urge politicians to initiate brisk changes, the latter tend to privilege continuity in their policy decisions. However, with the growing evidence that climate change is quite real with serious consequences, politicians increasingly (attempt to) blur the distinction between the two, presenting continuity as an enactment of change. The case of Canadian prime minister Justin Trudeau, a self-described champion of environmental issues, allows us to observe how he walks this blurry line.

Time in change and continuity: the case of United Nations' Sustainable Development Goals

The United Nations' Sustainable Development Goals (SDGs) are apt examples of discourse aiming at creating change to ensure continuity:[1] they are a strong invitation to political, institutional and business leaders to change the way we work, produce, consume and live, to preserve the continuity of our very lives on this planet. Such urgency is regularly repeated, as was the case in a 2020 UN broadcast: "On 25 September 2015 … 193 world leaders committed to the 17 Sustainable Development Goals … These are a series of ambitious objectives and targets to end extreme poverty and hunger, fight inequality and injustice, and tackle climate change, by 2030."[2] In this statement, we see how the SDGs are positioned temporally: they have a starting point – 2015 – and an end point – 2030 – whose pressing nature is stressed by the "ambitious" character of the objectives that were formulated.

In taking a constitutive view, we can see how the UN's statement performs a strategic discursive construction of an urgent, necessary demand for change, by configuring together the past, the present and the future: our past has failed to respond to grand societal challenges, and so our continuing future depends on urgent, ongoing changes. The seriousness of the issues at hand may give the impression that the situation's urgency is obvious. Yet, when closely observing the communication practices taking place in various international, national, and local institutions and organizations, we notice that counter-narratives emerge that suggest alternative paces and time horizons for these objectives. Indeed, as the UN's call for strategic change disseminates to other actors, it is also distorted and transformed into counter-narratives and other communicative practices that resist the UN's version of reality. These communication practices can be sorted out according to the three categories of *constitutive* discourse and communication identified above.

Strategic and resisting conceptions of time can be exemplified in Canadian prime minister Justin Trudeau's efforts, during the 2021 elections, to reconcile his defense of his country's oil and gas industry, with his claim to be an environmental champion. To do so, he operated a discursive repositioning, by which he committed to ensuring that the oil and gas industry reaches "carbon neutrality" by 2050, starting in 2022. Any new oil exploitation project would need to help attain these goals. Trudeau was also pressed to justify his government's 4.5-billion-dollar purchase of the TransMountain pipeline in 2018. To him, the purchase is justified because the government will "invest all the profits in the green transition," as reported in a newspaper article of the time (Shields,

2021). While, to some, Trudeau's position appears to adopt a hard line with the oil and gas industry, in fact these new commitments delay prior objectives and suggest that the countdown only starts in 2022 (while the UN's broadcast, above, positioned the starting point in 2015). As an expert commented in the same article, if we want to reach climate change goals by 2050 – not to mention the UN's 2030 – the oil and gas industry does not need to be carbon neutral, it needs to have all but disappeared. Trudeau's suggestion that buying a pipeline is a way of funding green projects also suggests a transitional period during which fossil fuels simultaneously cohabitate with a green transition, and therefore that change coexists with continuity.

The example of Prime Minister Trudeau thus illustrates how it is possible to discursively appear to pursue similar goals but to move the temporal signposts and to suggest simultaneity, all to delay action and resist the pace produced by others' strategic formulations. However, it also shows that others – such as experts – can provide alternatives, thus highlighting the multidirectional and collective nature of the discursive constitution of time and temporality.

Second, we can zoom in on the text/conversation interplay through which some actors negotiate the urgency of the SDGs, and such zooming in also allows us, third, to observe some interactional features this negotiation. The context of a debate between Canadian party leaders, which took place during the 2021 electoral campaign, offers a good opportunity to look at the way they communicatively conducted such negotiation regarding climate change in particular.[3] An obvious case of text/conversation interplay is offered by an opposition leader, Yves-François Blanchet, who criticized Trudeau's lack of action, by pointing out that "the Intergovernmental Panel on Climate Change has established that Canada is a very very bad student when it comes to climate change." Blanchet thus lends his voice to a text, the IPCC report, showing that his own critique in fact extends ongoing ones. Shortly after Blanchet's comment, a journalist, Paul Journet, asked Trudeau: "you wish to put a ceiling to gas and oil emissions, but you are still giving out drilling permits, including to Newfoundland. When will you put an end to new projects?" This intervention can be looked at both in terms of text/conversation interplay and interactionally. It presents both Trudeau's "wish" to put a ceiling and the fact that he hands out drilling permits as established texts (presumably based on party's program and on prior government decisions) and, by juxtaposing them, stresses the apparent contradiction between both. It then directly poses a question in temporal terms, asking *when* new projects will be barred. Trudeau's answer was that "we will continue being serious by pricing pollution and taking other necessary measures," which is vague but also illustrates that, for him, no change is necessary, since he can just *continue* with his current course of action. The journalist appears displeased with the answer, and insists with another question asked in temporal terms: "but, if I may, the ceiling starts on what year, and will decrease at what rhythm? It is a slow slope, or an abrupt one?" Journet insists that Trudeau commits to a clear temporal framework and to a pace of change. However, the prime minister, again, answers in terms of continuity, giving a temporal horizon moving towards the past, explaining that "the emissions have been capped for four or five years, and they won't be raised anymore."

The exchange between Trudeau, the opposition party leader and the journalist, thus illustrates the importance of the interaction itself as a time through which other temporalities are made relevant (as Journet's efforts show) and through which participants characterize their shared history (i.e. depicting Trudeau as either failing to commit to change or not). The exchange also highlights how different rhythms coexist, and that people reflexively revisit past texts (the IPCC report, electoral promises, government decisions, etc.) as they layer temporalities. Overall, the example of the SDGs and their negotiation in Canada shows how temporal horizons and the pacing of action are not intrinsic, but rather communicative accomplishments. As climate change objectives were reiterated communicatively on different occasions, their urgency was also renegotiated in subtle (and, at times, not so subtle) ways.

Implications for scholars and practitioners

Adopting a *constitutive* view of the role of communication and discourse in continuity and change has several implications for the way we understand these two related notions and their temporal underpinning. First, it sensitizes us to the fact that continuity and change are *becoming* together. Their joint evolution corresponds to entangled and open-ended relations, which are continuously reconfigured through communicative practices across actors and spaces *in, through* and *over* time (Plotnikof & Pedersen, 2019; Thomas et al., 2011; Vásquez et al., 2018). While this temporal underpinning is evident in much ODS and CCO literature, this chapter has explicated how a constitutive view on change and continuity as ever-shifting relations also recast new temporal arrangements, highlighting that time is never a given, but also communicatively and discursively performed.

As such, our view on communication alters our working assumptions about time and temporality, which in turn affect how we understand continuity and change. While a conventional, transmission-based view of communication (see Axley, 1984) emphasizes a step-by-step, intentional conception of change initiated by top managers, a constitutive view stresses a multilateral and fuzzy conception, where continuity and change are interwoven and joint accomplishments by multiple parties involved. This also entails that the organization's different parts may enact and construct time at different paces. When time is considered a communicative accomplishment, then, if people interact differently in their unit or department, they also constitute and pace time in their own way.

Putting communication and discourse at the center calls for a more critical and reflexive consideration of how we develop and mobilize temporal notions in our research. In more conventional perspectives on time, researchers can safely suppose that, no matter what they do, we are merely reporting on external phenomena. However, when we recognize that communication and discourse constitute continuity and change relations through multimodal, multidirectional, and multivocal pacings, then our own practices as researchers – which are also communication practices – indeed become consequential in determining *what* we observe, and how and why we observe it (Plotnikof & Mumby, 2023). In making such (more or less conscious) choices, we also privilege, in our accounts, some relations of change over others, and though those accounts, we also contribute to communicatively constituting them, and giving them materiality. Our research agenda, then, must become more temporally explicit about how time underpins (our studies of) the relations of organizational change and continuity.

For practitioners, considering that continuity and change are communicatively constituted allows them to better grasp their entangled nature. They can then perceive that their apparent opposition is but the result of a temporary emphasis that may be put on either one of them. When conventional models draw attention to one organizational state, the other may be set aside, but it does not disappear for that much. Concretely speaking, practitioners, such as change managers or strategic planners, must attune themselves to the meaning negotiations or counter-narratives through which organizational members may emphasize or struggle over one or the other, hence accepting the power-resistance dynamics inherent to attempts of affecting change and continuity. Similarly, focusing on text/conversation interplays and interactions provides a firm ground for observing the way people communicatively constitute continuity and change. Practitioners may look at the way change is promoted or stifled as organizational members jointly accelerate or slow down the pace of time. Rather than assuming that people have psychological or political motivations to resist change, practitioners may therefore gain richer insights by considering the interrelated dynamics of change and continuity, including power-resistance, and the way these are communicatively and collectively created.

Most importantly, though, practitioners must keep in mind that continuity and change – and resistance to them – cannot entirely be planned or intended. A communicative perspective, indeed, stresses the messy and precarious character of continuity and change. The practitioner's role, then, changes too: it becomes a matter of co-producing, engaging with, and facilitating the communicative and discursive practices through which people seek to effectuate change or hang on to continuity. The practitioner may try to identify how, in the way people talk, write, tell stories, or share experiences, they pace change or sustain organizing processes differently, and draw their attention to these effects. All stakeholders may thus gain a more critical and context-sensitive view of the ways in which their daily lives are always in the making of both change as well as continuity through discursive and communicative practices *in, over and through time.*

Notes

1. See https://www.un.org/sustainabledevelopment/sustainable-development-goals/.
2. See https://www.un.org/sustainabledevelopment/blog/2020/09/united-nations-releases -special-2020-broadcast-calling-for-collective-action/.
3. The debate took place in French, and is available at https://youtu.be/zMkGuQFVUS0 ?t=1732.

References

Axley, S. R. (1984). Managerial and organizational communication in terms of the conduit metaphor, *The Academy of Management Review*, 9(3), 428–37, https://doi .org/10.2307/258283.

Balogun, J., & Johnson, G. (2004). Organizational restructuring and middle manager sensemaking, *The Academy of Management Journal*, 47(4), 523–49, https:// doi .org/10.2307/20159600.

Basque, J., Bencherki, N., & Kuhn, T. R. (eds) (2022). *Routledge Handbook of the Communicative Constitution of Organization*, New York: Routledge.

Basque, J., Bencherki, N., & Rouleau, L. (2019, July 4). How people practically and communicatively constitute concerns as strategic over the years at a microbrewers' association, European Group for Organizational Studies, Edinburgh, UK.

Basque, J., & Langley, A. (2018). Invoking Alphonse: the founder figure as a historical resource for organizational identity work, *Organization Studies*, 39(12), 1685–708, https://doi.org/10.1177/0170840618789211.

Bencherki, N., Basque, J., & Rouleau, L. (2019). A sensemaking perspective on open strategy, in D. Seidl, R. Whittington & G. von Krogh (eds), *The Cambridge Handbook of Open Strategy* (pp. 241–58), Cambridge: Cambridge University Press.

Bencherki, N., & Iliadis, A. (2021). The constitution of organization as informational individuation, *Communication Theory*, 31(3), 442–62, https://doi.org/10.1093/ct/qtz018.

Bencherki, N., Sergi, V., Cooren, F., & Vásquez, C. (2021). How strategy comes to matter: strategizing as the communicative materialization of matters of concern, *Strategic Organization*, 19(4), 608–35, https://doi.org/10.1177/1476127019890380.

Benoit-Barné, C., & Martine, T. (eds) (2022). *Speaking with One Voice: Multivocality and Univocality in Organizing*, London: Routledge.

Bourgoin, A., & Muniesa, F. (2016). Building a rock-solid slide: management consulting, PowerPoint, and the craft of signification, *Management Communication Quarterly*, 30(3), 390–410, https://doi.org/10.1177/0893318916629562.

Brown, A. D., Colville, I., & Pye, A. (2015). Making sense of sensemaking in organization studies, *Organization Studies*, 36(2), 265–77, https://doi.org/10.1177/0170840614559259.

Buchanan, D., & Dawson, P. (2007). Discourse and audience: organizational change as multi-story process, *Journal of Management Studies*, 44(5), 669–86, https://doi.org/10.1111/j.1467-6486.2006.00669.x.

Chaput, M., Brummans, B. H. J. M., & Cooren, F. (2011). The role of organizational identification in the communicative constitution of an organization: a study of consubstantialization in a young political party, *Management Communication Quarterly*, 25(2), 252–82, https://doi.org/10.1177/0893318910386719.

Chia, R., & Tsoukas, H. (2003). Everything flows and nothing abides: towards a "rhizomic" model of organizational change, transformation and action, *Process Studies*, 32(2), 196–224, https://doi.org/10.5840/process20033223.

Clark, C., & Pinch, T. (2010). Some major organisational consequences of some 'minor', organised conduct: evidence from a video analysis of pre-verbal service encounters in a showroom retail store', in N. Llewellyn & J. Hindmarsh (eds), *Organisation, Interaction and Practice: Studies of Ethnomethodology and Conversation Analysis* (pp. 140–71), Cambridge: Cambridge University Press.

Cooren, F. (ed.) (2007). *Interacting and Organizing: Analyses of a Management Meeting*, Mahwah, NJ: Lawrence Erlbaum Associates.

Cooren, F. (2010). *Action and Agency in Dialogue: Passion, Ventriloquism and Incarnation*, Amsterdam: John Benjamins.

Cooren, F. (2012). Communication theory at the center: ventriloquism and the communicative constitution of reality, *Journal of Communication*, 62(1), 1–20, https://doi.org/10.1111/j.1460-2466.2011.01622.x.

Cooren, F. (2015). In the name of law: ventriloquism and juridical matters, in K. McGee (ed.), *Latour and the Passage of Law* (pp. 235–72), Edinburgh: Edinburgh University Press.

Cooren, F. (2018). Materializing communication: making the case for a relational ontology, *Journal of Communication*, 68(2), 278–88, https://doi.org/10.1093/joc/jqx014.

Cooren, F., Bencherki, N., Chaput, M., & Vásquez, C. (2015). The communicative constitution of strategy-making: exploring fleeting moments of strategy, in D. Golsorkhi, L. Rouleau, D. Seidl & E. Vaara (eds), *The Cambridge Handbook of Strategy As Practice* (pp. 370–93), Cambridge: Cambridge University Press.

DePamphilis, D. (2015). *Mergers, Acquisitions, and Other Restructuring Activities*, 8th edition, Cambridge, MA: Academic Press.

Doerfel, M. L., & Harris, J. L. (2017). Resilience processes, in *The International Encyclopedia of Organizational Communication* (pp. 1–6), American Cancer Society, https://doi.org/10.1002/9781118955567.wbieoc178.

Frandsen, S., Kuhn, T., & Lundholt, M. W. (eds) (2018). *Counter-narratives and Organization*, New York: Routledge.

Garfinkel, H. (1967). *Studies in Ethnomethodology*, Hoboken, NJ: Prentice Hall.

Grant, D., & Marshak, R. J. (2011). Toward a discourse-centered understanding of organizational change, *The Journal of Applied Behavioral Science*, 47(2), 204–35, https://doi.org/10.1177/0021886310397612.

Grant, D., Michelson, G., Oswick, C., & Wailes, N. (2005). Guest editorial: discourse and organizational change, *Journal of Organizational Change Management*, 18(1), 6–15, https://doi.org/10.1108/09534810510579814.

Grothe-Hammer, M. (2022). The communicative constitution of the world: a Luhmannian view on communication, organizations, and society, in J. Basque, N. Bencherki & T. Kuhn (eds), *Routledge Handbook of the Communicative Constitution of Organization* (chapter 5), New York: Routledge.

Hardy, C., & Thomas, R. (2014). Strategy, discourse and practice: the intensification of power, *Journal of Management Studies*, 51(2), 320–48, https://doi.org/10.1111/joms.12005.

Heaphy, E. D. (2013). Repairing breaches with rules: maintaining institutions in the face of everyday disruptions, *Organization Science*, 24(5), 1291–315, https://doi.org/10.1287/orsc.1120.0798.

Hernes, T., Feddersen, J., & Schultz, M. (2021). Material temporality: how materiality 'does' time in food organizing, *Organization Studies*, 42(2), 351–71, https://doi.org/10.1177/0170840620909974.

Hjorth, D., & Dawson, A. (2016). The burden of history in the family business organization, *Organization Studies*, https://doi.org/0170840615613375.

Kaplan, S., & Orlikowski, W. J. (2013). Temporal work in strategy making, *Organization Science*, 24(4), 965–95, https://doi.org/10.1287/orsc.1120.0792.

Kim, K.-M. (1999). The management of temporality: ethnomethodology as historical reconstruction of practical action, *The Sociological Quarterly*, 40(3), 505–23.

Köhler, K., & Zerfass, A. (2019). Communicating the corporate strategy: an international benchmark study in the UK, the USA, and Germany, *Journal of Communication Management*, 23(4), 348–74, https://doi.org/10.1108/JCOM-10-2018-0106.

Koschmann, M. A., Kuhn, T., & Pfarrer, M. D. (2012). A communicative framework of value in cross-sector partnerships, *Academy of Management Review*, 37(3), 332–54, https://doi.org/10.5465/amr.2010.0314.

Kuhn, T. R. (2008). A communicative theory of the firm: developing an alternative perspective on intra-organizational power and stakeholder relationships, *Organization Studies*, 29(8–9), 1227–54, https://doi.org/10.1177/0170840608094778.

Kuhn, T. R., & Putnam, L. L. (2014). Discourse and communication, in P. Adler, P. du Gay, G. Morgan & M. Reed (eds), *The Oxford Handbook of Sociology, Social Theory, and Organization Studies* (pp. 414–46), Oxford: Oxford University Press, https://doi.org/10.1093/oxfordhb/9780199671083.013.0018.

Langley, A., Smallman, C., Tsoukas, H., & Van de Ven, A. H. (2013). Process studies of change in organization and management: unveiling temporality, activity, and flow, *Academy of Management Journal*, 56(1), 1–13, https://doi.org/10.5465/amj .2013.4001.

LeCouvie, K., & Pendergast, J. (2014). The opportunities and challenges of continuity, in K. LeCouvie & J. Pendergast (eds), *Family Business Succession: Your Roadmap to Continuity* (pp. 1–12), New York: Palgrave Macmillan, https://doi.org/10.1057/9781137280923_1.

Lewin, K. (1947). Frontiers in group dynamics: concept, method and reality in social science; social equilibria and social change, *Human Relations*, 1(1), 5–41, https://doi.org/10.1177/001872674700100103.

Lewis, L. K. (1999). Disseminating information and soliciting input during planned organizational change: implementers' targets, sources, and channels for communicating, *Management Communication Quarterly*, 13(1), 43–75, https://doi.org/10.1177/0893318999131002.

Llewellyn, N., & Butler, C. W. (2011). Walking out on air, *Research on Language and Social Interaction*, 44(1), 44–64, https://doi.org/10.1080/08351813.2011.544128.

Llewellyn, N., & Hindmarsh, J. (2010). *Organisation, Interaction and Practice: Studies in Ethnomethodology and Conversation Analysis*, Cambridge: Cambridge University Press.

Martine, T., Cooren, F., & Bartels, G. (2017). Evaluating creativity through the degrees of solidity of its assessment: a relational approach, *The Journal of Creative Behavior*, 53(4), 427–42, https://doi.org/10.1002/jocb.219.

Matte, F., & Bencherki, N. (2019). Materializing ethical matters of concern: practicing ethics in a refugee camp, *International Journal of Communication*, 13, 5870–89.

Mumby, D. K., & Plotnikof, M. (2019). Organizing power and resistance: from coercion, to consent, to governmentality, in J. McDonald & R. Mitra (eds), *Movements in Organizational Communication Research: Current Issues and Future Directions* (pp. 35–55), London: Routledge.

Phillips, N., & Oswick, C. (2012). Organizational discourse: domains, debates, and directions, *Academy of Management Annals*, 6(1), 435–81, https://doi.org/10.5465/19416520.2012.681558.

Plotnikof, M. (2015). Negotiating collaborative governance designs: a discursive approach, *Innovation Journal*, 20(3), 1–22.

Plotnikof, M. & Mumby, D. K. (2023). Temporal multimodality and performativity: exploring politics of time in the discursive, communicative constitution of organization, *Organization*, https://doi.org/10.1177/13505084221145649.

Plotnikof, M., & Pedersen, A. R. (2019). Exploring resistance in collaborative forms of governance: meaning negotiations and counter-narratives in a case from the Danish education sector, *Scandinavian Journal of Management*, 35(4), https://doi.org/10.1016/j.scaman.2019.101061.

Pomerantz, A., Sanders, R. E., & Bencherki, N. (2018). Communication as the study of social action: on the study of language and social interaction. An interview with Anita Pomerantz and Robert E. Sanders, by Nicolas Bencherki, *Communiquer. Revue de Communication Sociale et Publique*, 22, 103–18, https://doi.org/10.4000/communiquer.2786.

Rawls, A. W. (2005). Garfinkel's conception of time, *Time & Society*, 14(2–3), 163–90.

Robichaud, D. (2003). Narrative institutions we organize by: the case of a municipal administration, in B. Czarniawska & P. Gagliardi (eds), *Narratives We Organize By: Advances in Organization Studies* (pp. 37–54), Amsterdam: John Benjamins.

Robichaud, D., Giroux, H., & Taylor, J. R. (2004). The metaconversation: the recursive property of language as a key to organizing, *Academy of Management Review*, 29(4), 617–34, https://doi.org/10.5465/amr.2004.14497614.

Samra-Fredericks, D. (2010). Ethnomethodology and the moral accountability of interaction: navigating the conceptual terrain of 'face' and face-work, *Journal of Pragmatics*, 42(8), 2147–57, https://doi.org/10.1016/j.pragma.2009.12.019.

Schoeneborn, D., Kuhn, T. R., & Kärreman, D. (2019). The communicative constitution of organization, organizing, and organizationality, *Organization Studies*, 40(4), 475–96, https://doi.org/10.1177/0170840618782284.

Schultz, M., & Hernes, T. (2020). Temporal interplay between strategy and identity: punctuated, subsumed, and sustained modes, *Strategic Organization*, 18(1), 106–35, https://doi.org/10.1177/1476127019843834.

Schulz-Knappe, C., Koch, T., & Beckert, J. (2019). The importance of communicating change: identifying predictors for support and resistance toward organizational change processes, *Corporate Communications: An International Journal*, 24(4), 670–85, https://doi.org/10.1108/CCIJ-04-2019-0039.

Schutz, A. (1967). *The Phenomenology of the Social World*, Evanston, IL: Northwestern University Press.

Shields, A. (2021, August 31). Trudeau prêt à dire non au pétrole. *Le Devoir*, A4.

Taylor, J. R., Cooren, F., Giroux, N., & Robichaud, D. (1996). The communicational basis of organization: between the conversation and the text, *Communication Theory*, 6(1), 1–39, https://doi.org/10.1111/j.1468-2885.1996.tb00118.x.

Taylor, J. R., & Van Every, E. J. (2000). *The Emergent Organization: Communication as Its Site and Surface*, Mahwah, NJ: Lawrence Erlbaum Associates.

Thomas, R., & Davies, A. (2005). Theorizing the micro-politics of resistance: new public management and managerial identities in the UK public services, *Organization Studies*, 26(5), 683–706, https://doi.org/10.1177/0170840605051821.

Thomas, R., Sargent, L. D., & Hardy, C. (2011). Managing organizational change: negotiating meaning and power-resistance relations, *Organization Science*, 22(1), 22–41, https://doi.org/10.1287/orsc.1090.0520.

Vaara, E., Sonenshein, S., & Boje, D. (2016). Narratives as sources of stability and change in organizations: approaches and directions for future research, *Academy of Management Annals*, 10(1), 495–560, https://doi.org/10.5465/19416520.2016.1120963.

Vásquez, C., Bencherki, N., Cooren, F., & Sergi, V. (2018). From 'matters of concern' to 'matters of authority': reflecting on the performativity of strategy in writing a strategic plan, *Long-Range Planning*, 51(3), 417–35, https://doi.org/10.1016/j.lrp.2017.01.001.

Vásquez, C., & Kuhn, T. R. (eds) (2019). *Dis/organization as Communication: Exploring the Disordering, Disruptive and Chaotic Properties of Communication*, London: Routledge.

Vásquez, C., Kuhn, T. R., & Plotnikof, M. (2022). Disrupting CCO thinking: a communicative ontology of dis/organization, in J. Basque, N. Bencherki & T. R. Kuhn (eds), *Routledge Handbook of the Communicative Constitution of Organization* (chapter 7), London: Routledge.

Vásquez, C., Schoeneborn, D., & Sergi, V. (2016). Summoning the spirits: organizational texts and the (dis)ordering properties of communication, *Human Relations*, 69(3), 629–59, https://doi.org/10.1177/0018726715589422.

Weick, K. E., & Quinn, R. E. (1999). Organizational change and development, *Annual Review of Psychology*, 50, 361–86, https://doi.org/10.1146/annurev.psych.50.1.361.

Wenzel, M., Krämer, H., Koch, J., & Reckwitz, A. (2020). Future and organization studies: on the rediscovery of a problematic temporal category in organizations, *Organization Studies*, https://doi.org/10.1177/0170840620912977.

7 Imaginary practices as the nexus between continuity and disruptive change

Iben Sandal Stjerne, Anders Buch and Matthias Wenzel

Introduction

> Through collective efforts, we will manage to soon transform Mecklenburg-Western Pomerania, Saxony-Anhalt, Brandenburg, Saxony, and Thuringia [the federal states of the German Democratic Republic] into blooming landscapes in which it is worth living and working.
> *Helmut Kohl, speech on the currency, economic, and social union of Western and Eastern Germany, July 1, 1990*

History shows us that disruptive change in large arrays of activity is rare but possible, and that such change typically starts with imagining a future that differs from the present. By "disruptive change in large arrays of activity," we refer to processes that involve breaking with the *continuity* of currently performed practices that are broadly shared within and across organizations, so as to give room for *change*. In this view, "continuity" refers to the reproduction of social and organizational life through the (n)ever-same performance of practices, whereas "change" refers to the performance of practices that differ markedly from the ones currently performed. In the case of the German reunification, a disruptive change in large arrays of activity meant breaking with broadly performed socialist practices in state-owned companies, amongst others, which gave room for the privatization of GDR's economy, as well as incisive shifts toward the performance of capitalist practices.

Practice theory is central for understanding disruptive change in large arrays of activity, as it seeks to explain both continuity and change as an outcome of performing practices (e.g. Reckwitz, 2002; Schatzki, 2002). However, similar to established understandings of disruption (e.g. Christensen, 2006; Kumaraswamy et al., 2018) and field-level change (e.g. Feront & Bertels, 2021; Suddaby et al., 2007) in management and organization studies, practice-based work tends to portray change as a process that happens incrementally. This

127

work does so by showing that small variations in the situated performance of current practices can cumulatively contribute to the emergence of new practices (e.g. Feldman et al., 2016; Vaara & Whittington, 2012). At the same time, practice theory clarifies that practices not only contribute to incremental change, but also generate continuity in that their performance can reproduce social and organizational life, rather than gradually altering it (e.g. Reckwitz, 2002; Schatzki, 2002). This continuity, however, leaves us with an incomplete understanding of the ways in which actors' performance of practices occasionally, even though rarely, produce disruptive change in large arrays of activity as an attempt to break with this continuity. Therefore, we ask: How can the performance of practices contribute to breaking with the continuity of current practices to initiate and enact disruptive change in large arrays of activity?

In this chapter, we seek to outline opportunities for disruptive change in large arrays of activity as a matter of central practices being embedded in and, at the same time, informed by and reflecting on imaginaries that contribute to organizing broadly performed practices in new ways. Specifically, we make a case for imaginary practices as key ways of creating disruptive change in large arrays of activity. We refer to "imaginary practices" as *ways of continuing and organizing activity that anticipate and deliberate possible lines of action, and foreshadow responsive strategies of action that are guided by values and norms that differ from the ones organized by established habits and customs.* Imagination has not played a central role in practice-theoretical accounts of change. Therefore, we elaborate our understanding of imaginary practices by inspiring accounts of practice theory with classical American pragmatism, notably John Dewey. In doing so, we argue that imaginary practices are essential in accounting for disruptive change in large arrays of activity. It is in and through imaginary practices through which actors expand the environment of situated activity and experiment with rules and principles in a playful way. As we posit, these features of imaginary practices help actors break with the continuity of current practices and, in doing so, give room for disruptive change in large arrays of activity.

We illustrate the imaginary practices in the case of the Dogma 95 movement in the Danish filmmaking industry. Dogma 95 contributed to putting Denmark on the map as film avantgarde within a short period of time and became a strong reference point for many practitioners in the industry up until today. How did actors in the Danish filmmaking industry break with the continuity of established practices? In this case, disruptive change in the practices of cinematography started with a few players who imagined a future for filmmaking that markedly differed from the practices performed in this industry at that time. Based on this observation, we illustrate how a delicate blend of locally situated and broadly shared practices is actualized and transformed through imaginative experience and activity.

Our chapter contributes to debates on organizational continuity and change by extending understanding of how disruptive change in large arrays of activity is performed in practice. Specifically, building on insights from practice theory as well as an illustrative case, we begin to draw attention to how the performance of imaginary practices contributes to breaking with the continuity of current practices through the production of alternative futures and, in doing so, gives room to the performance of practices that differ markedly from the ones currently performed not only within, but across organizations. In doing so, we position imaginary practices as a key concept for furthering our understanding of how disruptive change in large arrays of activity happens.

Practice theory

According to practice theories, practices organize and structure social activity. Agency is thus neither located in sovereign individuals nor in overarching deterministic social structures, but resides in practices. Practices, broadly defined, are collectively enacted patterns of activity, made up of individuals' actions that guide actions but do not determine any single individual's actions (Reckwitz, 2002; Schatzki, 2002). Practices manifest themselves as patterns of social activities that are organized and normatively sanctioned in particular ways by the individuals who enact the practices. Theodore Schatzki's version of practice theory envisions practices as "an open-ended, spatially-temporally, dispersed nexus of doings and sayings" (Schatzki, 2012, p. 14). He finds practices to be open-ended as he construes the theory within a Heideggarian event ontology that considers human activity to be indeterminate. Activity is not fixed until it has been carried out in time, and activity could in fact be enacted in different ways. However, according to Schatzki, activity is not random or confined to individual concerns. The social nature of human beings orients people to coordinate and organize their activities in practices that guide activity.

According to Schatzki (2012), the coordination of efforts in the performance of a practice is based on normative adjustments and agreements on how to go on enacting that practice. As Schatzki argues, such coordination occurs through four elements of practices: practical understandings, rules, teleoaffective structures, and general understandings. Practitioners have a practical understanding – a feel for the game and knowledge on how to carry out desired actions

– that enables them to continue their activities "in the right way." Sometimes, actions might also be guided by explicit rules and procedures that prescribe action. Teleoaffective structures imply guiding practices through collectively held ends, prescriptions, and purposes for activity. In turn, general under-standings are practitioners' convictions or *Weltanschauung*, which frame the overall purposes of tasks and projects.

While social practices guide practitioners' activities, they are also constrained and afforded by material arrangements. Activity is performed in space and time as well as among and through material objects, artifacts, human bodies, and other biological organisms. Material arrangements set limits for activities and tend to channel and shape activities in different ways. Some activities are more feasible and easier to accomplish than others given the restraints set by the material arrangements. And as Schatzki (2016a) argues, practices and material arrangements are bundled up with one another to form larger constellations, or nexuses, of practices and material arrangements. Accordingly, against the background of practice theory, large social phenomena "are large nexuses of practice-arrangement bundles or spatially far-flung sets of aspects thereof. These nexuses and sets are what there is in the world to such phenomena as governments, economic systems, energy provision systems, corporations, and educational establishments" (Schatzki, 2016b, p. 14). Therefore, "disruptive change in large arrays of activity" implies breaking with the continuity of practices currently performed within these nexuses to give room for the per-formance of practices that differ markedly from the ones currently performed.

Continuity and change of practices

Notably, Schatzki does not consider nexuses of practices to be stable by bringing closure to activity. Nexuses of practices and material arrangements are prone to change, as "novelty and innovation can burst forth anytime and, although inextricably tied to the past and present, set developments in new directions unanticipated by present actors" (Schatzki, 2016a, p. 39). However, even though Schatzki's practice-theoretical account installs indeterminacy and change as inherent in human activity and material existence, nexuses of practices tend to produce continuity by prefiguring future activity. Specifically, moments of stability are accomplished through the reenactment of practices. There is a sluggishness to change practices, as these are internalized to guide our sense of judgment of what is "good" and "bad," accepted or unaccepted, and belonging or not belonging to a specific practice. These practical sensibilities are interwoven into larger nexuses, textures, or connective tissue of practices that overlap and exist in codependent or even competing ways.

When looking at change and continuity from a practice perspective, the premise for acting in the world is the indeterminacy of action. Practices contribute to stabilizing action because dispositions are learned and internalized into teleoaffective structures that pierce through every emotion, sense, and belief of practitioners. At the same time, change is gradually but unavoidably happening as no practice will fully stay the same over time. This is so because practitioners are not fully able to perform the same practice in the exact same way over time and enact desires to refine practices in response to situations at hand. Even though every community includes some actors who attempt to protect certain practices as "core" by defining what is accepted as belonging and what is discarded as not belonging to these practices, this power structure may change over time or even become disrupted by competing enactments. The practical understandings, fundamental for knowing how to go on, are learned by practitioners as they are stirred into social practice, and continuity and discontinuities of performing the practice are negotiated. These negotiations, then, culminate in a duality of continuity and change in which practices are both stabilized and gradually changed in and through their situated performance.

Thus, from a practice perspective, social change involves action even when it is materially mediated (Schatzki, 2019). As action is guided by practices, the configuration of practices must eventually differ for change in large arrays of activity to emerge. By decentering individual actors and focusing on the transformations in and among social practices and material arrangements, practice theoreticians "offer […] a 'tool kit' of symbols, stories, rituals, and worldviews, which people may use in varying configurations to solve different kinds of problems" (Swidler, 1986, p. 273). Changes in practices – and *a fortiori* change in large arrays of activity – occur when the elements of practices change or become related to one another in new constellations and setups, and when the interlinking of social practices and material arrangements is altered. Therefore, analyzing change from a practice perspective amounts to analyzing the effects of social actions as these are organized in social practices and their interconnections with material arrangements, nexuses of practices, and wider constellations of nexuses of practices.

Consequently, change in large arrays of activity of any kind (driving, cooking, art, etc.) is a complex process because it relies on the interplay and configuration of multiple elements of nexuses of practices and material arrangements, and may be initiated by multiple of these elements (cf. Shove, 2022). Yet, while extant practice-based understandings of the dynamics of continuity and change draw our attention to the simultaneous continual reproduction and gradual change of social and organizational life, we know much less about how actors "break away" from current practices so as to enact disruptive change in large arrays of activity. Actors' "breaking away" from current practices occurs in different situations, and depends on different circumstances, and, therefore, may be grounded in many different (e.g. psychological) reasons. However, focusing on the plane of *social practices*, we argue, enables us to draw particular attention to imaginary practices as a way of understanding how the continuity of ongoing activity enables disruptive change in large arrays of activity.

Imaginary practices

In traditional folk psychology, 'imagination' is understood as a mental faculty or capacity of individuals that spurs creative activity.[1] The individualistic orientation of this common understanding of imagination sits uncomfortably with practice theories, which center on "practices" as their unit of analysis. Accordingly, within the practice-theoretical tradition, Charles Taylor has introduced the notion of "social imaginaries" to characterize "that common understanding that makes possible common practices and a widely shared sense of legitimacy" (Taylor, 2004, p. 23). Taylor's conception of social imagination is thus radically different from the mentalistic and individualistic notion of imagination held by traditional psychology. In this view, social imaginaries form a pre-reflexive "background" or "framework" (Taylor, 2002, p. 115) that bind actions together in practices and make them mutably intelligible. It is a characteristic of social imaginaries that they are widely shared (though not necessarily unanimously held by all) and not easily transformed. However, they are by no means static.

In Taylor's account, social imaginaries play a significant role in epochal, historical transformations of societies. As Taylor highlights: "Western modernity on this view is inseparable from a certain kind of social imaginary, and the differences among today's multiple modernities need to be understood in terms of the divergent social imaginaries involved" (Taylor, 2004, p. 2). Social imaginaries thus have a transformative role in large arrays of activity. To explain the rise of modernity in the West, Taylor describes how central ideas of influential individuals acting in a nexus of markets, legal rights, and divisions between the public and private sphere are able to infiltrate, transmute, and potentially breach existing imaginaries to become a discursive resource for new social imaginaries.

However, Taylor's construal of social imaginaries as pre-reflexive backgrounds only provides a vague characterization of how imagination connects with activity in social practices. Practice theory is not a theory of everything. It only provides a general background account of social activity and it must be combined with other theories to address more specific domains of human life such as experience, learning, interaction, cognition, and more (Schatzki 2021, p. 120). We thus turn to John Dewey to substantiate the connections between imagination and social practices.

In the tradition of American pragmatism, John Dewey assigns a prominent role to imagination in accounting for human conduct and experience. Whereas Taylor's account of social imagination is primarily related to the broad and deep framework of ideas and linguistic practices that shape our interpretative horizons, Dewey's account is much more mundane and related to human conduct and action in concrete (cultural) contexts. For Dewey, human beings are biological organisms and cultural beings that are situated in a dynamic interplay with their material environments and symbolic surroundings. It is in these situations that experience comes about – not as passive perception, but through an active, engaged, and directed process of interaction, trial, and experimentation. Experience is thus intimately and teleologically connected with action:

> Experience [...] is primarily what is undergone in connexion with activities whose import lies in their objective consequences – their bearing upon future experiences. Organic functions deal with things as things in course, in operation, in a state of affairs not yet given or completed. What is done with, what is just 'there', is of concern only in the potentialities which it may indicate. As ended, as wholly given, it is of no account. But as a sign of what may come, it becomes an indispensable factor in behavior dealing with changes, the outcome of which is not yet determined. (Dewey, 2011/1917, p. 117)

The course of experience is a temporal organization of activity through habits and customs. The process of habituation organizes our responsiveness to the environment to form avenues of conduct, that is, "predisposition[s] to ways or modes of response" (Dewey, 2007/1922, p. 42) that guide human conduct. Customs are formed as habits are collectivized through persistent processes of group interactions based upon prior customs. This renders experiencing through habituation and adoption of collective customs an iterative and accumulative process. Imagination plays a central role in the process of experience as we temporally orient ourselves to the world. For Dewey, imagination is that which expands our habits to other and new situations and integrates our actions to become patternlike. When we act (in the present), we anticipate the consequences of our actions (in the future) by deliberating possible outcomes of activities. Similarly, past activities are interpreted and integrated with the present situation to establish continuity. Dewey writes:

> Deliberation is an experiment in finding out what the various lines of possible action are really like. It is an experiment in making various combinations of selected elements of habits and impulses, to see what the resultant action would be like if it were entered upon. But the trial is in imagination, not in overt fact. The experiment is carried on by tentative rehearsals in thought which do not affect physical facts outside the body. Thought runs ahead and foresees outcomes, and thereby avoids having to wait the instruction of actual failure and disaster. An act overtly tried out is irrevocable, its consequences cannot be blotted out. An act tried out in imagination is not final or fatal. It is retrievable. (Dewey, 2007/1922, p. 190)

Imagination is thus a fundamental and pervasive feature of human conduct that enables us to anticipate and deliberate possible lines of action. It expands the environment that we respond to by envisioning possible future lines of actions and considering their consequences. The deliberative and expansive phase in human conduct is essential for Dewey. We are often put in situations where we consider how best to proceed, and which values would best serve as principles for future conduct. Values and norms thus become essential for our activities. Dewey sees norms, values, rules, and principles as instruments or hypotheses that can guide our actions, not as shared rules that govern activity:

> Principles are methods of inquiry and forecast which require verification by the event; and the time honored effort to assimilate morals to mathematics is only a way of bolstering up an old dogmatic authority, or putting a new one upon the throne of the old. But the experimental character of moral judgment does not mean complete uncertainty and fluidity. Principles exist as hypotheses with which to experiment. [...] The problem is one of continuous, vital readaptation. (Dewey, 2007/1922, p. 205)

Rules do not have an inherent power to propel and determine our actions, but they can play a significant role in our deliberative efforts to transcend and break with established habits. Based on Dewey's characterization of the role played by imagination in experience, we are able to conceptualize imaginary practices. We conceive imaginary practices as ways of continuing and organizing activity that anticipate and deliberate possible lines of action and foreshadow responsive strategies of action that are guided by values and norms that differ from the ones organized by established habits and customs.

In what follows, we draw on the case of Dogma 95 to illustrate how disruptive change in large arrays of activity can happen through the performance of imaginary practices. Prior filmmaking practices were guarded by experts who would explicate and distinguish "good" from "bad" filmmaking and, in that way, reproduce continuity. We illustrate how the Dogma 95 movement started with an imaginary practice that both explicated and challenged the continuity of established filmmaking practices through adopting 10 vows of chastity. These vows served as an experimental explication of hypotheses that guided directors' imaginative inquiry into the change of cinematography and eventually contributed to transforming the filmmaking practices of the entire industry.

Illustration: Dogma 95 and the disruptive change of cinematography

Dogma 1995 was a movement that sought to provoke and disrupt large arrays of activity in the Danish filmmaking industry. At the time, 15 years of mainstream commercial comedies had dominated this industry. Danish film production ensued from a film-subsidy agreement between the Danish Filmmaking industry and The Danish Ministry of Culture. The subsidy allowed films with promising commercial appeal to get 50 percent of the total budget, with an upper limit, covered by public funding. These movies were often based on stories that drew on a national cultural heritage back from the 1950s and 1960s, book series and epic historical dramas based on World War II events, and popular historical figures that would attract a broad audience. Internationally, the filmmaking industry was primarily dominated by the Hollywood film aesthetics. As stated by Birgitte Hald, the CEO and founder of a production company that was a front runner in the Dogma 95 movement, this type of aesthetics had a commercial appeal, which implied a "lack of focus on the dramaturgical storytelling" (interview) as well as using techniques that would artificially "wrap or dress" the film by adding music, props, makeup, and lighting. Hence, extant nexuses of filmmaking practices were not very experimental; neither in their aesthetical expressional style nor in their production process, and therefore did not allow for much variety in artistic expression.

In the early 1990s, there was a generation change in the Danish filmmaking industry, with a new wave of debuting directors, actors, and producers. This group of newbies felt a severe lack of artistic freedom. As stated by Lars von Trier, the front runner of the Dogma 95 movement:

> In the beginning of my career, I was not given any freedom at all, and also the actors, they all looked like props. (Interview, YouTube, Lars from 1-10)
> I think 99 percent of all the films that are produced in the world today are pure nonsense because these are films that nobody wants to direct. These are films that are made only for the market. (Interview Cannes, YouTube, 1998)

The new-wavers perceived the mainstream comedies to be of little artistic quality. Therefore, they created a new movement, which manifested in the Dogma 1995 Manifesto. Dogma 95 ushered in a new era of filmmaking in Denmark, as the manifesto was a verbal expression of an imaginary practice that leaned on other practices performed in creative industries, for example playfulness, intended obstructions, curiosity, and artistic provocation, as well as the use of rule-based dogmas seen in prior art movements. In a playful manner, Dogma 95 twisted nexuses of established filmmaking practices in the Danish filmmaking industry while, at the same time, being ideologically driven and political at its core. As stated by the second founder of Dogma 95, Thomas Vinterberg:

> The rules of Dogma were a game! It was an ideology, it was politics, it was a provocation, it was arrogance, but it was also playfulness. An example could be no[t to include] music. I invented that rule because it was the most fearful thing to do, to cut away the music. (Thomas Vinterberg, interview, YouTube)

The disruption of nexuses of practices that dominated the Danish filmmaking industry happened through various imaginary practices that emerged along the way through various events. The new wavers organized activity in ways that anticipated and deliberated alternative possible lines of action rather than sticking to the status quo of a "stalemate" filmmaking industry. In fact, the imaginary of the new wavers differed from the ones dominant in established habits and customs in the filmmaking industry at the time. Three of the most central events that disrupted established filmmaking industry practices were (1) experimenting with dogmas, (2) manifesting Dogma 95 in rules, and (3) branding the new movement.

Experimenting with Dogmas in "The Kingdom"

The run-up to Dogma 95 happened over several years. The first attempt happened in a TV series called "The Kingdom" broadcast in 1994, directed by Lars von Trier. It was a low-prestige, low-budget production, and the people recruited were newbies in the filmmaking industry. However, the project quickly turned into a stage-setting TV series that emptied the streets of Denmark during airtime. During production, von Trier experimented with some new principles: (1) All ideas are good ideas; (2) Use handheld cameras and only strip light as lighting – a revolt against the technical dominance back then; (3) Let coincidence rule; and (4) Drop the acting, which implied adding plots that would trick real emotions in actors. This resulted in unusual new practices emerging across all filmic functions.

Molly Marlene, the film editor, stated that she experienced the material she had received as something very unusual; especially the first four episodes of the series were very much like "shot from the hip" (interview). This unusual appeal required new film-editing practices and experimentation with aesthetics. Such experimentation resulted in a characteristic Dogma 95 aesthetic, which was entirely unexplored at the time. As the film editor described:

> The more hectic the story became, the more we edited to make it look as uneasy as possible … One of the new things was that, at the time, it was pretty unusual to edit forth and back between one up-front picture of one person to another. In general, we just rejected all editing rules, and yet, nobody actually had a problem with following the scenes … And we have developed that further since then. At first, it was very demonstrative and something people should notice, whereas now, it's more a way to see how much the audience follows. (Behind the scenes documentary, 2005)

One of the episodes where this break with established filmmaking practices, by enforcing the second principle, became clear to the cinematographer was a scene during production, where handheld filming practices seemed to provide very limited pictures that would not make any sense, at least not within established nexuses of filmmaking practices. In these particular situations, von Trier encouraged people to film in the new ways even when facing severe resistance. The principle guided practitioners toward a new practice that had yet to emerge and manifest in concrete activity. For example, a cinematographer told a story of a scene where two actors were getting into a car. This scene rendered following established principles of handheld filming difficult, as there was not enough space to even film a full face:

> Lars wanted me to get in the car with the handheld camera and film. I told him that this could not be done. Lars got really mad and yelled, 'What is not possible? Give me that camera!' He pulled the camera away, got in the car, squeezed the camera in, and filmed quarter of an eye of one and half of an eye of the other actor. And I had to recognize that yes, it actually cannot be done, but let's do it anyway, it's just another aesthetic. That approach has followed me ever since. (Erik Kress, Soundvenue.com, 2014)

Hence, imagining a different, liberal way of producing film and aesthetics cul-minated in breaking with the established practice of filming only in environ-ments where the camera had enough space. Likewise, acting changed as actors should not pay attention to traditional appropriate camera angles.

This event provided the emergence of what later became the Dogma 95 movement in that it became a guiding theme in the ensuing production of The Kingdom. The first part of The Kingdom was broadcast in November and December 1994 and unexpectedly became a huge success, first nationally and subsequently internationally. Imagining and enacting different ways of film production and aesthetics in The Kingdom was, therefore, the first step of breaking with the traditional nexuses of filmmaking practices that had domi-nated the cinema scene since the 1960s.

Manifesting Dogma 95 in rules: the 10 vows of chastity

Not long after The Kingdom, von Trier met with his colleague, Thomas Vinterberg. Together, they sat for half an hour to write down the Dogma 95 Manifesto, intending to initiate a broader industry-wide debate on the poten-tial and core of filmmaking. At the time, von Trier was inspired by the French New Wave, which had successfully set out to disrupt established nexuses of filmmaking practices in France years earlier. As he stated, the Dogma 95 "Is a French New Wave knock off" (interview in Cannes, 1998). This French New Wave movement, often referred to as one of the most influential movements in the history of cinema, was a self-conscious rejection of the traditional film conventions that had dominated France up until the 1950s. Since this French new wave movement led by film director, producer, and critic François Truffaut, and stated in an essay-style manifesto in 1954 no other film mani-festos had been made. As a consequence, fostering creativity through dogmas that criticize the status quo became part of the standard repertoire taught in film schools around the world, including Denmark. However, there had been no such manifesto statement in the filmmaking industry ever since the French New Wave.

Inspired by the French New Wave, the Dogma 95 Manifesto was a framework that explicated 10 filmmaking rules. These rules, referred to as the "The ten vows of chastity," asking what one usually does and what not to do anymore. Vinterberg explained this in the following way:

> And we said, 'What do we normally do to "wrap" our film, to dress a film?' We dress it with makeup, prop, strings, and lighting. And we just prohibited it. (Interview, documentary "Looking back at The Celebration," 1998)

The other 10 vows of chastity, referred to as Dogma 95, were developed in the same opposing manner, as rules that prohibit the usual ways of filmmaking, such as:

> Shooting must be done on location. Props and sets must not be brought in.
> The sound must never be produced apart from the images or vice versa.
> The camera must be handheld. Any movement or immobility attainable in the hand
> is permitted. (www.Dogme95.dk)

As von Trier reflected: "The Dogma rules are very much … orders to myself to not do that what I have been doing for a long time" (von Trier, interview). Hence, keeping the formulate rules meant breaking with established nexuses of filmmaking practices, as the articulated ways in which films were to be produced according to these rules differed markedly from established ones in the Danish filmmaking industry.

Yet, at the same time, the Dogma 95 Manifesto invited filmmakers to explore new avenues. As von Trier stated:

> Every good director has some rules they follow. Even if they are not written down, the rules help you say, 'These are the rules, let's work with them … If you have rules like that, then you are forced to use your imagination.' … We put down these 10 (rules), it could have been nine or five or (any number) … (Interview, YouTube)

Hence, working with these rules meant performing imaginary practices at a broader scale, inviting filmmakers across the entire industry to anticipate and deliberate nexuses of filmmaking practices that differed markedly from established ones. Therefore, the ten rules of the Dogma manifesto became a means for experimentation that helped actors in the Danish filmmaking industry break with established nexuses of filmmaking practices. Some experienced the manifesto as a direct provocation, while others found it liberating. In any case, it stirred up the debate and contributed to imagining alternatives and changing nexuses of practices within the community of art-house film. Some of the Dogma-inspired movies won several international awards, and still today, new filmmakers claim to be inspired by the Dogma rules.

Branding the new movement

During the spring of 1995, von Trier was invited to participate in an international symposium in Paris named "Le cinéma vers son deuxième siècle" ("Cinema moving into its second century"), organized by the French Ministry of Culture. At about the same time, celebrations were underway to mark the 100th anniversary of the birth of film. This provided an opportunity to further stir up the debate and present the Dogma 95 Manifesto as a humorous provocation of a stalemate cinema.

Von Trier had been asked to present where cinema is now and where it is heading. Yet, when von Trier stepped on stage, he presented a humorous, artistic performance that set Dogma 95 as a new agenda. On behalf of the Dogma 95 group, von Trier read their manifesto aloud and after he had finished, he

> kicked things off on the balcony of Paris's Odéon Theater by scattering hundreds of red flyers on which were inscribed a ten-point manifesto bashed out in less than an hour. (Green, 2016, www.empireonline.com)

He then left the stage with no further elaboration. This ceremony made journalists keen to hear more. Von Trier declared that he had the group's permission to present the text but not to discuss it. Hence, the journalists and the news created public curiosity about the manifesto, almost like a cliff hanger when reading an interesting book.

Von Trier and Vinterberg considered the celebration "an ironic event ... But the best part of the joke was that von Trier and Vinterberg were in earnest" (Peter Schepelern, www.Dogme95.dk). As this event created broad attention for the Dogma 95 movement, it branded and promoted the movement as a revolutionary one that intended to disrupt the stalemate filmmaking industry through a rule-based performance of imaginary practices. Consequently, the disruptive effects of imaginary practices rapidly expanded beyond the realms of the Danish filmmaking industry.

Reflections: imaginary practices and disruptive change of large arrays of activity in the Danish filmmaking industry

There is no doubt that the proclamation of the Dogma 95 Manifesto has turned out to be key events in the course of the history of Danish and international filmmaking. The question is rather whether these events contributed to the reproduction and continual transformation of filmmaking practices in *significant* ways, and which features and elements in the Dogma movement should be stressed in explaining the impact they made. From a practice-theoretical perspective, continuity and change equally call for explanation, and due to the complexity of the filmmaking industry, many explanations may qualify as pertinent. In fact, in the flow of events, there are many candidates for explaining change in large arrays of activity (Schatzki, 2019). However, explanation does not amount to listing the totality of contributing elements in this flow, but rather to "… fashion […] overviews (*Übersichten*; see Wittgenstein […]) of the large and complex nexuses that lead to them" (Schatzki, 2022, p. 50). Singling out the entrepreneurial role of von Trier in initiating the Dogma 95 movement and highlighting the imaginary practices that were enacted by proponents of the Dogma 95 movement, we argue, are good candidates for explaining the transformation of the filmmaking industry that took place in the 1990s.

Therefore, our inquiry has focused on illustrating the role of imaginary practices in the disruptive change of the Danish filmmaking industry instigated by the Dogma 95 movement. We argue that the Dogma 95 movement contributed significantly to disruptive changes in large arrays of activity in the filmmaking industry, and that this disruption was initiated by, and enacted through, the performance of imaginary practices as part of von Trier and other central directors' general dissatisfaction with the mainstream aesthetics of the Danish and Hollywood filmmaking industry. The Dogma 95 movement averred an ideal of authenticity and an ambition to reinstall curiosity and playfulness in film as a storytelling medium. The impact of the Dogma 95 movement thus started with the imaginary of a different kind of future for cinematography and film production. But how did this imaginary of a different kind of future become resources for the transformation of central practices within the filmmaking industry? According to Taylor, social imaginaries are effective in transmuting culture by supplying discursive resources. This suggestion, though plausible in principle, lacks specificity. We therefore turned to Dewey's suggestion that imagination is integral in human conduct: Imaginary practices help us expand the environment of habits and customs by making them objects for examination and experimentation.

Although the vision of a different kind of future was earnest and personal, the Dogma 95 proponents had no idea that this would be taken seriously by others and that they would succeed in making a movement. For them, it was a funny, experimental, and playful exercise to set themselves free and stir up the debate in order to envision alternative and more authentic ways of cinematography and filmmaking. In fact, the Dogma 95 movement started more or less as a "joke" for von Trier: an imaginative and playful suggestion that the 10 rules might eventually bring about more authentic and explorative filmmaking. Ten years later, the funny idea had become a milestone for film, and Danish film art became internationally renowned for the Dogma 95 movement. It has been described by a Danish national newsletter as "a creative boost, and a reminder that you don't need to possess giddy amounts, gigantic decorations, ruinously expensive special effects, to produce strong and relevant movies" (Berlingske, Dk Culture). Yet, while the disruptive change in the Danish filmmaking industry is widely recognized as such, our chapter shows that this process is nevertheless just that: a process, instead of a moment-to-moment shift from one to another constellation of practices. As we argue, it is the experimental and playful engagement in imaginary practices that opens courses of action, ones that would remain disclosed in attempts to induce one-off changes.

In the case of Dogma 95, the enactment of imaginary practices played a central role in the process of "breaking with" the established practices to enable disruptive change in large arrays of activity. Imaginary practices provided an expansion of the future horizon enacted at various events (e.g. experimenting manifesting and branding that would become a movement). Von Trier imagined a different future that would break out of the straitjacket of the production era to allow more creative freedom. This was the normative starting point for several playful events that led to massive changes in the nexuses of practices in the filmmaking industry. This experience guided practitioners in their course of actions, as they responded to the environment and produced new collective patterns for the filmmaking industry. At first, the movement stemmed from a practice that was taught in the Danish film school and highly accepted within the Danish filmmaking industry, namely, setting up dogmas and challenging the current filmic language, however, usually not in such disruptive ways. This practice allowed von Trier to engage in imaginary practices to experiment with the Dogmas for a larger disruption of filmmaking. Developing the 10 vows of chastity implied, firstly, the fixation of a rather static and explicated picture of what the current filmmaking practice and its inherent norms and values were (even though it could be argued that these established practices also evolved incrementally over time). Secondly, creating rules for future action that deliberately break with current nexuses of practices; and hence, thirdly, forcing a disruption of action into a future of exploring new practices for the entire filmmaking industry.

However, since the Dogma 95 disruption, filmmaking practices have, of course, continued to evolve, and even von Trier claims the need to continuously work with new dogmas based on one's own *learning* process. Hence, despite this continuously evolving aesthetic expression through dogmas, this has become the "new normal" of filmmaking practices, and no longer marks significant differences that allow disruption of large arrays of practices as such. It is rather a new era of continuous change. Accordingly, as we show, continuity and change are not opposites in practice, but rather they are interdependent aspects of disruptive change.

Conclusion

As we argue in this chapter, the performance of imaginary practices creates room for disruptive change in large arrays of activity because it produces an image of "things-that-might-be" and an "engaging with a situation's possibilities" that at that moment in time is not yet transformed into a "shown thing." In that moment, imaginary practices are realizing "what is not present" but ought to be. In order for the idea to transform and be "shown," it takes proleptic reasoning, that is, engaging in a pursuit before the value of this pursuit is fully grasped (prior to action). Imagination, in other words, signifies "the capacity to concretely perceive what is before us in light of what could be" (John Dewey in Fesmire, 2003, p. 65) and can bring to light undisclosed possibilities inherent in the situation at hand. The image created by imaginary practices guides the direction for actions.

Our account of imaginary practices does not imply that an individual agent (e.g. von Trier) by the stroke of genius transformed the filmmaking industry. Rather, we argue that imaginary practices are thoroughly social, collective, and contingent, and that imaginary practices *befall* actors and contribute, among many other social circumstances and material conditions, to bringing about change in both small and large arrays of activity. Hence, through the concept of imaginary practices, we contour the connection between imagination and practices. As illustrated in the case, we provide insights on the connection between the individual agents trying out potential ideas, and the link to practices that connects those ideas to potential valuable activity, holding situated potentials to disrupt established nexuses of practices. This implies that imaginary practices involve a tacit understanding of established practices so as to find "the right way" of "breaking with" them. Hence, for disruptive change in large arrays of activity to emerge, it must be routed in and, in a sense, continue established practices in order to find efficacious ways of disrupting them. Hence, change emerged from continuity. Entrepreneurs must thus find an appropriate balance between sensemaking and sensebreaking (cf. Pendelton-Jullian & Brown, 2018). The normative appropriateness is, however, contingent upon subsequent sanctioning of other actors in relevant nexuses of practices. Consequently, disruption from a practice-theoretical perspective is a skillful act of performing imaginary practices that cannot be reduced to individual entrepreneurs alone, as imaginary practices are normative and social. Therefore, disruption demands "breaking in the right way" by engaging with both continuity and change in any given event. Imaginary practices are expansions of the imagined actionable potentiality of engaging with a situation's possibilities, which happens at events that hold the potentiality of both practicing continuity and disruptively breaking with practice. Imaginary practice is, thus that what connects and enables actions for enacting futures that differ significantly from the past.

Importantly, the expectations raised through imaginary practices are not necessarily fulfilled in action. For example, in the case of the German reunification, many people were disappointed as the metaphor of "blooming landscapes" was not materialized as such. The key point is that imaginary practices inspire action that would otherwise be unthinkable, even when original hopes and desires are not fulfilled. We, therefore, argue that future research should examine more fully the interplay between hopes, desires, expectations, aspirations, and actions, in the production and enactment of imaginary practices as catalysts for disruptive change in large arrays of activity.

Note

1.   Mark Johnson (1987) has examined the evolution of "imagination" in the Western intellectual tradition from Plato and Aristotle to contemporary cognitive science.

References

Christensen, C. M. (2006). The ongoing process of building a theory of disruption, *Journal of Product Innovation Management*, 23(1), 39–55.

Dewey, J. (2007/1922). *Human Nature and Conduct: An Introduction to Social Psychology*, Cosimo.

Dewey, J. (2011/1917). The need for a recovery of philosophy, in R. B. Talisse & S. F. Aikin (eds), *The Pragmatism Reader: From Peirce through the Present*, Princeton University Press.

Feldman, M. S., Pentland, B. T., D'Adderio, L., & Lazaric, N. (2016). Beyond routines as things, *Organization Science*, 27(3), 505–13.

Feront, C., & Bertels, S. (2021). The impact of frame ambiguity on field-level change, *Organization Studies*, 42(7), 1135–65.

Fesmire, S. (2003). *John Dewey and Moral Imagination: Pragmatism in Ethics*, Indiana University Press.

Johnson, M. (1987). *The Body in the Mind. The Bodily Basis of Meaning, Imagination, and Reason*. The University of Chicago Press.

Kumaraswamy, A., Garud, R., & Ansari, S. (2018). Perspectives on disruptive innovations, *Journal of Management Studies*, 55(7), 1025–42.

Pendelton-Jullian, A. & Brown, J. S. (2018). *Design Unbound: Designing for a White Water World – Ecologies of Change*, MIT Press.

Reckwitz, A. (2002). Toward a theory of social practices: a development in culturalist theorizing, *European Journal of Social Theory*, 5(2), 243–63.

Schatzki, T. R. (2002). *The Site of the Social: A Philosophical Account of the Constitution of Social Life and Change*, Pennsylvania State University Press.

Schatzki. T. R. (2012). A primer on practices: theory and research, in J. Higgs, R. Barnett, S. Billett, M. Hutchings & F. Trede (eds), *Practice-based Education: Perspectives and Strategies* (pp. 13–26), Sense Publishers.

Schatzki, T. R. (2016a). Practice theory as flat ontology, in G. Spaargaren, D. Weenink & M. Lamers (eds), *Practice Theory and Research: Exploring the Dynamics of Social Life* (pp. 26–40), Routledge.

Schatzki, T. R. (2016b). Keeping track of large phenomena, *Geographisches Zeitschrift*, H.1, 4–24.

Schatzki, T. R. (2019). *Social Change in a Material World*, Routledge.

Schatzki, T. R. (2021). Forming alliances, in M. Lounsbury, D. A. Anderson & P. Spee (eds), *On Practice and Institution: Theorizing the Interface* (pp. 119–37), Emerald Publishing.

Schatzki, T. R. (2022). The determinants for social change, including entrepreneurs, in N. Thompson, O. Byrne, A. Jenkins & B. Teague (eds), *Research Handbook on Entrepreneurship as Practice* (pp. 40–53), Edward Elgar Publishing.

Shove, E. (2022). *Connecting Practices: Large Topics in Society and Social Theory*, Routledge.

Suddaby, R., Cooper, D. J., & Greenwood, R. (2007). Transnational regulation of professional services: governance dynamics of field level organizational change, *Accounting, Organizations, and Society*, 32(4–5), 333–62.

Swidler, A. (1986). Culture in action: symbols and strategies, *American Sociological Review*, 51(2), 273–86.

Taylor, C. (2002). Modern social imaginaries, *Public Culture*, 14(1), 91–124.

Taylor, C. (2004). *Modern Social Imaginaries*, Duke University Press.

Vaara, E., & Whittington, R. (2012). Strategy-as-practice: taking social practices seriously, *Academy of Management Annals*, 6(1), 285–336.

8 Narrative habitus: how actors connect episodic and continuous change in the moment

Henrik Koll and Astrid Jensen

Introduction

Recent developments within organization and management studies have increasingly turned towards the role of time and temporality when trying to understand organizational phenomena. These developments have given way to the emergence of two distinct research streams known respectively as "the historic turn" and "a turn towards temporality" (Reinecke et al., 2021). These studies have firmly established the lens of time as a conceivable and workable way of understanding processes of organizational change by moving beyond conventional understandings of time as objective clock-time that exists exogenously to events and processes (Hernes & Maitlis, 2012; Koll & Jensen, 2021). Consequently, with time being inherent to the very definition of change (Noss, 2002; Van de Ven & Poole, 1995, 2005; Weick & Quinn, 1999), studies of organizational change have displayed a growing recognition of the interrelation between the definitions we apply to time, as either objective or subjective, and the way we understand change as either episodic or continuous (e.g. Hernes, 2014, 2020; Suddaby & Foster, 2017). Accordingly, objective time is generally associated with a linear chronology captured by clocks and calendars, whereas the subjective time view is connected to more multidirectional perspectives on time (Koll, 2021; Shipp & Cole, 2015). It follows that the lens of time has emerged as the prime baseline for discussions concerning the constitution of change as either episodic or continuous since the two are underpinned respectively by a sequential and a process time view. By the same token, episodic change and continuous change have conventionally been deemed ontologically incompatible (Hernes et al., 2021; Hussenot & Missonier, 2016; Tsoukas & Chia, 2002).

Recently, however, Hernes et al. (2021) took promising steps towards integrating episodic and continuous change into the same ontological framework by applying an event-based process view. The authors achieve integration by conceptualizing episodic change not as objective events fixed once occurred, but as events continuously in the making as actors draw inspiration from past events of change and reinterpret them in the present. In so doing, the event-based process view draws attention to the way in which actors continuously enact past events of episodic change while practicing continuous change in the moment, hence providing an unprecedented opportunity to analyse episodic and continuous change together as two dimensions of the same movement through time. In the same vein, the authors also follow an emerging trend in organization and management studies of conceptualizing the past as a temporal resource at the disposal of agentic actors (e.g. Carroll, 2002; Suddaby et al., 2010; Wadhwani et al., 2018), emphasizing how the past is constantly in the making and redefined as actors move through time (Hernes et al., 2021, p. 735). However, by focusing on how actors narrate and enact the past in the present, this literature tends to foreground the efforts of actors in shaping the past and downplay how the agency of actors to engage in these efforts is informed by the past in its habitual aspect (Emirbayer & Mische, 1998). More specifically, we believe that the literature tends to lose sight of how actors' inclination and ability to make the past active in the face of present problems is only possible if their own past predisposes them to do so and endows them with the appropriate competencies to make it function (Bourdieu, 1981). In other words, through social engagement in certain practices over time, actors become embedded in temporal structures that in a habitual sense inform their actions, even when those actions are attempts to influence those very structures (Hernes & Schultz, 2020; Schultz & Hernes, 2013).

Accordingly, we argue that the way actors enact the past, which past events that emerge as significant to them, which narratives they construct about these events, and their ability to appropriate these narratives, is not merely a product of conscious and deliberate engagement with the past. Rather, there is also the habitual aspect in play – an embodied disposition that keeps a sense of continuity by recalling and reactivating past experiences. In other words, the past is both subjective and objective, and it works simultaneously as a structured and structuring structure (Koll & Ernst, 2022; Koll & Jensen, 2021).

Thus, in this chapter, we aim to extend the event-based view (Hernes et al., 2021) with a perspective on time that embeds actors' narrations and enactments of past events in the configuration of a practice associated with a past. We outline a framework that accommodates how enacting the past engages simultaneously with perceptions of time as narrations of past events, and with perceptions shaped by time as embodied dispositions acquired as actors move through time (Oberg et al., 2017). To this end, we build on and further develop the construct of *narrative habitus* (Ernst & Jensen, 2021; Fleetwood, 2016; Frank, 2010; Koll & Jensen, 2021) by drawing together Bourdieu's concept of habitus (1990) with an embedded and embodied narrative perspective (e.g. Cunliffe et al., 2004; Menary, 2008; Ricœur, 1980, 2002).

Our aim is to extend the event-based view in two ways. Firstly, by theorizing the processes through which actors connect past episodic events of change and continuous change in the moment as narratives constructed out of embodied experience and perception (Menary, 2008); secondly, by embedding these processes in the configuration of a practice that in a habitual sense makes some connections 'possible' and others 'impossible' (Koll, 2021; Koll & Jensen, 2021). Narrative habitus in this sense directs attention to how actors' narrations and enactments of past events and the objective dimensions of past events exist in duality (Fleetwood, 2016). Accordingly, narrative habitus offers a perspective on change and continuity as inherently intertwined because actors' inclination to perceive events as episodic change, and the competencies of actors to narrate them as such are shaped by actors' engagement in certain practices over time.

The chapter is organized as follows: next, we introduce the theoretical basis for our discussion by explaining how episodic and continuous change has been conceived through the lens of time. Then, we unfold our theoretical framework by drawing together Bourdieu's concept of habitus with an embodied and embedded narrative perspective. The construct of narrative habitus is further unfolded through two empirical illustrations before we round off the chapter by specifying our contribution to the research agenda on organizational continuity and change. In conclusion, we outline suggestions for future research.

The incompatibility of episodic and continuous change seen through the lens of time

Organization and management studies span two radically different ontological stances on organizational change, which reveal themselves through the lens of time as an objective–subjective time dichotomy (Dawson, 2014; Dawson & Sykes, 2016; Tsoukas & Chia, 2002). According to Hernes et al. (2021), extant understandings of continuity and change in organizations have consequently been hampered by this ontological divide between episodic and continuous change views. The former understands change as isolated happenings observable from the outside as a difference before and after a certain point in time (Van de Ven & Poole, 1995, 2005). The latter in contrast understands change as an ongoing process of becoming, experienced from within by practitioners as an unfolding process in time (Tsoukas & Chia, 2002).

The establishment of the lens of time as a viable way of understanding organizational continuity and change has been accompanied by an emergent agenda of moving organizational scholarship beyond objective notions of clock time (e.g. Chia, 1999; Tsoukas & Chia, 2002; Wiebe, 2010) and assumptions of objectivity in historical narrations of the past (Reinecke et al., 2021). In other words, organization and management studies have looked to break with conventional episodic understandings of change by promoting more subjective conceptions of time. The prevalence of subjective time has been salient in studies within the research stream of *temporal work* (Kaplan & Orlikowski, 2013) also known as *strategic organization of time* (Bansal et al., 2022), which for instance includes studies on *uses of the past* (Wadhwani et al., 2018) and *rhetorical history* (Suddaby et al., 2010). Inspired by a process view of time, this line of work is based on a shared understanding of the past as a temporal resource that can be appropriated by actors to serve a wide array of purposes in the present.

As an alternative to objective conceptions of time, the notion of temporal work has opened up new avenues of understanding how actors create organizational continuity or change through narrations and re-enactments of past events. However, this perspective has also contributed to reducing the past to a malleable substance, which actors mould and shape almost as they wish (Blagoev et al., 2018; Lubinski, 2018), amounting to a resource deployed as a tool by managers to achieve strategic outcomes (Brunninge, 2009; Foster et al., 2017; Suddaby & Foster, 2017). Consequently, the way narrations and enactments of the past is informed by the past in its habitual aspect has largely been neglected (Thomassen & Ødegård, 2022; Wadhwani et al., 2018).

Episodic change

The episodic change view rests on assumptions about time as an objective and external measure of processes that flows independently of human experience or, in other words, as a sequential view of time (Hernes et al., 2021). Thus, classical models of change tend to represent the past as states or events ordered chronologically along a fixed timeline (Dawson & Sykes, 2016; Hernes, 2022). Following this linear line of thought, the relation between events is often explained through a causal logic (Hernes, 2017; Hussenot & Missonier, 2016). This is, for example, captured by the notion of path dependence, which suggests that future strategic choices are shaped deterministically by the path organizations travel through time (Ericson, 2006). In this view, the cumulative passage of time creates a sedimentary accumulation of past events and experiences (Suddaby & Foster, 2017). Another example of this logic is found in prescriptive change management stage-models where the sequential order of managerial activities is seen as critical for advancing the organization to the next planned stages and where a misstep in a prior stage becomes determinant of the envisioned change outcome (Dawson & Sykes, 2016). In this sense, the episodic change view ascribes a high degree of objectivity to the past to an extent where it becomes a constraining influence on change. It follows that little agency is left for actors to reconstruct the past or imagine alternate futures (Suddaby & Foster, 2017).

Continuous change

The continuous change view subscribes to a process ontological view of time. The emphasis here is on emergence, constant flux, or the ongoingness of time (Langley et al., 2009). Change is seen as an ongoing process of *becoming* as organizations are constantly in the process of becoming something else. This implies that there is no beginning and end of time but only unfolding moments and ongoing transformation (Tsoukas & Chia, 2002). The continuous change view has traditionally been very critical of the episodic change view, calling it a 'snapshot view' arguing that it only captures isolated moments in time and, thus, ironically, not change or movement itself, but frozen snapshots of reality. The episodic change view is, thus, incapable of capturing the ongoing small or incremental change that goes on continuously in organizations (Tsoukas & Chia, 2002). Hence, because episodic change per definition is defined by observable beginnings and endpoints in time, it does not correspond to the process view of time, and consequently, it makes little sense to talk about change as episodic from a continuous change view. In contrast to the episodic change view, process time emphasizes time as *experienced*, thereby, making the past as well as the future open to reinterpretation, and accommodating the possibility of multiple pasts, and multiple futures (Reinecke & Ansari, 2017). As an ontological stance, a process time view invites us to consider how flows are stabilized, bent or deflected by actors themselves, which means that the past is considered much more malleable and subjective. Accordingly, reinterpretations of the past, thus, become consequential for future acts (Hernes, 2014).

Event-based (process) view

While the general tendency, as shown above, has been to reject the episodic view as a purely realist ontology, Hernes et al. (2021) recently broke with this convention by proposing integration of the episodic and continuous change views. The authors approach integration by extending the continuous change view advocated by, for example, Tsoukas and Chia (2002) and Orlikowski (1996) with an event-based process view. Where the continuous change view emphasizes actors' experience of change in the present, the event-based view adds emphasis on how past and future are enacted in the present (Hernes et al., 2021). By applying a process view of events to events of change in actors' pasts or futures, Hernes et al. (2021) argue that it is possible to integrate episodic and continuous change within the same ontological framework. They consequently promote a different understanding of events, where events are not understood as accomplished occurrences fixed forever as particular occurrences at specific moments in time. Rather, the event-based view defines events by their becoming an event, even after the actual unfolding of the events, and define the duration of events by the time it takes events to become events (Hernes, 2020). Accordingly, episodic change is conceptualized as 'breaks' in an 'immanent temporal trajectory' (Hernes et al., 2021, p. 744), with the present as a vantage point for past episodic change and possible future change. Events are conceived as continuously in the making as 'temporal resources available for actors' (p. 743) as actors enact a temporality constantly redefined in the 'now' (Hussenot et al., 2020, p. 58).

Episodic change is, thus, not objectively observable from the outside, as per the traditional episodic change view, but conceptualized as *experienced* breaks that mark a difference between a perceived 'before' and 'after' on actors' temporal trajectories. Part of the argument here is that as actors continuously ascribe new meaning and definition to episodic changes in the past or future, these reenactments become part of actors' experience of continuous change in the moment. Conversely, activities in the moment associated with continuous change enable actors 'to be selective of which [past or future] changes to address' and draw upon in the present (Hernes et al., 2021).

From our perspective, the event-based view offers a novel integrative approach that enables analyses of the interplay between episodic and continuous change in the moment. At the same time, however, by arguing that actors 'selectively' choose which past events to address, the event-based view is at risk of neglecting how actors' inclinations towards specific events, and certain ways of narrating those events, are shaped by actors' engagement in a particular practice over time. By developing the construct of narrative habitus, we offer an alternative perspective on the relationship between continuity and change, where the past is neither an objective, external determinant nor a subjective, malleable, strategic resource. Rather, we define the past as a structuring and structured structure – a mutual interplay between narrations of the past and historically embodied dispositions (Koll & Jensen, 2021). Thereby, we extend the integration of episodic and continuous change, outlined by the event-based view, with a view of time that is more explicitly attentive to the duality of the past. We unfold the construct and its implications below.

Integrating episodic and continuous change views through narrative habitus

In the following, we present our approach to integrating episodic and continuous change views into the same ontological framework. Our starting point is Bourdieu's (1990, 2000) theory of social practice combined with the construct of narrative habitus (Ernst & Jensen, 2021; Fleetwood, 2016; Jones, 1998; Koll & Jensen, 2021), which is based on the idea that narratives structure action, and that actors draw on the narratives pertaining to the fields of practice in which they are invested and socialized. As an example offered by Fleetwood (2016, p. 182), 'the narrative of a drug dealer', who has dealing as his/her livelihood, 'would not be credible in a criminal justice setting such as a court, [but] clearly belong to the street field' (Fleetwood, 2016, p. 182). We emphasize in particular how narrative habitus inherently accommodates how narrations of the past simultaneously shape, and are shaped, by temporally embedded practices. The construct of narrative habitus first emerged in socio-narratology (Frank, 2010) and later in narrative criminology research (Fleetwood, 2016). To our knowledge, Ernst and Jensen (2021) and Koll and Jensen (2021) are the first studies in organization and management to adopt and develop the construct. Based on these studies, we look to make the construct more theoretically robust and unfold its potential for developing new understandings of continuity and change in organizations.

Habitus, continuity and change: recalling and reactivating the past

Bourdieu's theory of social practice is based on an integrative temporal view, which we define here as a habitus-based conceptualization of temporality (Koll, 2020; Robinson et al., 2022; Thomassen & Ødegård, 2022). Bourdieu's temporal view is integrative in the sense that social practices are seen to transpire through ongoing mutual adjustments between subjective and objective temporal structures, encapsulated by the concepts of habitus and field (Bourdieu, 2000).

Defined as a 'durable and transposable set of dispositions', habitus is essentially embodied socialization that forms dispositions for perceiving the world and acting in it (Bourdieu, 1990, p. 52). Habitus is both collective and individual as it brings a level of stability of identity to individuals as well as groups of actors (Bourdieu & Chartier, 2015; Chia & Holt, 2006; Frank, 2010). Because it is acquired in a field of practice over time, habitus has a double historicity to it in the sense that it accommodates that actors are products of historical structures and simultaneously put these historical structures to work in action. Thereby, practice becomes the product of a habitus, which is itself a product of the embodiment of the objectified historical structures of the field (Bourdieu & Wacquant, 1992). Yet, importantly, while actors on the one hand internalize social structures into their habitus, they do not just respond passively to these structures, but also have the power to change them by applying the habitus in new and creative ways in action (Bourdieu, 1990).

Fields of practice are social arenas occupied by groups of actors engaged in struggles or social games over resources that are perceived as relevant and essential in order to have success in the game (Robinson et al., 2022). Over time, as a habitus adjusts to the structuring principles of a field, also known as the rules of the game, actors develop a practical sense or feel for the game that enables them to navigate and strategize seamlessly through everyday problems (Bourdieu, 1990). In this way, practical sense can be described as the intuitive feel that enables the basketball player to adjust not to what he sees but to what he anticipates (i.e. sees in advance in the perceived present). As an example, player A knows exactly where on the floor the ball is going to find him before his teammate player B releases the ball (Bourdieu, 1990). Thus, as a modus operandi, habitus is rooted in both the past, the present, and the anticipated future (Thomassen & Ødegård, 2022). When habitus and field are in sync with one another, practice becomes acts of temporalization, where actors 'transcend the immediate present via practical mobilization of the past and practical anticipation of the future inscribed in the present in a state of objective potentiality' (Bourdieu & Wacquant, 1992, p. 138). In this sense, by pre-perceptively recalling or reactivating past experiences in action, habitus ensures a continuity or constancy of practices over time (Bourdieu, 1990; Chia & Holt, 2006; Thomassen & Ødegård, 2022).

Habitus, field and change

The fact that habitus is a product of social conditions and is *often* adjusted to the structures that produce it, has generated criticism of Bourdieu's framework as a theory of reproduction rather than change (Gorski, 2013; Yang, 2014). However, one of the most defining characteristics of habitus is the idea of improvisation within defined limits (Steinmetz, 2011) – an ability to act and adapt unthinkingly to contingent local demands (Chia & Holt, 2006). Habitus thus brings a sense of continuity to the present moment, not as a blind social programming of behaviour, or obedience to rules, but 'as principles which generate and organize practices and representations that can be objectively adapted to their outcomes without presupposing a conscious aiming at ends or an express mastery of the operations necessary in order to attain them' (Bourdieu, 1990, p. 53). The strategies and maneuverings actors undertake are not fully inscribed in the logic of the situation they are facing, or in their habitus, but emerge through processes of adjustment that are located neither entirely in the unconscious nor entirely in conscious decision-making (Steinmetz, 2011). Without expressed calculation, habitus defines responsive actions, things to do or not to do, things to say or not to say, by connecting the past to a probable upcoming future (Bourdieu, 1990). In other words, as an unspoken principle of choice, habitus regulates only the range and variety of possible actions without selecting specific actions (Steinmetz, 2011). Habitus is thus always in transition and alteration, however, for the most part in slow and incremental ways (Thomassen & Ødegård, 2022).

The subtle, continuous change that occurs in the moment of everyday practices is therefore easily subsumed within the ongoing mutual adjustments between habitus and field where habitus internalizes the structuring principles of the field and simultaneously puts these structures to work in action (Hardy, 2008).

Habitus and radical change

While processes of adjustment accounts for continuous change, the concept of habitus was first introduced by Bourdieu in order to understand and explain radical change (Steinmetz, 2011). In Bourdieusian terms, radical change is seen as disruptions in the routine adjustment between objective and subjective structures, causing a mismatch between habitus and the requirements of a current situation (Bourdieu, 2000; Hardy, 2008). According to Bourdieu, 'habitus, accounts equally well for cases in which dispositions function out of phase and practices are objectively ill-adapted to the present conditions because they are objectively adjusted to conditions that no longer obtain' (1990, p. 62). Since habitus is both enduring and adaptable, the responses to these situations vary from misadaptation as well as adaptation, to revolt as well as resignation (Bourdieu, 2000). It follows that some actors seize the opportunity to adapt their habitus to new field conditions while others fail to do it and are left with a destabilized habitus, that is, a state of ambivalence, contradiction, and suffering, because the positions occupied by actors require dispositions that are different from those socialized (Bourdieu, 2000).

Narrative habitus: connecting the current moment with past events of change

The construct of *narrative habitus* zooms in on the processes through which actors use narratives to connect past and future episodic events of change to their experience of continuous change in the moment, and embeds these processes in configurations of practice that enable and constrain them.

In the following we will develop the theoretical construct of narrative habitus and offer empirical illustrations from two previous studies undertaken by Koll (2021) and Koll and Jensen (2021). These studies were part of a larger study of organizational change in the Scandinavian telecommunications company, Telco (pseudonym), which was conducted by the first author over a two-year span from 2016 to 2018. As a result of market liberalization across the EU nations, the company had been privatized almost a quarter century prior to the study. Yet, despite growing market competition, it still found itself in transition from a monopolistic working culture to a more business-oriented working culture. Through participant observation and interviews, the study followed a group of increasingly cross-pressured frontline managers in their efforts to raise the level of performance in their respective teams and to instil a performance-consciousness in their subordinates.

Narrative habitus: a theoretical construct

Drawing on an embedded and embodied narrative perspective (e.g. Bruner, 1991; Menary, 2008; Ricœur, 1980), we understand narratives as temporal unfolding of events connecting the past, the present, and the future, hence, linking past experiences with what may come (Bruner, 2001). Narratives, thus, are a basic human strategy for coming to terms with time and change (Herman, 2009), where actors draw on their past in order to make sense of the present. This means that performed narratives are not just retrospective accounts of past events, rather, they involve active attempts to shape the present and the future (Linell, 2009).

When coupling the narrative constructions of actors with habitus, we argue that narratives are fundamental to habitus, and habitus is infused with narratives (Jones, 1998). In other words, we understand narratives as embodied, learned, and generative, and as products of a narrative habitus (Fleetwood, 2016; Koll & Jensen, 2021), where narratives can be understood as social action rooted in social structure, generated by pre-verbal dispositions for perceiving the world and acting in it (Fleetwood, 2016; Koll & Jensen, 2021; Menary, 2008). It follows, that narratives shape not only actors' understanding of their own lives and the events that happen in them, but also the fields of practice in which actors are invested (Jones, 1998). Consequently, in the same way that Bourdieu understands habitus as the internalization of one's position in the field, narrative habitus is the internalization of the narratives pertaining to the field, including actors', goals, circumstances, conflicts, values, vocabulary, symbolic systems, collective memory, and temporal character (Bourdieu, 1991; Fleetwood, 2016; Ricœur, 1980; Jones, 1998). Thus, narratives can be seen as embodied cultural resources used by actors to define and perform activities in the field; as dynamic language forms, grounded in the world of action (Bruner, 1990; Ricœur, 1980). In response to current events, actors create order and coherence through narrative processes of emplotment, that is, by embedding events within an overall 'plot' that links events into a familiar trajectory (Ricœur, 2002). The ways actors structure these trajectories and experience past, present, or future events as continuity or change is dependent on the positions actors occupy in the respective field of practice and how well-adjusted their habitus has been to the rules and regularities of the field (Koll, 2021).

Drawing on two studies of organizational change in the Scandinavian telecommunications company, Telco, Koll (2021) and Koll and Jensen (2021), we offer two empirical illustrations of how actors connect episodic and continuous change through their narrative habitus. In the first example (A), we show how two different groups of actors (technicians and shop stewards) ascribe different narratives to the same change event relative to their position in the field and to how well their habitus is adjusted to the rules of the game. In the second example (B), we demonstrate, how actors' appropriation of certain narratives is based on an embodied disposition acquired over time, on the position actors currently occupy in the field, and on the narratives prevailing in the current field of practice.

Empirical illustration A: narrating different trajectories in response to misalignment

In his study, Koll (2021) showed how technicians and shop stewards, in Telco, responded differently to events that created a misalignment between their civil servant habitus, which they had acquired when the company was a state-owned monopoly, and the structures, which had been inserted and enforced through a series of strategic initiatives after the company was privatized and no longer had monopoly of their market. The study showed how technicians used nostalgic narratives as a strategy to sustain the old structures, of which their habitus was a product, and thereby, refusing to adapt to the new rules of the game. The shop stewards, on the other hand, managed to reshape their habitus to accommodate both former and new rules of the game by forging a narrative of themselves as a crucial link between management and technicians during a time of change. As a past event of change, privatization became significant for actors' current experience of the strategic change initiatives as they used the event to imagine different trajectories into the past and future. The technicians longed for the 'good old days' and had difficulties projecting themselves into the future, whereas the shop stewards embraced the opportunity to assume a role as a kind of deputy to the frontline managers while simultaneously retaining the trust and confidence of their peers. Because the event of privatization could not be readily subsumed under the routine everyday adjustments between habitus and field, the event left significant traces through time as a historical point of reference experienced by actors as a difference between before and after.

Empirical illustration B: appropriating dominant narratives

In the following example taken from a study of frontline managers attempts to implement change in the wake of privatization of Telco, Koll and Jensen (2021) demonstrated how the dominant narrative of senior management was appropriated by the frontline managers as a strategy to safeguard their position by showing official allegiance with the new rules of the game. The frontline managers displayed a noticeable ability to sense when to accommodate new and former rules of the game respectively by adhering more or less to the dominant narrative.

Senior management had threatened to outsource the department unless the level of performance was raised significantly. The threat was accompanied by the emergence of a narrative of urgency to discard practices of the past in order to avoid outsourcing, and thereby keeping a sense of continuity, while pursuing a bright new future imbued with a new performance culture. In the wake of privatization, managerial idealization of the future and disdain for the past, also known as 'managerial postalgia' (Ybema, 2010, p. 486) became the prevailing narrative as the new company structure empowered management and disempowered their subordinate technicians and the union.

The study showed how frontline managers adjusted to the new rules of the game by appropriating the prevailing narrative of abandoning the past, where the past was constructed as an obstacle to reaching the new performance targets and, thus, to securing the projected future of the department. The appropriation of this particular narrative emerged as a strategy for frontline managers to show allegiance to the future projected by senior management, while also providing themselves with an explanation for their own failures to change the culture among their subordinates and bring performance up to par.

While on the one hand adhering to the dominant narrative of abandoning the past, the frontline managers also used elements of the past to solve their day-to-day problems of implementing the new performance culture. A salient course of action was to use shop stewards to convey messages to the technicians and collaborate with them in ways that accommodated former rules of the game without exposing a withdrawal of allegiance to the new rules of the game promoted by the prevailing postalgic narrative of senior management. At management meetings, for example, the frontline managers would explicitly adhere to the narrative of abandoning the past, but in other situations, they would compromise and accommodate former ways of working by using the shop stewards as a line of communications to the technicians in order to get on with tasks at hand and avoid direct conflict with the subordinates.

The study showed how the narrative habitus of frontline managers endowed them with an intuitive feel for which narratives they were expected to abide to according to their position in the game. This feel for the game also included an ability to operationalize these narratives on appropriate occasions and down-play them on other occasions by intuitively predicting how other actors might react to them. Thereby, narratives emerged as a way for frontline managers to connect past events of change to their practice and experience of continuous change in the moment. Rather than just discarding the past, the frontline managers brought a sense of continuity to the lived moment through continuous enactment and recalling of past rules of the game by collaborating with the shop stewards even though this alliance conflicted with the prevailing narrative of the field.

Based on this study, we argue that the sense of continuity, which was brought into the current moment of practitioners through their use of narratives, was not merely the product of selective and deliberate engagement with the past, rather, we see it as deriving from an embodied disposition acquired over time in the field of practice.

Summary

As demonstrated by both studies mentioned above, the way in which the past defines actors' narrative habitus is connected to the collective aspect of habitus (Thomassen & Ødegård, 2022), that is, how members of groups, occupying similar positions and having similar stakes in the game, embody similar inclinations and strategic preferences towards certain events and narratives. In this sense, narrative habitus adds to our understanding of why certain events emerge as significant on actors' temporal trajectory. By representing past events both as reenactments and as embodied dispositions, we assert that narrative habitus adds more dimensions to the interplay between continuity and change, because narratives are those actions that structure actors' experiences as continuity or change and simultaneously are structured by dispositions acquired as actors move through time. Narrative habitus inherently intertwines continuity and change because the inclination to perceive an event as change, and narrate it as such, is shaped by actors' involvement in a particular practice over time. Thus, as a habitus in each present moment is subject to experience and, by the same token, transformed by these experiences (Bourdieu & Chartier, 2015), the past is the time dimension most constitutive in habitus-formation because it is written in the bodies of actors (Bourdieu, 1990).

Contribution

The emergence of the lens of time in organizational scholarship has been key in shaping discussions of change as episodic or continuous, and mostly to deem them as ontologically incompatible. At the same time, there has been a tendency in organization and management studies to promote a process view of time, and thereby explicitly distance oneself from a sequential view of time. While this shift has moved continuity and change research forward, we believe that the argument for subjective time has been pushed too far. Consequently, there has been a tendency to reduce the past to a temporal resource at actors' disposal and thereby foreground actors' subjective experiences over the more embedded and embodied dimensions of the past (Koll, 2020).

Hernes et al. (2021) extend the continuous change view by introducing a definition of change as an 'immanent temporal trajectory' where past and future episodic events of change are continuously redefined in the present. By connecting remembered or imagined events of episodic change to the current moment, actors bring a sense of continuity to the lived present. Constant reenactment of events becomes part of actors' experience of continuous change as they continuously ascribe new meaning and definition to episodic changes in the past or future. In this sense, the event-based view takes the present as a vantage point from which actors' own subjective views determine what counts as episodic change. Thereby, the event-based view foregrounds a subjective view of the past. In this chapter, we offer an extension of the event-based view through the construct of narrative habitus, our aim being to integrate episodic and continuous change while accommodating both objective and subjective dimensions of the past.

Similar to the event-based view, narrative habitus highlights how actors use narrations of the past as a point of reference to make sense of the present and to create a sense of continuity or change. In other words, through narratives, actors connect past events of episodic change to their experience of continuous change in the present. However, narrative habitus adds to the event-based view by directing attention to the way actors' ability to perform and enact these narrations of the past is shaped by embodied dispositions acquired through engagement in a particular practice over time. In this sense, narrative habitus shows how, on the one hand, the past can be seen as events in the making, a structured structure, shaped by actors' narrations of past events. On the other hand, the past is also a system of dispositions, a structuring structure, which in its habitual aspect places limits on actors' appropriation of the past by making some actions seem possible and others impossible. Narrative habitus, thus, provides a way to integrate episodic and continuous change into the same ontological framework, but it does so without reducing the past to a subjective, malleable substance or to an objective, external determinant. Rather, because actors are embedded in temporal structures that in a habitual sense inform their actions, continuity and change emerge through processes of adjustment that are located neither entirely in the unconscious nor entirely in conscious decision-making.

Conclusion

In this chapter, we have demonstrated the potential of narrative habitus as an integrative temporal framework that connects subjective and objective dimensions of time. Through this temporal view, we have argued that change and continuity are mutually intertwined because the inclination to perceive an event as change, and narrate it as such, is shaped by dispositions acquired as actors move through time. By accommodating the duality of the past as simultaneously *acting* and *enacted*, narrative habitus offers a temporal view distinct from prevalent process time views promoted by the temporal work perspective and extended by the event-based view. In this sense, the construct adds a new perspective to discussions concerning continuity and change in organizations. We have used empirical illustrations to demonstrate how the perceived significance of certain events, and the use of narratives pertaining to those events, are embedded in the configuration of particular fields of practice. However, we believe that more empirical research is needed in order to unlock the full potential of narrative habitus and to further its contribution to the research field.

References

Bansal, P., Reinecke, J., Suddaby, R., & Langley, A. (2022). Temporal work: the strategic organization of time, *Strategic Organization*, 20(1), 6–19.

Blagoev, B., Felten, S., & Kahn, R. (2018). The career of a catalogue: organizational memory, materiality and the dual nature of the past at the British Museum (1970–today), *Organization Studies*, 39(12), 1757–83.

Bourdieu, P. (1981). Men and machines, in K. Knorr-Cetina & A. V. Cicourel (eds), *Advances in Social Theory and Methodology* (pp. 304–17), London: Routledge and Kegan Paul.

Bourdieu, P. (1990). Time perspectives of the Kabyle, in *The Sociology of Time* (pp. 219–37), Cham: Springer. (Original work published 1963)

Bourdieu, P. (1990). *The Logic of Practice*, Cambridge: Polity.

Bourdieu, P. (1991). Identity and representation, in J. B. Thompson (ed.), *Language and Symbolic Power*, Cambridge: Polity.

Bourdieu, P. (2000). *Pascalian Meditations*, Stanford, CA: Stanford University Press.

Bourdieu, P., & Chartier, R. (2015). *The Sociologist and the Historian*, Chichester: John Wiley & Sons.

Bourdieu, P., & Wacquant, L. J. D. (1992). *An Invitation to Reflexive Sociology*, Cambridge: Polity.

Bruner, J. (1990). *Acts of Meaning* (vol. 3), Cambridge, MA: Harvard University Press.

Bruner, J. (1991). The narrative construction of reality, *Critical Inquiry*, 18(1), 1–21.

Bruner, J. (2001). Self-making and world-making, in J. Brockmeier & D. Carbaugh (eds), *Narrative and Identity: Studies in Autobiography, Self, and Culture* (pp. 25–37), Amsterdam: John Benjamins.

Brunninge, O. (2009). Using history in organizations: how managers make purposeful reference to history in strategy processes, *Journal of Organizational Change Management*, 22(1), 8–26.

Carroll, C. E. (2002). The strategic use of the past and future in organizational change –introduction, *Journal of Organizational Change Management*, 15(6), 556–62.

Chia, R. (1999). A 'rhizomic' model of organizational change and transformation: perspective from a metaphysics of change, *British Journal of Management*, 10(3), 209–27.

Chia, R., & Holt, R. (2006). Strategy as practical coping: a Heideggerian perspective, *Organization Studies*, 27(5), 635–55.

Cunliffe, A. L., Luhman, J. T., & Boje, D. M. (2004). Narrative temporality: implications for organizational research, *Organization Studies*, 25(2), 261–86.

Dawson, P. (2014). Reflections: on time, temporality and change in organizations, *Journal of Change Management*, 14(3), 285–308.

Dawson, P., & Sykes, C. (2016). *Organizational Change and Temporality: Bending the Arrow of Time*, Abingdon: Routledge.

Ericson, M. (2006). Exploring the future exploiting the past, *Journal of Management History*, 12(2), 121–36.

Emirbayer, M., & Mische, A. (1998). What is agency? *American Journal of Sociology*, 103(4), 962–1023.

Ernst, J., & Jensen, A. (2021). Organizational identity struggles and reconstruction during organizational change: narratives as symbolic, emotional and practical glue, *Organization Studies*, 42(6), 891–910.

Fleetwood, J. (2016). Narrative habitus: thinking through structure/agency in the narratives of offenders, *Crime, Media, Culture: An International Journal*, 12(2), 173–92.

Foster, W. M., Coraiola, D. M., Suddaby, R., Kroezen, J., & Chandler, D. (2017). The strategic use of historical narratives: a theoretical framework, *Business History*, 59(8), 1176–200.

Frank, A. W. (2010). *Letting Stories Breathe: A Socio-Narratology*, Chicago, IL: University of Chicago Press.

Gorski, P. S. (2013). *Bourdieu and Historical Analysis*, Durham, NC: Duke University Press.

Hardy, C. (2008). Hysteresis, in M. Grenfell (ed.), *Pierre Bourdieu: Key Concepts* (pp. 131–48), Durham, UK: Acumen.

Herman, D. (2009). Cognitive narratology, in *Handbook of Narratology* (pp. 30–43), Berlin: De Gruyter.

Hernes, T. (2014). *A Process Theory of Organization*, Oxford: Oxford University Press.

Hernes, T. (2017). Process as the becoming of temporal trajectory, in A. Langley & H. Tsoukas (eds), *The Sage Handbook of Process Organization Studies* (pp. 601–7), Thousand Oaks, CA: Sage.

Hernes, T. (2020). Events and the becoming of organizational temporality, in J. Reinecke, R. Suddaby, A. Langley & H. Tsoukas (eds), *Time, Temporality, and History in Process Organization Studies* (pp. 29–43), Oxford: Oxford University Press.

Hernes, T. (2022). *Organization and Time*, Oxford: Oxford University Press.

Hernes, T., Hussenot, A., & Pulk, K. (2021). Time and temporality of change processes: applying an event-based view to integrate episodic and continuous change, in M. S. Poole & A. Van de Ven (eds), *The Oxford Handbook of Organizational Change and Innovation* (pp. 731–50), Oxford: Oxford University Press.

Hernes, T., & Maitlis, S. (2012). *Process, Sensemaking, and Organizing*, Oxford: Oxford University Press.

Hernes, T., & Schultz, M. (2020). Translating the distant into the present: how actors address distant past and future events through situated activity, *Organization Theory*, 1(1), https://doi.org/2631787719900999.

Hussenot, A., Hernes, T., & Bouty, I. (2020). Studying organization from the perspective of the ontology of temporality, in J. Reinecke, R. Suddaby, A. Langley & H. Tsoukas (eds), *Time, Temporality, and History in Process Organization Studies* (pp. 50–68), Oxford: Oxford University Press.

Hussenot, A., & Missonier, S. (2016). Encompassing stability and novelty in organization studies: an events-based approach, *Organization Studies*, 37(4), 523–46.

Jones, B. (1998). Customers are consumers of library resources and services—or are they? *The Australian Library Journal*, 47(2), 131–44.

Kaplan, S., & Orlikowski, W. J. (2013). Temporal work in strategy making, *Organization Science*, 24(4), 965–95.

Koll, H. (2020). Bourdieu and the strategic organization of time in organizations, *Praktiske grunde. Tidsskrift for kultur og samfunnsvitenskab*, 3–4, 5–30.

Koll, H. (2021). Bridging the dialectical histories in organizational change: hysteresis in Scandinavian telecommunications privatization, *Nordic Journal of Working Life Studies*, 11(3), https://doi.org/10.18291/njwls.123602.

Koll, H., & Ernst, J. (2022). Caught between times: explaining resistance to change through the tale of Don Quixote, in S. Robinson, J. Ernst, K. Larsen & O. J. Thomassen (eds), *Pierre Bourdieu in Studies of Organization and Management: Societal Change and Transforming Fields* (pp. 23–40), London: Routledge.

Koll, H., & Jensen, A. (2021). Appropriating the past in organizational change management: abandoning and embracing history, in J. Reinecke, R. Suddaby, A. Langley & H. Tsoukas (eds), *Time, Temporality, and History in Process Organization Studies* (pp. 220–39), Oxford: Oxford University Press.

Langley, A., Smallman, C., Tsoukas, H., & Van de Ven, A. H. (2009). Process studies of change in organization and management, *Academy of Management Journal*, 52(5), 1069–70.

Linell, P. (2009). *Rethinking Language, Mind, and World Dialogically*, Charlotte, NC: Information Age Publishing.

Lubinski, C. (2018). From 'history as told' to 'history as experienced': contextualizing the uses of the past, *Organization Studies*, 39(12), 1785–809.

Menary, R. (2008). Embodied narratives, *Journal of Consciousness Studies*, 15(6), 63–84.

Noss, C. (2002). Taking time seriously: organizational change, flexibility, and the present time in a new perspective, in R. Whipp, B. Adam & I. Sabelis (eds), *Making Time: Time and Management in Modern Organizations* (pp. 46–60), Oxford: Oxford University Press.

Oberg, A., Drori, G. S., & Delmestri, G. (2017). Where history, visuality, and identity meet: institutional paths to visual diversity among organizations. In M. A. Höllerer, T. Daudigeos & D. Janscary (eds), *Multimodality, Meaning, and Institutions* (chapter 3), Bingley: Emerald Publishing.

Orlikowski, W. J. (1996). Improvising organizational transformation over time: a situated change perspective, *Information Systems Research*, 7(1), 63–92.

Reinecke, J., & Ansari, S. (2017). Time, temporality and process studies, in A. Langley & H. Tsoukas (eds), *The Sage Handbook of Process Organization Studies* (pp. 402–16), Thousand Oaks, CA: Sage.

Reinecke, J., Suddaby, R., Tsoukas, H., & Langley, A. (eds) (2021). Time, temporality, and history in process organization studies: an introduction, in *Time, Temporality, and History in Process Organization Studies* (pp. 1–14), Oxford: Oxford University Press.

Ricœur, P. (1980). Narrative time, *Critical Inquiry*, 7(1), 169–90.

Ricœur, P. (2002). Narrative time, in B. Richardson (ed.), *Narrative Dynamics: Essays on Time, Plot, Closure, and Frames* (pp. 35–46), Columbus: Ohio State University Press.

Robinson, S., Ernst, J., Thomassen, O. J., & Larsen, K. (2022). Introduction: taking Bourdieu further into studies of organizations and management, in S. Robinson, J. Ernst, K. Larsen & O. J. Thomassen (eds), *Pierre Bourdieu in Studies of Organization and Management: Societal Change and Transforming Fields* (pp. 1–20), London: Routledge.

Schultz, M., & Hernes, T. (2013). A temporal perspective on organizational identity, *Organization Science*, 24(1), 1–21.

Shipp, A. J., & Cole, M. S. (2015). Time in individual-level organizational studies: what is it, how is it used, and why isn't it exploited more often? *Annual Review of Organizational Psychology and Organizational Behavior*, 2(1), 237–60.

Steinmetz, G. (2011). Bourdieu, historicity, and historical sociology, *Cultural Sociology*, 5(1), 45–66.

Suddaby, R., & Foster, W. M. (2017). History and organizational change, *Journal of Management*, 43(1), 19–38.

Suddaby, R., Foster, W. M., & Trank, C. Q. (2010). Rhetorical history as a source of competitive advantage, *Advances in Strategic Management*, 27, 147–73.

Thomassen, O. J., & Ødegård, A. (2022). Recalling or reactivating the past? A habitus-based conceptualisation of temporality in organisations, in S. Robinson, J. Ernst, K. Larsen & O. J. Thomassen (eds), *Pierre Bourdieu in Studies of Organization and Management: Societal Change and Transforming Fields* (pp. 41–57), London: Routledge.

Tsoukas, H., & Chia, R. (2002). On organizational becoming: rethinking organizational change, *Organization Science*, 13(5), 567–82.

Van de Ven, A. H., & Poole, M. S. (1995). Explaining development and change in organizations, *Academy of Management Review*, 20(3), 510–40.

Van de Ven, A. H., & Poole, M. S. (2005). Alternative approaches for studying organizational change, *Organization Studies*, 26(9), 1377–404.

Wadhwani, R. D., Suddaby, R., Mordhorst, M., & Popp, A. (2018). History as organizing: uses of the past in organization studies, *Organization Studies*, 39(12), 1663–83.

Weick, K. E., & Quinn, R. E. (1999). Organizational change and development, *Annual Review of Psychology*, 50(1), 361–86.

Wiebe, E. (2010). Temporal sensemaking: managers' use of time to frame organizational change, *Process, Sensemaking, and Organizing*, 1, 213–41.

Yang, Y. (2014). Bourdieu, practice and change: beyond the criticism of determinism, *Educational Philosophy and Theory*, 46(14), 1522–40.

Ybema, S. (2010). Talk of change: temporal contrasts and collective identities, *Organization Studies*, 31(4), 481–503.

9 Towards a nuanced explanation of historically conditioned continuity: interdependent action patterns as enacted history

Blagoy Blagoev and Waldemar Kremser

Introduction

The phenomenon of historically conditioned continuity in organizations, often discussed under labels such as path dependence (Sydow et al., 2009, 2020) or structural inertia (Hannan & Freeman, 1984), has been demonstrated empirically numerous times (e.g. Burgelman, 2002; Koch, 2011; Tripsas, 2009). Historically conditioned continuity refers to (often counterproductive) organizational "pattern[s] of action and reflection" (Koch, 2011, p. 339) that persist counterfactually (i.e. despite pressure for change or repeated change efforts). It poses a critical challenge for many organizations, especially in times of disruptive change (Christensen, 1997). While there are many different explanations of such "puzzling persistencies" (Sydow et al., 2009, p. 695) to be found in organization theory, all of them are at least implicitly based on the assumption that past events are objectively given and, therefore, can, under certain conditions, exert causal influence on present actions by creating irreversible "turning points" (Abbott, 2001) in the history of an organization.

In direct contradiction to such established explanations for historically conditioned stability, recent research on time and temporality in organizations (Hatch & Schultz, 2017; Hernes & Schultz, 2020; Kaplan & Orlikowski, 2013; Schultz & Hernes, 2013) argues that the past (just like the future) is not objectively given, but instead a socially constructed and therefore always malleable horizon of actions situated in the present (see also, e.g. Mead, 1934). And just as with historically conditioned continuity, there are already a number of empirical studies that support this view of the past as a socially constructed,

167

ever-changing time horizon (e.g. Blagoev et al., 2018; Hatch & Schultz, 2017; Schultz & Hernes, 2013).

Looked at in combination, these two research streams pose a fascinating conceptual puzzle for scholars of organizational change and continuity. How is it possible that many organizations apparently fail to overcome long established patterns, if the past is an always malleable horizon of the present? Shouldn't organizational actors be able to shed off undesirable legacies from the past by simply reconstructing their history in ways that are more pertinent to present or future contingencies?

The purpose of this chapter is to outline a new theoretical perspective that helps us resolve this conceptual puzzle. In short, we argue that history is not merely a socially constructed horizon (i.e. a narrated memory of the past) but also a situated, socio-material enactment of interdependencies among multiple action patterns in the present. In its narrated form, the focus of prior research, history appears as accounts of past events that actors draw upon to make sense of their present(s) (Blagoev et al., 2018; Hatch & Schultz, 2017). In its enacted form, the focus of our paper, history appears as a specific and non-random pattern of interdependence among multiple socio-material patterns of action enacted in the present: structural couplings. We use the term structural coupling to designate a relation among two or more action patterns, whereby enacting one pattern has constraining, enabling, or orienting effects (Cardinale, 2018) on the enactment of other patterns (Rosa et al., 2021). As we develop below, seeing enacted history as structural couplings enables us to resolve the puzzle of historically conditioned continuity in organizations. It does so by shifting research attention from the ways in which actors imagine and narrate the past toward how structurally coupled patterns of action enact each other's past in the present.

By developing the notion of structural couplings as enacted history, we deepen research on organizational continuity and change in two ways. First, we advance an understanding of structural coupling as a temporal concept, that is, how one action pattern's situated enactment in an ongoing present makes references to the past (and the future) of specific other action patterns. We discuss how such an understanding can enable organizational scholars to develop novel, and more sound explanations of the different modes through which continuity is enacted in organizational life. Second, we show that distinct forms of enacted interdependence create distinct forms of continuity. Our theorizing thus enables organizational scholars to see a wider variety of different action patterns and forms of interdependence, thus offering many opportunities for future research.

Narrated history and historically conditioned continuity in organizations

Over the past two decades, there has been a surge of interest in time and temporality across various sub-fields of management and organization studies (Ancona et al., 2001; Hernes & Schultz, 2020; Kaplan & Orlikowski, 2013; Kunisch et al., 2017; Orlikowski & Yates, 2002; Shipp & Jansen, 2021; Staudenmayer et al., 2002). This line of research has increasingly advocated an event-based view of time (not to be mistaken with event time), whereby the past (just like the future) is seen as a dimension of the present. As such, the past can orient – but does not and cannot exert a casual influence on – the performance of actions situated in the present: "In this mode of thinking, things, people, past, future, etc. only exist here and now in the living present, i.e. in the actual event" (Hussenot & Missonier, 2016, p. 528). For example, in a meeting (event), actors might refer to topics discussed, or decisions made, in previous meetings (the dimension of the past) as well as anticipate decisions that need to be made in other meetings that are still to come (the dimension of the future). In its most radical version, this argument implies that neither the past nor the future have an ontological existence separate from how they are brought into the present: The past no longer "is," whereas the future "cannot begin" (Luhmann, 1976; St. Augustine, 1992); the present, including the present past and the present future, is the only time we can have.

The emphasis of this recent scholarship can, therefore, be summed up as "narrated history." This emphasis has been particularly strong in research on "the uses of the past" in organizations (Wadhwani et al., 2018). This line of research has advanced a view of (narratives about) the past as a resource that enables novel courses of action in the present rather than constraining the latter (Blagoev et al., 2018; Hatch & Schultz, 2017; Suddaby & Foster, 2017). In this narrative view, the past is assumed to be almost infinitely "malleable": actors arguably can re-imagine the past almost as they wish. The assumed malleability of narrated history, in turn, implies that if phenomena such as historically conditioned continuity occurred, they could be easily overcome by re-narrating the past.

This assumption of malleability has already been challenged by studies that underscore materiality as a constraining and orienting factor for what happens in the present (Abbott, 2001; Blagoev et al., 2018). For instance, in a study of the British Museum, Blagoev et al. (2018) found that materials inherited from the past actively constrained and oriented how organizational actors approached the digitalization of the museum's collections. Materiality actively drew actors toward certain courses of action rather than others. This finding led the authors to introduce the notion of "the dual nature of the past" as existing in the present both as narratives and as a material reality inherited from previous times.

However, even this increased attention to materiality, does not suffice to explain why organizations sometimes struggle with historically conditioned continuity. That is, a situation in which their present reality cannot simply be "imagined" or "narrated" away and instead is experienced as irreversible or unavoidable (Blagoev & Schreyögg, 2019; Kremser, 2017). In such situations, the past appears not only as a dimension of present agency that can be freely re-interpreted but also as a complex socio-material enactment in which actors feel "trapped" (Michel, 2011, p. 355). While the "'stickiness' of past material reality" (Abbott, 2001, p. 222) plays an important role here, we argue that interdependence among organizational action patterns constitutes an even more significant, but only poorly understood factor. In unfolding this argument, we complement the focus on narrated history in prior work with an explicit consideration of what we call enacted history (see Figure 9.1 for an overview of our framework).

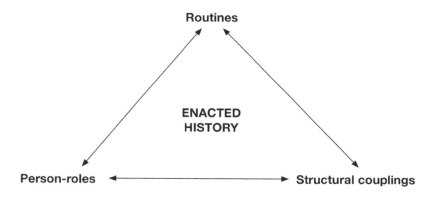

Figure 9.1   Theoretical framework

Routine interdependence and enacted history

In what follows, we develop the concept of enacted history by, first, drawing on research on routine dynamics (Feldman et al., 2016; Feldman & Pentland, 2003) and routine interdependence (Kremser & Schreyögg, 2016; Rosa et al., 2021), and second, the concept of structural couplings (Maturana & Varela, 1992).

Routine dynamics and routine interdependence

Organizational routines are "repetitive, recognizable pattern[s] of interdependent actions, involving multiple actors" (Feldman & Pentland, 2003, p. 96) that are oriented toward the accomplishment of a "day-to-day operational task" (Rerup & Feldman, 2011, p. 584) and emerge as their constituent actions become reflective of each other (Kremser et al., 2019). Organizational routines seldom exist in isolation. In real-life organizational contexts, multiple routines often work together to achieve larger organizational outcomes and, therefore, come to form networks of interdependent routines (Rosa et al., 2021). Importantly, the dynamics among interdependent routines can be markedly different from the dynamics observed within single routines; for example, we might observe change within the performances of a focal routine while, at the same time, observing continuity in the overall cluster that routine is part of (Kremser & Schreyögg, 2016).

Routines – and by implication also networks of interdependent routines – are temporal phenomena (Turner, 2014; Turner & Rindova, 2018). On the most fundamental level, they are temporally patterned as sequences of actions, in the sense that the specific sequential order in which actions are performed is meaningful (Goh & Pentland, 2019). In practice, this means that each action within the performance of a routine draws its meaning from the actions it precedes and/or succeeds in accomplishing a given task. In addition, routines also exhibit their own narrated history to the extent that actors who contribute to a focal routine will co-construct expectations about the pattern of a routine based on their experiences with past performances of that routine (Dittrich et al., 2016). Within routine dynamics research, the outcome of such reflections has been traditionally referred to as the "ostensive aspect" of routines (Feldman & Pentland, 2003), that is, the routine pattern in the abstract. For example, by observing that a focal routine is performed again and again at a specific point in time (e.g. 9 a.m.), a focal actor might infer expectations that their contribution to that routine is usually performed around that time and act accordingly (Kremser & Blagoev, 2021; Turner & Rindova, 2018). In addition, actors might discuss and narrate deviations from such expectations with other involved actors, thus contributing to the emergence of a shared collective understanding of the routine pattern. In any case, such an understanding encompasses narrated accounts about past routine performances, which, in turn, inform what actors do and say in the present.

Enacting history by performing structural couplings

By contrast, the enacted history of a focal routine shifts attention away from what happens (or has happened) in that routine, to those routines with which the focal routine is interdependent. More specifically, we argue that the enacted history of a focal routine is constituted not in the past but in its ongoing present through patterns enacted in other, interdependent routines.

The key insight here is that, over time, interdependencies among action patterns can result in what Maturana and Varela (1992) have called "structural couplings" (see also Kremser, 2017), which generally refers to the way that the structure of one system is dependent on, or influenced by, the structure of another system. In our specific context, structural couplings can be understood as adjustments within a focal action pattern through which that action pattern becomes sensitive to specific (i.e. not all) perturbations from other patterns. In a small diner, for example, the serving routine might become sensitive (i.e. adapt) to the rhythm of the cooking routine (see below), while remaining unaffected, for example, by the specifics of how Hash Browns are prepared. For structural couplings to emerge, mutual perturbations need to be patterned, so that the pattern of one routine – as opposed to a specific, singular performance – forms partly as a reaction to the pattern of another, and vice versa. In our small diner, for example, some aspects of the pattern of the serving routine (e.g. how often a waiter will usually check the pass-through for completed orders) will – over the course of multiple performances – likely become adjusted to some aspects of the cooking routine (e.g. how long the kitchen usually takes to prepare specific items on the menu) and vice versa. A waiter might not adjust their enactment of the serving routine altogether only because one order arrived late once. But they might consider doing just that if they develop an expectation that it happens on a regular basis, for example by checking the pass-through less frequently and informing their guests that certain dishes tend to take a bit longer.

As one form of enacted interdependence, structural couplings have important implications for change and continuity. More specifically, those parts of a focal action pattern which couple it structurally to another pattern will typically change at a slower pace than other parts of that focal pattern (see also Simon, 1962). This is the case because variations that affect structural couplings are less likely to "stick" as they do not only have to satisfy the requirements of the focal pattern but also those of other, interdependent patterns. In our small diner, for example, the temporal aspects of the pattern of the cooking routine might not just need to support the accomplishment of the cooking task (e.g. through enough time for high quality cooking), but also the accomplishment of the serving task (e.g. by enabling quick service of ordered meals). In so far as that happens, the (endogenous) drift of the temporal aspects of the overall pattern of the cooking routine will be characterized by less "degrees of freedom" – fewer of all possible variations in its performance are likely to "stick" and become part of the pattern – because of its structural coupling with the serving routine and not (only) because of how the cooking team constructs narratives of its own history. Even if the cooking team would start to construct its own history in such a way that a much slower pace of the cooking routine would appear to be a good thing, the disturbances that this will create in the serving routine would lead the kitchen team to re-evaluate that specific interpretation of the cooking routine's history over the course of just a few performances. A variation to that part of the pattern is not very likely to "stick," even if it does occur. As a result of structural couplings between two routines, the present performances of one routine – rather than only the social construction of the past – can exert a stabilizing effect on the performance of another.

The implications of structural couplings among routines for enacted history

As a consequence of this emergent continuity, structural couplings among routines can also be understood as a form of enacted history. We propose that the enacted history of routines – as opposed to the enacted history of other types of action patterns in organizations – will be especially helpful in explaining specific cases of historically conditioned continuity which have been referred to as "routine rigidity" (Gilbert, 2005). Routine rigidity denotes situations in which an organization appears unable to change its way of accomplishing specific tasks, or, more abstractly, its capabilities. For example, Kremser and Schreyögg (2016, p. 698) demonstrated how structural couplings, what they label as "programmed interfaces," can result from actors' efforts to realize complementarities among routines. Realizing complementarities then triggers the formation of routine clusters. The authors go on to suggest that this specific form of enacted interdependence among routines will "amount to a trajectory which guides the cluster's future shape when challenged to adapt to new developments" (Kremser & Schreyögg, 2016, p. 702). Put differently, when new routines ought to be integrated into an established cluster (e.g. in order to react to innovative new technology), they will be accepted, adapted, or rejected based on how well the fit into the established cluster. This suggests that the continuity emanating from structural couplings is not limited to the coupled routines, but also extends to the capacity of the cluster to integrate new routines. They can create a learning trajectory not just for specific routines, but also for organizational capabilities, defined as "collection[s] of routines" (Winter, 2003, p. 991).

In sum, structural couplings among routines stabilize that part of an organization's enacted history which concerns what an organization can and cannot do (i.e. what commonly is referred to as organizational capabilities) (Winter, 2003). Enacted history helps us to explain historically conditioned continuity as an effect not of the past per se (e.g. "That's how we have always done things around here!") but rather of situated performances of interdependence among routines (e.g. "We tried to change that thing, but the other team immediately started complaining about all the problems that this caused in their work").

There are, however, other parts of enacted history within an organization that are less concerned with an organization's capabilities and more focused on the normative question of what and who is considered important or valuable to the organization, what will often result in a characteristic pattern of resource allocation within an organization (Gilbert, 2005). To be able to theorize how these parts of enacted history become stabilized, we need to turn our attention towards another central action pattern in organizations: organizational roles.

Enacted history in role-routine ecologies

In this section, we further develop the concept of enacted history by drawing on interactionist role-theory (Turner, 1990) and the concept of person-roles (Hernes, 2014). In so doing, we enhance our argument by discussing the consequences of a second form of enacted interdependence: role-routine couplings.

Person-roles and role-routine ecologies

Interactionist role theory suggests that organizational roles are patterns of action "tied together only by their emanation from a single individual who is oriented to a single status during the period of his action" (Turner, 1990, pp. 88–9). Understood as an action pattern, a role is likely to become increasingly specific to the person who enacts it. To emphasize this important feature of all organizational roles, we will speak of person-roles here (see also e.g. Hernes, 2014). Person-roles are patterned with regard to two relational aspects: functional responsibilities and relative social positions. Functional responsibilities relate a focal person-role's expected involvement in different tasks (routines) to other person-roles, that is, the "task requirements of different roles and how they relate to one another" (Okhuysen and Bechky, 2009, p. 476). Relative social positions, in turn, "refer to the relations of deference that connect a focal role to other roles within its role set" (Kremser & Blagoev,

2021, p. 343). Person-roles thus enable actors to performatively accomplish and negotiate social relationships to other actors in their role set during episodes of role-taking and role-making (Katz & Kahn, 1978).

Role-taking denotes the process through which actors "select" their own action by taking the roles of significant others (Dionysiou & Tsoukas, 2013). For instance, actors performing the serving routine in a diner are likely to take the role of the kitchen chef – who is known to want food to be served hot at the customers' tables – and act accordingly, thereby also establishing a structural coupling of the role of the kitchen chef and the service routine. By contrast, role-making denotes a process through which actors collectively and usually only partially (re-)negotiate the functional accountabilities and relative social positions of one or more person-roles within a given role-set. For example, if a waiter is always too slow in serving food, the kitchen chef might engage in role-making to influence the ways in which the waiter performs his contributions to the serving routine. Importantly, role performances – even though they always only concern specific aspects of specific person-roles – also enact a normative order that defines who and what is important within a specific organizational context. If the kitchen chef, for example, repeatedly succeeds at influencing how the waiter acts within the serving routine, the chef and their preferences might increasingly become regraded as more important than those of the waiter. The dynamics of person-roles, thus, enable us to analyze how questions about what and who is considered important or valuable to an organization are handled and addressed within a specific work context.

As alluded to in the previous paragraph, the dynamics of person-roles and routines often intersect in organizations. Over time, these intersecting patterns are likely to become structurally coupled to each other in so far as social relations become an important premise for how specific tasks are performed and vice versa: In these instances, getting things done is as important as getting along with each other. And while such couplings can arise as a reaction to explicit (organizational) design decisions (e.g. when a person's job profile includes contributions to specific routines), they will likely also emerge through everyday interaction and conflict resolution in organizations. It is therefore analytically useful to conceptualize complex organizational settings not simply as networks of routines, but as role-routine ecologies, that is, "complex system[s] of two different yet intersecting action patterns, person-roles and organizational routines" (Kremser & Blagoev, 2021, p. 366). The concept of role-routine ecologies is especially relevant for our theorizing precisely because it highlights that interdependencies can exist not only among routines (as developed above) but also among a variety of different types of action patterns, such as routines and roles. Below we spell out the implications of this insight for our theorizing of enacted history.

The implications of role-routine couplings for enacted history

Role-routine couplings emerge when "the pattern of a focal routine is adjusted to better fit the preferences of a specific person-role" (Kremser & Blagoev, 2021, p. 368). This means that the enacted history of a person-role can be found in parts of routine patterns that have been previously adjusted in response to the preferences of that person-role. In our diner example, the parts of the serving routine that have been adjusted to better fit the temporal preferences of the kitchen chef (faster performance) represent the enacted history of that person-role. If, for example, the chef were to work at a slower pace than the accelerated service routine requires, it would be more likely than before that their person-role would be subject to role-making performances from others ("*Are we a bit on the slow side today*?!") directed at establishing more continuity in that person-role.

Importantly, role-routine couplings result in a normative (re-)shaping of routines where person-roles have a normative influence on organizational routines. For example, if a person-role considered important or powerful (e.g. the kitchen chef) contributes to a focal routine (e.g. the cooking routine), that routine is likely to be considered more important, too, and accordingly is likely to be allocated more resources (e.g. higher salaries, better equipment). This, in turn, would increase continuity by reinforcing the powerful position of the kitchen chef. But role-routine couplings might also create continuity in the normative ordering of actors and tasks in other ways. For example, Kremser and Blagoev (2021) observed how management consultants had to adapt the pattern of their presentation preparation routine to the consistently delayed contributions by clients, which however were essential for a successful routine performance. Clients – who were not members of the consulting firm – consistently ignored consultants' attempt to engage in role-making (i.e. to make them contribute on time by setting deadlines). Consultants, in turn, over time abandoned such attempts altogether, and instead adjusted the timing of the routine to the delayed contributions by clients. This contributed to continuity of the normative ordering of actors and tasks in the consulting project as it established in practice that client-side work routines will generally be prioritized over the routines of the consulting project.

In sum, we argue that role-routine couplings represent a form of enacted interdependence that is particularly important for understanding those parts of an organization's enacted history that concern the normative ordering of actors and tasks. Over time, the repeated enactment of role-routine couplings can stabilize a specific normative order that defines who and what is considered valuable or important within an organization. Hence, role-routine couplings constitute an additional form of enacted interdependence among actions patterns that plays an important role in understanding another form of historically conditioned stability. Whereas interdependence among routines enables us to explain the task-related parts of enacted history (i.e. those that concern the organization's capabilities), interdependence between routines and person-roles over time enacts the normative ordering of actors and tasks in an organization (i.e. who and what is important).

Therefore, we expect role-routine couplings to be particularly important for explaining what has been referred to as "resource rigidity" (Gilbert, 2005), that is, cases of historically conditioned continuity in established resource allocation patterns. For example, by deciding to let person A and task B wait yet another time, a focal actor willingly or unwillingly reproduces a specific normative ordering of actors and tasks; whatever and whoever must wait is obviously not important enough: "Tasks that are always at a disadvantage must in the end be devalued and ranked as less important in order to reconcile fate and meaning" (Luhmann, 1971, p. 148). Thus, the performance of role-routine couplings amounts to the enactment of those parts of an organization's history that concern questions about the value and worth of tasks. And the (patterned) ways in which such questions are typically addressed in a specific organization is likely to inform how this organization allocates resources among different actors and tasks.

Our approach therefore implies that structural couplings of routines and of person-roles and routines stabilize two distinct parts of enacted history. Structural couplings of routines stabilize what operative tasks an organization can perform and how (i.e. its capabilities). It lets us explain historically conditioned continuity in the evolution of organizational capabilities that cannot be overcome by merely re-narrating the past. By contrast, structural couplings of person-roles and routines enable us to explain historically conditioned continuity that becomes visible when organizations are confronted with novel regimes of value that call for a radical reconfiguration of the existing normative order of an organization's capability set, for example when tasks considered unimportant in the past suddenly appear as crucial and valuable and vice versa.

In both cases, paying attention to interdependent action patterns as enacted history helps us resolve the puzzle of historically conditioned continuity without re-introducing an objectivist view of the past as a fixed constraint. The concept suggests a clear and precise empirical form of historically conditioned continuity in the present: structural couplings among action patterns. This implies that the degree of continuity of a focal pattern depends not only on how the actors performing that pattern narrate its history. In addition, it will depend on what happens in other, structurally coupled patterns. The higher the complexity of this web (i.e. the higher the number of patterns and relationships of interdependence among them), the harder it will be for actors to control what happens within it.

Discussion

In this chapter, we set out to explore the puzzle of historically conditioned continuity in organizations. To do so we introduced and developed the concept of enacted history as a counterpart to prior work's focus on narrated history. We demonstrated how enacted history can be viewed in terms of structural couplings among different types of action patterns, using organizational routines and person-roles as examples (see Figure 9.2 for an overview). We then theorized the distinct stabilizing effects of two different structural couplings (couplings among routines and role-routines couplings) as two different forms

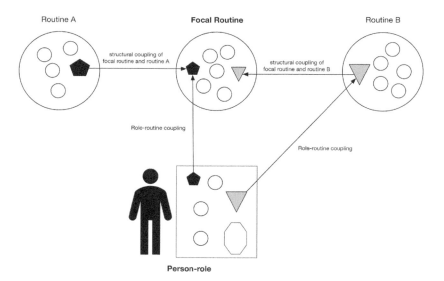

Figure 9.2   The enactment of history through structural couplings among routines and roles

of enacted history. In what follows, we develop how enacted history contributes to research on organizational continuity and change.

The temporal dimension of structural couplings

The idea of enacted history deepens current research on organizational temporality and uses of the past (Kaplan & Orlikowski, 2013; Schultz & Hernes, 2013; Wadhwani et al., 2018) by suggesting that history appears in organizations not only as narration but also as a specific type of socio-material enactment of interdependence among action patterns: structural couplings. This specific form of enacted interdependence enables us to explain those "sticky" aspects of the present that actors seem to be unable to narrate away.

The structural coupling of action patterns can be seen as a crucial, yet often invisible way in which action patterns enact each other's past in the present. This fosters historically conditioned continuity as it will become more challenging to change those aspects of a focal pattern that couple it structurally to other patterns. The reason is that variations that affect structural couplings have to satisfy the requirements of multiple patterns in order to "stick," otherwise these variations, even if they occur, will not change the overall pattern. Furthermore, considering the important differences between different actions patterns enables researchers – and practitioners – to better understand the differences between various modes of historically conditioned continuity in practice. Its core implication is that in addition to focusing on how actors narrate the past in present, we should consider the ways in which structural couplings among action patterns are enacted in organizations.

The relevance of these insights is emphasized by the observation that, whereas narration and enactment of the past might overlap in some cases, this does not need to be the case. Often, actors would be inclined to narrate failed attempts at changing certain patterns by referring to history, for example by pointing toward events that have happened in the past and construing the effect of those events on the present as irreversible (Granqvist & Gustafsson, 2016). Still, such narratives might be nothing more than a social defense mechanism that serves to keep actors away from questioning and changing the actual ways in which continuity is maintained in everyday action (Padavic et al., 2020). By drawing on the concept of enacted history, scholars could move one step closer to unravelling the puzzle of historically conditioned continuity as a phenomenon that exists and is thus also produced and reproduced in the present.

Interdependence, continuity and change

Our study also adds to research on organizational continuity and change (e.g. Farjoun, 2010; Feldman et al., 2021; Feldman & Pentland, 2003) by demonstrating how structural couplings among different types of patterns can help us to explain different forms of continuity in organizational life. We specifically discussed the consequences of structural couplings among routines as well as role-routine couplings. Interdependencies among routines could manifest as disruptions in the accomplishment of operative tasks, for example a change in how one task is performed disrupts the accomplishment of another. Addressing such disruptions likely contributes to the emergence of structural couplings among routines in the form of mutually adapted patterns of task accomplishment (e.g. performing the routines within a specific timeframe, using specific tools, being especially sensitive to certain mistakes yet less sensitive to others). Conversely, interdependencies among person-roles and routines could manifest as disruptions in social relations, for example (covert or overt) conflicts about what and who ought to be prioritized. Addressing such disruptions likely contributes to the emergence of role-routine couplings that amount not merely to a specific way of accomplishing tasks, but to a larger pattern of deference among person-roles and routines, that is, a hierarchy of actors and tasks.

A logical consequence of this insight is that each type of structural coupling enacts a different type of continuity. We developed that structural couplings among routines facilitate the emergence of continuity in evolution of organizational capabilities. By contrast, structural couplings among routines and roles facilitate the emergence of continuity in patterns of resource allocation. This insight enables scholars to be more precise in unpacking how the specific actions, performed by specific actors, at specific places and specific times contribute to the different forms of organizational change and continuity. Moreover, it suggests that change and continuity in organizations are mutually constitutive to the extent that change in one pattern can manifest as disruption in another and, hence, motivate actions oriented toward maintaining continuity.

These two forms concerned only two types of action patterns in organizations: routines and person-roles. Of course, organizations are replete with many types of patterns. For example, time-use patterns can become an important for understanding interdependence, particularly when routine performances are time-sensitive (Gardner et al., 2017; Geiger et al., 2021). In addition, we expect larger organizational patterns – such as strategy and identity (Schultz & Hernes, 2020) – to become entangled with routines and person-roles in non-trivial ways. Future research can build on our theorizing to examine empirically and conceptually how different forms of interdependence among different patterns can become carriers and manifestations of history as a socio-material enactment in organizations. In addition, we believe that cross-couplings among different types of patterns (e.g. between person-roles and time-use patterns) provide important avenues for future research. Finally, scholars could also further explore how enacted and narrated history influence each other. For example, an organization might try to re-narrate its history in order to establish continuity with a new, future-oriented identity as a sustainable company. However, enacting this identity might be constrained by the enacted patterns of interdependence which constitute that organization's enacted history.

Conclusion

Whether we see history as a narration or an enactment has important consequences for how we study organizations and what we mean when we say that "history matters." Whereas much past research has taken either an objectivist stance, thereby taking the past's causal effect on the present for granted, or a subjectivist view that sees history as a narration of the past in the present, our chapter offers an alternative view: history appears in organization as a situated, socio-material enactment of interdependence among action patterns. This enables us to resolve the puzzle of historically conditioned continuity in organizations and see the latter as temporalized social systems that crucially depend on their capacity to remember the past both through narration *and* enactment. These insights enable researchers to see issues such as organizational inertia, continuity, and change in new and more complex ways. This should, in turn, afford novel approaches for acting upon and changing persistent patterns of action and reflection in organizations.

References

Abbott, Andrew (2001). *Time Matters*, Chicago, IL and London: University of Chicago Press.

Ancona, Deborah G., Okhuysen, Gerardo A., & Perlow, Leslie A. (2001). Taking Time to Integrate Temporal Research, *The Academy of Management Review*, 26(4), 512.

Blagoev, Blagoy, Felten, Sebastian, & Kahn, Rebecca (2018). The Career of a Catalogue: Organizational Memory, Materiality and the Dual Nature of the Past at the British Museum (1970–Today), *Organization Studies*, 39(12), 1757–83.

Blagoev, Blagoy, & Schreyögg, Georg (2019). Why Do Extreme Work Hours Persist? Temporal Uncoupling as a New Way of Seeing, *Academy of Management Journal*, 62(6), 1818–47.

Burgelman, Robert A. (2002). Strategy as Vector and the Inertia of Coevolutionary Lock-in, *Administrative Science Quarterly*, 47(2), 325–57.

Cardinale, Ivano (2018). Beyond Constraining and Enabling: Toward New Microfoundations for Institutional Theory, *Academy of Management Review*, 43(1), 132–55.

Christensen, Clayton M. (1997). *The Innovator's Dilemma: When New Technologies Cause Great Firms to Fail*, Boston, MA: Harvard Business School Press.

Dionysiou, Dionysios D., & Tsoukas, Haridimos (2013). Understanding the (Re) Creation of Routines from Within: A Symbolic Interactionist Perspective, *Academy of Management Review*, 38(2), 181–205.

Dittrich, Katharina, Guérard, Stéphane, & Seidl, David (2016). Talking About Routines: The Role of Reflective Talk in Routine Change, *Organization Science*, 27(3), 678–97.

Farjoun, Moshe (2010). Beyond Dualism: Stability and Change as a Duality, *Academy of Management Review*, 35(2), 202–25.

Feldman, Martha S., & Pentland, Brian T. (2003). Reconceptualizing Organizational Routines as a Source of Flexibility and Change, *Administrative Science Quarterly*, 48, 94–118.

Feldman, Martha S., Pentland, Brian T., D'Adderio, Luciana, & Lazaric, Nathalie (2016). Beyond Routines as Things: Introduction to the Special Issue on Routine Dynamics, *Organization Science*, 27(3), 505–13.

Feldman, Martha S., Worline, Monica, Baker, Natalie, & Lowerson Bredow, Victoria (2021). Continuity as Patterning: A Process Perspective on Continuity, *Strategic Organization*, 20(1), 80–109.

Gardner, John W., Boyer, Kenneth K., & Ward, Peter T. (2017). Achieving Time-Sensitive Organizational Performance Through Mindful Use of Technologies and Routines, *Organization Science*, 28(6), 1061–79.

Geiger, Daniel, Danner-Schröder, Anja, & Kremser, Waldemar (2021). Getting Ahead of Time—Performing Temporal Boundaries to Coordinate Routines under Temporal Uncertainty, *Administrative Science Quarterly*, 66(1), 220–64.

Gilbert, Clark G. (2005). Unbundling the Structure of Inertia: Resource versus Routine Rigidity, *Academy of Management Journal*, 48(5), 741–63.

Goh, Kenneth T., & Pentland, Brian T. (2019). From Actions to Paths to Patterning: Toward a Dynamic Theory of Patterning in Routines, *Academy of Management Journal*, 62(6), 1901–29.

Granqvist, Nina, & Gustafsson, Robin (2016). Temporal Institutional Work, *Academy of Management Journal*, 59(3), 1009–35.

Hannan, Michael T, & Freeman, John (1984). Structural Inertia and Organizational Change, *American Sociological Review*, 49(2), 149–64.

Hatch, Mary Jo, & Schultz, Majken (2017). Toward a Theory of Using History Authentically: Historicizing in the Carlsberg Group, *Administrative Science Quarterly*, 62(4), 657–97.

Hernes, Tor (2014). *A Process Theory of Organization* (1st edition), Oxford: Oxford University Press.

Hernes, Tor, & Schultz, Majken (2020). Translating the Distant into the Present: How Actors Address Distant Past and Future Events Through Situated Activity, *Organization Theory*, 1(1), 1–20.

Hussenot, Anthony, & Missonier, Stéphanie (2016). Encompassing Stability and Novelty in Organization Studies: An Events-based Approach, *Organization Studies*, 37(4), 523–46.

Kaplan, Sarah, & Orlikowski, Wanda J. (2013). Temporal Work in Strategy Making, *Organization Science*, 24(4), 965–95.

Katz, Daniel, & Kahn, Robert L. (1978). *The Social Psychology of Organizations*, 2nd edition, New York: Wiley.

Koch, Jochen (2011). Inscribed Strategies: Exploring the Organizational Nature of Strategic Lock-in, *Organization Studies*, 32(3), 337–63.

Kremser, Waldemar (2017). *Interdependente Routinen*, Wiesbaden: Springer Fachmedien Wiesbaden.

Kremser, Waldemar, & Blagoev, Blagoy (2021). The Dynamics of Prioritizing: How Actors Temporally Pattern Complex Role–Routine Ecologies, *Administrative Science Quarterly*, 66(2), 339–79.

Kremser, Waldemar, Pentland, Brian, & Brunswicker, Sabine (2019). Interdependence Within and Between Routines: A Performative Perspective, in M. S. Feldman, L. D'Aderio, K. Dittrich & P. Jarzabkowski (eds), *Routine Dynamics in Action: Replication and Transformation* (Research in the Sociology of Organizations, vol. 61) (pp. 79–98), Bingley: Emerald Publishing.

Kremser, Waldemar, & Schreyögg, Georg (2016). The Dynamics of Interrelated Routines: Introducing the Cluster Level, *Organization Science*, 27(3), 698–721.

Kunisch, Sven, Bartunek, Jean M., Mueller, Johanna, & Huy, Quy N. (2017). Time in Strategic Change Research, *Academy of Management Annals*, 11(2), 1005–64.

Luhmann, Niklas (1971). Die Knappheit der Zeit und die Vordringlichkeit des Befristeten, in N. Luhmann (ed.), *Politische Planung* (1st edition, pp. 143–64), Opladen: Westdeutscher Verlag.

Luhmann, Niklas. (1976). The Future Cannot Begin: Temporal Structures in Modern Society, *Social Research*, 43(1), 130–52.

Maturana, Humberto R., & Varela, Francisco J. (1992). *The Tree of Knowledge: The Biological Roots of Human Understanding* (revised edition), New York: Shambhala.

Mead, George Herbert (1934). *Mind, Self & Society*, Chicago, IL: University of Chicago Press.

Michel, Alexandra (2011). Transcending Socialization: A Nine-Year Ethnography of the Body's Role in Organizational Control and Knowledge Workers' Transformation, *Administrative Science Quarterly*, 56(3), 325–68.

Okhuysen, G. A., & Bechky, B. A. (2009). Coordination in Organizations: An Integrative Perspective, *The Academy of Management Annals*, 3(1), 463–502, https://doi.org/10.1080/19416520903047533.

Orlikowski, Wanda J., & Yates, JoAnne (2002). It's About Time: Temporal Structuring in Organizations, *Organization Science*, 13(6), 684–700.

Padavic, Irene, Ely, Robin J., & Reid, Erin M. (2020). Explaining the Persistence of Gender Inequality: The Work–Family Narrative as a Social Defense against the 24/7 Work Culture, *Administrative Science Quarterly*, 65(1), 61–111.

Rerup, Claus, & Feldman, Martha S. (2011). Routines as a Source of Change in Organizational Schemata: The Role of Trial-and-Error Learning, *Academy of Management Journal*, 54(3), 577–610.

Rosa, Rodrigo A., Kremser, Waldemar, & Bulgacov, Sergio (2021). Routine Interdependence: Intersections, Clusters, Ecologies and Bundles, in L. D'Aderio, K. Dittrich, M. S. Feldman, B. T. Pentland, C. Rerup & D. Seidl (eds), *Cambridge*

Handbook of Routine Dynamics (pp. 244–54), Cambridge, UK and Malden, MA: Cambridge University Press.

Schultz, Majken, & Hernes, Tor (2013). A Temporal Perspective on Organizational Identity, *Organization Science*, 24(1), 1–21.

Schultz, Majken, & Hernes, Tor (2020). Temporal Interplay Between Strategy and Identity: Punctuated, Subsumed, and Sustained Modes, *Strategic Organization*, 18(1), 106–35.

Shipp, Abbie J., & Jansen, Karen J. (2021). The "Other" Time: A Review of the Subjective Experience of Time in Organizations, *Academy of Management Annals*, 15(1), 299–334.

Simon, H. A. (1962). The Architecture of Complexity, *Proceedings of the American Philosophical Society*, 106(6), 467–82.

St Augustine (1992). *Confessions*, Oxford: Oxford University Press.

Staudenmayer, Nancy, Tyre, Marcie, & Perlow, Leslie (2002). Time to Change: Temporal Shifts as Enablers of Organizational Change, *Organization Science*, 13(5), 583–97.

Suddaby, Roy, & Foster, William M. (2017). History and Organizational Change, *Journal of Management*, 43(1), 19–38.

Sydow, J., Schreyögg, Georg, & Koch, Jochen (2009). Organizational Path Dependence: Opening the Black Box, *Academy of Management Review*, 34(4), 689–709.

Sydow, J., Schreyögg, Georg, & Koch, Jochen (2020). On the Theory of Organizational Path Dependence: Clarifications, Replies to Objections, and Extensions, *Academy of Management Review*, 45(4), 717–34.

Tripsas, Mary (2009). Technology, Identity, and Inertia Through the Lens of "The Digital Photography Company", *Organization Science*, 20(2), 441–60.

Turner, R. H. (1990). Role Taking: Process versus Conformity, in D. Brissett & C. Edgley (eds), *Life as Theater* (2nd edition), Berlin: Aldine de Gruyter.

Turner, Scott F. (2014). The Temporal Dimension of Routines and Their Outcomes, in Abbie J. Shipp & Yitzhak Fried (eds), *Time and Work, Volume 2* (pp. 115–45), London and New York: Psychology Press.

Turner, Scott F., & Rindova, Violina P. (2018). Watching the Clock: Action Timing, Patterning, and Routine Performance, *Academy of Management Journal*, 61(4), 1253–80.

Wadhwani, R. Daniel, Suddaby, Roy, Mordhorst, Mads, & Popp, Andrew (2018). History as Organizing: Uses of the Past in Organization Studies, *Organization Studies*, 39(12), 1663–83.

Winter, S. G. (2003). Understanding dynamic capabilities, *Strategic Management Journal*, 24(10), 991–5, https://doi.org/10.1002/smj.318.

10 Re-embracing a rejected past in the flow of time: the shifting roles of nostalgia and nostophobia

Are Branstad and Ansgar Ødegård

Introduction

The concepts of continuity and change have long been considered opposites by a majority of organisational change scholars (Huy, 2002; Jarzabkowski, 2003; Kunisch et al., 2017). However, this logic is arguably sensible only in an essentialist and linear view of time (Ancona et al., 2001; Langley et al. 2013). For change managers, it also creates a mode of thinking and talking about change that can stir up much unnecessary resistance and conflict within the changing organisation. Much organisation change research advances the dualistic view that change disrupts continuity and that a need for continuity merely hinders change. The dominant paradigm seems to be that knowledge of the organisation's past is only useful for people who want to resist changes. Another assumption is that people's temporal orientations are contingent on their organisational position – typically that while employees are averse to change, top managers eagerly seek it (Gouldner, 1954; Nichols & Beynon, 1977; Gabriel, 1993). The alternative, which we adopt in this chapter, is, consistently with the aims of this book, to locate continuity in change and emphasise the mutual relationship between change and continuity in organisational life. Thus, we hope to deepen our knowledge of how changes in the role of the past can occur in organisations and what that could mean for managerial change in practice.

We start by discussing the need for a process-oriented understanding of organisations' pasts. Based on a process view of organisational change, we claim that the events that make up the past and the mode of remembering the past matter to people's understanding of the organisation's "living present" (Hernes, 2014). Two concepts in particular – nostalgia and nostophobia – are then presented. We go on to describe our methods of collecting and analysing the data that constitute our two-case longitudinal study of organisational adaptation to government reform of the electrical power sector in Norway. After presenting our findings in three interconnected phases of development, we discuss our findings against other studies and research streams.

Theoretical underpinnings

During the last two decades, organisation scholars have increasingly sought to understand the role of time in the dynamics of organisational life (Ancona et al., 2001; Langley et al., 2013; Cloutier & Langley, 2020; Schultz & Hernes, 2019; Hernes, 2022) and strategic change (Schultz & Hernes, 2013; Kunisch et al., 2017). This development in organisation theory urges scholars to view change processes as on-going and inseparable from processes of continuity (Hernes, 2022; March, 1981). The view that change and continuity are mutually constitutive categories alerts us to how organisational members can recall past events in order to influence future expected events, thus shaping strategic planning and design. To this end, the concept of temporal work was defined as 'negotiating and resolving tensions among different understandings of what has happened in the past, what is at stake in the present, and what might emerge in the future' (Kaplan & Orlikowski, 2013, p. 965).

The concept of continuity can be understood as a state of uninterrupted existence. Continuity can also the involve the return of something that once was, as when a product or a story is rediscovered and revived in organisations to cast new light on current events (Hatch & Schultz, 2017). In organisations, continuity could stem from people who have been with the organisation for a long time (Dibble, 1999), long-time customers, historic narratives, or brand names (Schultz & Hernes, 2013), or rules and work ethics (Strangleman, 1999), that is, things and ideas that create links between 'then' and 'now'. Continuity thus necessitates memory and going back in history (i.e. modes of thinking associated with nostalgia). As a temporal orientation, nostalgia can therefore be constructive of the notion of continuity in change.

There is no single established definition of what constitutes an organisational past event. However, we conceptualise organisational pasts as recollected events that can be used to make sense of or influence decisions and plans in organisations. Thus, we think of past events as communicable recollections, related to artefacts or concepts. Events can be *official* (the founding of a firm or its bankruptcy), retrievable in organisational records, or *symbolic* (stories and catchphrases) and shared in emotive language. Since an event, arguably, is something that stands out from the everyday stream of routines, the concept signals change and would normally undermine the notion of continuity. Past events are often represented in the literature as discontinuous punctuations between discrete states such as beginnings, peaks, and endings of organisational processes. However, such renderings often ignore the fact that past events are often used for sensemaking in the present. Past events can also include more habitual processes, such as routines and work practices (Gehman et al., 2013). Though arguably less 'eventful', these more continuous forms of events are elements around which organisational memory of the past evolves into organisational capabilities (Howard-Grenville & Rerup, 2016).

Historically-oriented organisation scholars have argued for the importance of distant organisational pasts (Pettigrew, 1990; Brunninge, 2009; Suddaby, Foster, & Trank, 2010; Lasewicz, 2015) and biography (Kimberly & Bouchikhi, 1995) for understanding strategy processes. In management, a study of Carlsberg (Hatch & Schultz, 2017) shows the importance of history when establishing claims to authenticity and how history becomes relevant to present and future activities. Narration increases the power of history (Brunninge, 2009) and becomes a powerful resource in supporting or weakening future strategies. For instance, Ybema (2010) showed in his study of a Dutch newspaper how history became a 'discursive battlefield' between protagonists and antagonists of organisational change. In this perspective, the past is open to interpretations that can shape what is experienced in the present and expected in the future (Wadhwani et al., 2018). Strangleman (1999, p. 729) argues that '(…) the past, history and identity are almost infinitely malleable and are used by management, and government, to win consent for change, or at least marginalise criticism, among workers, management, and the public'. Thus, the meaning of events is mutable and re-negotiable over time. Events are used in a social context and can be constructed to align with present interests, needs, or self-images (Suddaby et al., 2010).

Nostalgia and nostophobia in organisational change studies

By combining the words nostos ('return home') and algia ('longing') Johannes Hofer coined the term *nostalgia* in 1688 (Anspach, 1934). Historically, nostalgia was considered an honourable emotion, but the meaning of the term changed and became rather associated with negative human characteristics such as being reactionary, or sentimentally idealising the past (Baake-Hansen, 2015). Nostalgia is thus primarily concerned with time and the mode of looking backwards. The concept of nostalgia was further developed by Boym (2008), who distinguished between *restorative* and *reflective* nostalgia. *Restorative* nostalgia is a kind of dogmatic feeling which emerges through an objective (accurate) reconstruction of the past and longing for the past that once existed. *Reflective* nostalgia, by contrast, allows the coexistence of longing and critical reflection in which aspirations and dreams for the future can take place.

Organisational nostalgia is typically seen as a reaction to organisational change processes (Fineman, 2000; Gabriel, 1993; Strangleman, 1999). Examples can be found in earlier works within industrial sociology (Gouldner, 1954; Nichols & Beynon, 1977). Gabriel (1993) interprets nostalgia as a reaction to feeling marginalised, or as a comforting escape to a 'golden past' from the uncertainty of organisational change. These studies suggest that workers' attitudes are profoundly rooted in past experiences, and that managers fail to acknowledge how workers remember their former times.

Nostophobia is the opposite of nostalgia; a feeling of disgust for the past or a denial that anything interesting can come from it (Baake-Hansen, 2015). As a concept in organisational research, nostophobia was used by Strangleman (1999) in his study of New Public Management reforms in British Railways. Similarly, Munro (1998) used the phrase 'rubbishing the past', which means to delegitimise tradition as a sensemaking tool. Thus, what nostophobia and nostalgia commonly lead to is focusing on certain aspects of the past (Kunisch et al., 2017; Lubinski, 2018). Acts of remembering in organisations can therefore be seen as 'performed realities' (i.e. ways of presenting the past to shape the present and the future) (Ramsey, 2005). As performances, nostalgia cleans up the past, while nostophobia revels in exposing its dirt.

A concept similar in meaning to nostophobia is *postalgia*, coined in Ybema (2010). Here, managerial postalgia refers to the 'idealisation of the future and disdain for the past, and the concomitant condemning of the past-in-the-present/future (…)' (Ybema, 2010, p. 486). According to Bate, top management speech often displays a 'preference for forward-looking concepts, such as planning, mission, vision, or goal-setting' (Bate, 1997, p. 1155). Thus, postalgia draws attention to overly future-oriented thinking, which may be linked to a shunning of the past (i.e. nostophobia). Although postalgia is an interesting and apt concept for studying organisational change processes, we will continue using nostalgia and nostophobia here for the sake of conceptual neatness and staying focused on the role of the past.

From rejecting to appreciating the past over the course of time

In the following, we will describe the processes in two power utilities who, shortly after a radical reform of the power industry, distanced themselves from practices that, in their view, belonged to pre-reform times, performing an early form of nostophobia. They wanted to move away from what they considered a drab and unwanted pre-reform past. However, 20 years later they found their pre-reform past to be more relevant for staking out a course for the future, which we may associate with a reflective nostalgia.

Our case organisations, which we will call PowerEast and PowerWest,[1] are electrical power utilities established in the early 1900s, at the birth of the new age of hydropower (power production using waterfalls). Power utilities provide the electrical grids to distribute electricity to customers ranging from private households to power intensive industry. Until the 1990s, power utilities were owned by national, regional, and municipal government who also were responsible for maintaining and improving the power grid as well as selling the power to end consumers. The local municipalities were thus monopolistic providers of electricity within their county. This was the case for PowerEast and PowerWest in 1991, when the Norwegian government reformed the whole power industry. These two were among the very first utilities to adapt to the new market situation.

Our analysis of these two organisations builds on data from PowerEast and PowerWest collected over a period of 22 years, starting with a pilot research project in 1997, a main ethnographic study from 1999 to 2000, and a series of follow-up interviews from 2001 to 2019. In this period, the second author undertook 22 in-depth interviews (duration between 1.5 and 2.5 hours), 13 group interviews, and 82 informal interviews. The informants included top executives and employees and were typically with people who had been in the organisation for some time. The main ethnographic study also included participant observation in the two organisations, both in company offices and outdoors, each lasting 12 weeks. A collection of numerous media articles and internal news items also contributed to knowledge of important events, debates, and stakeholders in the electricity market.

In 1991, The Norwegian Parliament implemented a new Energy Act[2] (here-after The Market Reform), transforming this highly regulated electricity monopoly into a more liberalised market. It is still considered one of the most drastic industrial restructurings in post-war Norway (Midttun, 1995). In 1992, the CEO of the Norwegian Regulatory Agency said: 'This change is a revolution. Had someone told me five years ago that the industry would be in this situation I wouldn't have taken him seriously.' Electricity consumers could now choose freely between hydro-electric power suppliers. While keeping the power utilities in public ownership, the Act sought to improve the efficiency of the industry by separating electricity generation, distribution, and trading. PowerEast and PowerWest, were primarily technical power grid service suppliers, so their market became a competitive contract market in which each company had more strategic autonomy than before.

The Market Reform logic was that energy was a commodity (i.e. a product to be bought and sold on a free market). The liberalised market consisted of electricity trading and competition between power suppliers so that they could deliver large volumes of electricity through interconnected power grids. By large contract bidding, power plants could increase utilisation and drive down unit costs. This logic of commodification disrupted society's old conception of electricity being essentially a form of public infrastructure akin to roads and water pipelines. Moreover, the logic of commodification was seen as a 180 degree turn from the social consciousness and work ethic that had permeated the electricity workers' emphasis on high technical quality standards and power grid security.

1990–2000: PowerEast and PowerWest abandon parts of their pasts

During the first years after the Market Reform, PowerEast and PowerWest took it upon themselves to lead the way to the new frontier. Many constraints on power utilities' roles were now being lifted and future possibilities for strategic management opening up. The management of these two organisations responded with more urgency and determination than most other power utilities. As the Market Reform was effectuated, the top management and board representatives wanted to develop their business capacities and market positions to become the largest and most proactive players in the business. From the policy change agents' point of view, the pre-reform monopolies seemed sluggish and mundane, lacking initiative and entrepreneurial spirit. The top management of PowerEast and PowerWest sought to distance themselves from such labels in favour of more dynamic self-images that would help them exploit future opportunities for profit and growth.

They replaced their chief executives with business-oriented and entrepreneurial leaders from private sector backgrounds. In 1992, PowerEast's board appointed a new CEO from outside the electricity industry, known for his entrepreneurial agility. PowerWest appointed an experienced business manager and energy engineer as their new CEO. The two opened the utilities to owners from other sectors and people with different backgrounds took seats on the board. Both utilities became groups of corporations, splitting up power-grid management functions and installation services in separate daughter companies. Finally, both utilities' boards and top managers sought to change their organisations' self-images to become more progressive, modern, and entrepreneurial.

Everyone in the two organisations was affected by these changes. We noted in particular how employees and top managers started accusing one another of nostophobia or nostalgia. In 1999 Power East's CEO, espoused a Welchian[3] dedication to change, saying: 'There is no way back to the past. It is the future that is of interest. The world is changing, and we have to be future-oriented.' He claimed that employees, union representatives, and even leaders of other power utilities at the time were nostalgically afraid to take the necessary steps into the future market situation. In PowerWest, the CEO exhibited an equally strong motivation for change, explaining to us the dynamics and need for his organisation to embrace transformation: 'I have registered that some employees prefer stability over change. Stability promotes inertia.' The top level's attitude was that nothing strategically useful could be gleaned from the monopoly setting they were emerging from.

The commodification of power led to incentives to cut costs and increase profitability. Spending money on the best available materials or equipment (as done in the past) was seen by the upper echelons as wasteful, and something that belonged to the extinct monopolies. Eventually, many employees, especially technical workers and engineers complained about the new resource management ideas. In 1999 a union representative commented that 'There is too much focus on profit at the expense of anything else. We have to reduce our professional standards.' He felt the top management were putting pressure on them to reduce maintenance standards as well as the technical quality of new electricity systems. The increasing commitment to economic efficiency was commonly problematised by long-term employees who had been taught to view electricity as a societal infrastructure. It went against their professional standards to leave installations, plants, grid poles and wires in a less than an optimal state. Employees would sometimes use a common sarcastic saying: 'Let the poles stand 'till they fall over', parodying top managements' attitude towards grid maintenance.

Before the Market Reform, questions of cost efficiency had seldom been raised, allowing a professional culture of meticulousness and quality consciousness to develop among the technical staff. The totality of the power grid's technical quality, reliability, and robustness became symbolic of the professional work values. As the chief union representative for the technicians said, 'The [power] grid is in our soul.' The prevailing free market logic saw these values come under pressure.

From the point of view of resource management, it seems reasonable to obtain appropriate profits from a technical optimum created by previous investments. However, the technical staff saw it as a sign of management myopia. During an interview with four quality inspectors, the expression 'penny-wise and pound-foolish' was used to describe their thoughts on cost efficiency in grid maintenance. Seemingly ideal from the point of view of strategic management, cost savings came to represent the exciting new future, while meticulousness and quality standards came to stand for a drab past belonging to a bygone era.

2000–2010: PowerEast returns to core business, while PowerWest moves further away from it

During the first 10 years after the Market Reform, the top managers of both organisations saw the power industry as a diversifying market. In their view, strategic business expansion was the way of the future, in line with power utilities' new societal role. Interestingly, the top managers began to embrace the organisations' more distant pasts in terms of how they had pioneered changes before. The manager of PowerEast for instance, referred to how they had initiated mergers between electricity utilities as early as in the 1950s. PowerWest's managers also found they had always been a progressive organisation. We can see here the emergence of a form of reflective nostalgia. For example, a middle manager from a trade and commercial division remembered: 'We were innovators within the industry. Today [1999], several utilities consider becoming for-profit as we did back in 1981.' Top managers were not at all nostophobic about the past that concerned corporate strategy, only the part of the past that concerned the operational level. For instance, top managers would refer to the pre-reform days as a time when employees would borrow equipment and take materials home to work on private projects in work hours. Top managers of both organisations were simultaneously embracing their own past (having been strategic pioneers in the industry), while 'rubbishing' (Munro, 1998) the employees' work values as the progeny of traditional monopolism.

The ensuing acquisitions eventually transformed both organisations into complex groups of corporations, starting up business activities like offshore oil and gas and district heating. Many such activities had little connection to power utilities' traditional business. Once more, the resulting changes to the organisations, and their many subdivisions, provoked nostalgic reactions from workers and union representatives. A middle manager who was actively involved in the change processes claimed, 'We are merely occupied with increasing sales and becoming a big corporation. It doesn't seem to matter what kind of business we do anymore.' Investments were now happening in businesses far outside the core, introducing new groups of installation workers, and with them, new work values and practices. Now working alongside other operatives, the existing workers sensed a different attitude to work quality and thoroughness. To illustrate how important and ingrained the old work values were in these organisations, the technical staff explained that in the past, before getting a job as an energy installer, you had to sign a contract that you would, at all times, look out for such things as leaning trees, branches, heavy snow and so on, which could damage the power bars in stormy weather. Although belonging to the past, such stories mattered to the power grid technicians because they embodied events reminiscent of their work values.

Both organisations expanded extensively until the early 2000s. However, towards the close of 2010, PowerEast changed their management strategy to go in the opposite direction, divesting themselves of businesses outside core functions and returning to focus M&A activity solely on power distribution, as it had done in the distant past. In keeping with this restoration of the power distribution business, PowerEast recruited to executive positions staff and middle managers who had been employed since before the Market Reform had been instituted. Some long-timers even entered top management. 'We have a lot of those in leading roles', a senior executive said in 2013. Compared to PowerWest, PowerEast's management team included a considerable number of people who had direct experience from the pre- and post-reform periods.

Leading up to 2010, the attention of the board and senior management of PowerWest, however, was fully focused on future opportunities. During this period, the acquisitions led to huge growth for the company. 'On almost every board meeting, we were presented to a new potential takeover', said a senior employee and union representative on the board. At first, PowerWest sought to grow by acquiring other power utilities, but eventually acquired businesses in other sectors, such as two private local installation companies and companies in offshore oil and gas and district heating. Approximately 1,000 employees – more than half the staff – now came from various other sectors with different backgrounds, competences, and work values than the incumbent employees.

Dissatisfaction grew among PowerWest's long-term employees, who were no longer the major influential group in the organisation. Looking back at the previous decade a middle-manager said: '… growing into completely new and distanced businesses has been an economic catastrophe to us. In a way we have lost our soul.' He also complained of losing employees who could recall the pre-reform culture. A sentiment shared by many organisational members was that the top management had on several occasions ignored critical voices. These events were now interpreted as acts of suppression and a rejection of the pre-reform organisational identity. 'The old professional environment is getting watered down and you don't have the same feeling for the company anymore', a board member and representative of the union lamented.

2010–2020: PowerEast re-embraces the past while PowerWest distances itself further from it

Returning to the organisations in the period 2010 to 2019, the second author re-interviewed several key informants. Both organisations had overcome the initial nostophobic relationship with the pre-reform past in the sense that they now incorporated several key elements from the distant past. PowerEast, for instance, had now built a subsidiary company running distribution networks, infrastructure maintenance, and power construction. This company had grown organically from 50 to 500 employees and was rooted in the same type of core business activities as in the pre-reform years, although now operating in a free-market setting. Thus, rather than belonging to an outdated monopolistic past, the technical capabilities that existed before the reform were more relevant than ever.

In the last round of interviews, we noticed that, to the informants, the pre- and post-reform events seemed now to inhabit somewhat equally distant pasts. Ironically, the events that in 1991 had been classed as a 'revolution' were now collapsed into one temporal category, namely, the distant past. This quality of being in the distant past removed much of the remaining nostophobia tied to these events. The informants reflected on them in a new way, uninhibited by earlier internal politics, and critically re-examined their previous positions. A key informant said: 'In the earlier days we were very reliable and maybe even too reliable [chuckles]. Then the pendulum swung to the other side and maybe too much on commercial results, disregarding reliability to some extent.' Thus, in PowerEast, the past had become more accepted and useful as a resource of temporal understanding. The work values of the past were recast into the present competitive situation, finding nourishment in new buzzwords like 'quality control', 'contingency planning', and 'asset management'. Unlike the Market Reform period, when nostalgia and nostophobia permeated the organisation, the executives of PowerEast reflected on the work values, the professional standards, and the technical stability of the grid in terms of their here-and-now business challenges.

Another interesting observation from this period is that members of PowerEast invoked the distant past when discussing the present and future societal challenges. They remarked how climate change and extreme weather events were putting pressure on the stability of the power grids. Themes such as power grid quality, maintenance, and robustness were resurfacing with more positive overtones in the organisation at large. One employee said: '… then we return to focus on reliability and acknowledge it as a selling point; the supplier who is most reliable gets the contract. (…) That's where we are presently. We are back there now.' His anchoring of something urgently present (business contracts) in something fundamental that has long been overlooked invokes the organisation's view of its original capabilities in a compelling way. This way of talking is not a longing for the past – not a weak nostalgic yearning – but a re-embedding and revival of a quality that points ahead. It is, so to speak, 'continuity-talk'.

PowerWest, on the other hand, seemed to have lost its relationship with its distant past after years of sectoral expansion, reorganising, and downsizing. On a strategic level, PowerWest made the same moves as PowerEast. In 2015, they started divesting from businesses outside the core activity; a downscaling that slimmed the company down from 1,000 to about 200 employees. According to the CEO, this marked a return to a focus on the core activities of the pre-reform period. 'Our corporation produces a critical good to society, which is highly demanded and inherently progressive', the CEO of PowerWest told the regional newspaper in 2017. Accordingly, PowerWest's downsizing, and divestments could seem like a retreat from the former expansive strategy and a sort of reconciliation with the past. 'After an expansive period of acquisitions and establishment of construction companies, [PowerWest's] focus is again geared towards power.' However, this view was regarded as inauthentic by a key informant who said, 'I don't think it's a deliberate strategy of going back to the past. We have been forced to reverse [the expansion] a bit due to bad financial results.' His impression was supported by a union representative who spoke of the divestments as 'pure business' and not as an organisational re-embedding of the past. Despite positive remarks about the past from the organisation's management, a union member said, 'We used to be a power utility, now we are an industrial group of corporations.'

Summing up the development paths of the two case organisations, we could say that both have, in different ways, overcome those initial nostophobic reactions that characterised their strategic thinking and, over time, increasingly incorporated their heritage. To illustrate this development, we present in Figure 10.1 important change events on the societal and organisational levels during the timelines of our cases. From the standpoint of an external viewer, our two organisations appeared to be going through the same structural changes. However, these similarities were superficial because from 2005, PowerEast gradually incorporated more of their heritage into their strategic thinking, while PowerWest was still seeking, in various ways, to repress the past and grow into a larger corporation. Interestingly, it took PowerWest 12 more years to start making positive public references to the past.

Thus, underneath the similarities there were different organisational mindsets. The differences can be illustrated with the aid of Miller et al.'s (2019) types of strategic uses of the past. PowerEast's development pattern matches closely Miller et al.'s category of *strategy restoration*, in which a former strategy is revived *and* adapted to the present situation. On the other hand, PowerWest's development more closely resembles Miller et al.'s category of *strategy reversal*, which means simply cancelling a plan and returning to a previous one without revitalising or translating historic knowledge into the new future. This latter approach failed to provide a sense of continuity between the company's distant past and future growth aspirations. With relatively few remaining employees from the pre-reform era, PowerWest faces the disadvantage of having little access to relevant experiential memories embedded in organisational storytelling and informal talk that PowerEast seems to possess.

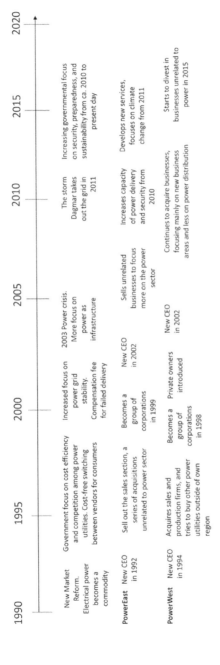

Figure 10.1   Theoretical framework

Discussion: overcoming nostophobia

We started our analysis by asking how the two case organisations had dealt with their pasts over the course of 30 years. We saw how the management of both organisations nostophobically rejected their recent past shortly after the Market Reform. However, with the passing of time, including major strategic changes, industrial restructuring, new societal demands, and natural crisis events, the distant past was cast in a different light by members with long histories in the organisation. Before concluding, we want to draw attention to the main insights that can be elicited from our research.

Taking a temporal perspective on organisational change, we found that the time that passes between events matters in terms of what those events mean. The main benefit gained from analysing the development of two organisations over this extensive period has been to observe how the past played different roles along the timeline of our study. A once abandoned and negative past re-emerged with restored relevance. This process of overcoming nostophobia was a relatively slow and subtle process. Nevertheless, it was beneficial to developing and implementing strategic changes. It was also a process of discovering continuity in change through narratives circulating within the organisation. As these narratives stretched out over decades, they provided glimpses of what time can do to the role of the past. Moreover, the narratives, discursive practices, and storytelling all constitute temporal work that may influence strategic thinking (Mantere, 2008; Crilly, 2017; Mcgivern et al., 2018).

As we observed in the interviews, an attribute of time is that as it passes it blurs distinctions and boundaries that once were crystal clear. The events' complexity and details are lost; lines of conflict become muddied, and sequences of events get shifted around. This feature can help a negative past to take on another meaning as it becomes more distant in time and exerts a profound effect on nostalgia and nostophobia. Returning to the same informants 15 and 30 years later, we noticed a change in their attitude towards the (then) distant past. The changes they once opposed now seemed more comprehensible, enabling them to reflect more freely and deeply on the nature of those change events. In the time right after the market reform there was a sentiment that the organisation was in the middle of a revolutionary change. In this time of temporal contraction, the difference between the recent past and the immanent future was huge. However, the revolutionary features of the initial change event faded as time passed and a sense of continuity emerged.

Research and practice show that the past may function as a type of organ-isational resource (Suddaby et al., 2010; Hatch & Schultz, 2017), and that reflective nostalgia provides a sense of continuity in organisational change (Reissner, 2011). However, the relevance of the past can also be actively rejected and repressed (Lasewicz, 2015; Strangleman, 1999). Both nostophobia and the term 'postalgia' (Ybema, 2004, 2010) are constituted by '*dis*continuity talk, discursively constructing a contrast between the "old" and the "new", between legacies from a common past and plans for the future' (Ybema, 2010, p. 481). Overcoming nostophobia (and possibly postalgia) in organisations, then, is about re-establishing a sense of continuity with a once discarded past. Thus, contributing to the literature on continuity in change (Hernes & Schulz, 2020) our study emphasises how this re-embracing of past events seems more feasible as they become more remote in time.

However, postalgia and nostophobia are conceptually distinct. While nost-ophobia shuns, rejects, and 'rubbishes' the past, postalgia also idealises the future. Furthermore, the two terms are fundamentally different when it comes to how they relate to the past. While nostophobia is characterised by knowing about the past but not being willing to use it as a resource, postalgia has a one-sided focus on the future which ignores the past entirely. Concentrating on the overcoming of nostophobia, we have aimed to understand how the past may come, over time, to function as an organisational resource. Future research could analyse the extent of the overlap in meaning between the two concepts and provide more nuanced insights to managerial change discourse. Both situations may be overcome, although perhaps through different means.

Nostalgia has almost exclusively been considered a hindrance to the willing-ness to change. However, furthering Boym's (2008) conceptualisation, we find that *reflective nostalgia* in narration involves jumping between and joining together past events with other past or present events in ways that emphasise a continuous flow of change. Our informants' narratives were riddled with fast-forward and rewinding jumps, creating highly complex webs of connec-tions between events and ideas that took place at different times. They would look back 20 years at what their younger selves thought would happen in the (then) future, compared to how things worked out some years later (which was then in their past). Only with intimate background knowledge about the organisation's long lines of transitions were we, the researchers, able to grasp some of the temporal complexity of these narratives.[4] Analysing this complex past–present–future reflexivity would exceed the limits of this chapter, but the point is that actors reflect constructively on the meaning of past events in the present, using such intricate temporal dynamics. Thus, there seems to be a close relationship between the extent of organisational collective memory shared between organisational members and their capacity for reflective nostalgia (Boym, 2008). In PowerEast in particular, we found that a capacity for reflective nostalgia increased with the passing of time, due to long-timers' use of experiential memory of past events to make sense of social and organisational changes. These findings suggest that an important feature of events in the past lies in their actuality and presence; their vividness, which is often found in organisational storytelling (Boje, 1991). Something in the present can breathe life into the stories of the distant past and reinvigorate memory and interpretation of historic events, often with the aid of narration (Barry & Elmes, 1997). Thus, the experiential 'memory bank' of the organisation can be re-opened by the voluntary nostalgia of those who can piece together elements from the past.

Boym's (2008) distinction between restorative and reflective nostalgia represents an avenue for further research on organisational change and a space of possibility for change managers. Moreover, its relationship with nostophobia has, to our knowledge, not been explored to a significant extent by either theorists or empirical studies before. Nostalgia is often associated with organisational culture and identity in organisations and thus viewed as antithetical to change. However, this study takes a few steps further in this new direction to show that developing reflective nostalgia might provide continuity to change processes in ways that support change. Growing attention is being paid to 'present pasts' (Huyssen, 2003). Thus, there is a need to consider how notions of the past change over time.

Lastly, we find that our study contributes to knowledge about the role of non-managerial change agents and middle-managers in influencing organisational change. Previous research has cast light on employees and middle managers as contributors to organisational continuity in change (Tucker, Hendy, & Barlow, 2012; Rouleau & Balogun, 2011; Huy, 2002). Huy (2002) for instance, contributes with a study that demonstrates the work by middle managers in securing the sense of continuity the organisation needs in order to implement radical changes. Building on these findings, Rouleau and Balogun (2011) show how middle managers' discursive practices give sense to change by 'performing the conversation' and 'setting the scene'. Our study approaches non-managerial agency from a temporal perspective, complementing these studies with longitudinal evidence of how continuity in change can be promoted by long-standing organisational members' discursive re-embracing of the past.

Managerial implications

When managers experience resistance to change, their response is often to emphasise the need for change and to try to make employees accept it by demanding they relinquish old practices and mentalities (Lasewicz, 2015). This is not necessarily the only valid position. Organisations do not consist of solely nostophobic or nostalgic people; it is more conducive to change management to develop sensitivity to how a loss of continuity in change can provoke resistance and counterproductive sensemaking. Furthermore, we argue that to do this, it should be assumed that change and continuity are not opposites, but interconnected and tangled processes.

The notion that continuity is integral to change processes suggests that rather than emphasising the ruptures between new and old, managers would be wise to look for narratives and discursive practices that circulate in the organisation. Such practices may reveal how nostalgia or nostophobia work in the organisation; knowing them might sensitise managers to how organisational members interpret plans and strategic actions. Because of its discontinuous nature, management nostophobia is often met with acts of resistance animated by nostalgia, and this could lead to an ever-widening tension. A way of overcoming this tension for managers could be to develop deeper organisational historic knowledge of narratives, practices, and values in their social surroundings at the time. This is not to say that managers must become organisation historians. However, interpreting and learning from informal discursive elements in the past can support managers' 'temporal anchoring' while they are continuously looking for opportunities and threats in the future. This point also has a bearing on strategic thinking and execution. Middle managers, if they have been in the organisation for a long time, may have historic knowledge or access to organisational memory that executives from outside the organisation do not possess. This key to unlock the past should not be taken for granted but rather be seen as a scarce internal resource and a prerequisite for reflective nostalgia.

Conclusion

This study has focused on the use of the relatively distant past and how the past contributes to the sense of continuity throughout periods of change. We have let time pass for three decades, and our findings underscore the constitutive role of time in organisational change processes (Ancona et al., 2001; Kunisch et al., 2017; Langley et al., 2013; Hernes, 2014). We have had the opportunity to observe how events take on different roles as they are pushed further back in time. This approach enabled us to study the organisational phenomenon that events in the distant past are often easier to come to terms with than events in the near past. We have studied how people reinterpret organisational changes and learned that the distancing of the past often allows it to be seen in a new light. Furthermore, the past might become a crucial resource for strategic thinking, not in a retrogressive sense in which strategies are reversed, but in a progressive sense in which strategic thinking is a continuous integration of past and future orientations.

Notes

1. Psuedonyms have been used.
2. Royal Ministry of Petroleum and Energy (1990), 'Proposition No. 43 (1989–90) to the Odelsting concerning an act relating to the generation, transmission, trading, and distribution of energy, etc. (The Energy Act). Recommendation from the Ministry of Petroleum and Energy, March 30th 1990' (approved in the Council of State on the same day), Oslo, Norway.
3. General Electric's CEO, Jack Welch, famously said: 'Forget the past, love the future.'
4. Gerard Genette (1983) spends an entire volume analysing variants of proleptic and analeptic narration in Marcel Proust's À la recherche du temps perdu. Proust's mastery of references to previous and coming events throughout the book was interestingly paralleled by how our informants spoke about events in different pasts. However it is beyond the limitations of this chapter to analyse such dynamics.

References

Anspach, C. K. (1934). Medical dissertation on nostalgia by Johannes Hofer 1688, *Bulletin of the Institute of the History of Medicine*, 2(6), 376–91.

Ancona, D. G., Goodman, P. S., Lawrence, B. S., & Tushman, M. L. (2001). Time: a new research lens, *Academy of Management Review*, 26(4), 645–63.

Baake-Hansen, M. (2015). Nostalgia and nostophobia: emotional memory, in D. Sharma & F. Tygstrup J. (eds), *Structures of Feeling: Affectivity and the Study of Culture* (pp. 11–35), De Gruyter.

Barry, D., & Elmes, B. (1997). Strategy retold: toward a narrative view of strategic discourse, *The Academy of Management Review*, 22(2), 429–52.

Bate, S. P. (1997). Whatever happened to organizational anthropology? A review of the field of organizational ethnography and anthropological studies, *Human Relations*, 50(9), 1147–71.

Boje, D. M. (1991). The storytelling organization: a study of story performance in an office-supply firm, *Administrative Science Quarterly*, 36(1), 106–26.

Boym, S. (2008). *The Future of Nostalgia*, Basic Books.

Brunninge, O. (2009). Using history in organizations: how managers make purposeful reference to history in strategy processes, *Journal of Organizational Change Management*, 22(1), 8–26.

Cloutier, C., & Langley, A. (2020). What makes a process theoretical contribution? *Organization Theory*, 1(1), 1–32.

Crilly, D. (2017). Time and space in strategy discourse: implications for intertemporal choice, *Strategic Management Journal*, 38(12), 2370–89.

Dibble, S. (1999). *Keeping Your Valuable Employees: Retention Strategies for Your Organisation's Most Important Resource*, John Wiley & Sons.

Fineman, S. (2000). *Emotion in Organisations*, 2nd edition, Sage.

Gabriel, Y. (1993). Organisational nostalgia: reflections on "the golden age", in S. Fineman (ed.), *Emotion in Organisations* (pp. 118–41), Sage.

Gehman, J., Trevino, L. K., & Garud, R. (2013). Values work: a process study of the emergence and performance of organizational values practices, *Academy of Management Journal*, 56(1), 84–112.

Genette, G. (1983). *Narrative Discourse: An Essay in Method* (vol. 3), Cornell University Press.

Gouldner, A. W. (1954). *Patterns of Industrial Bureaucracy*, The Free Press.

Hatch, M. J., & Schultz, M. (2017). Toward a theory of using history authentically: historicizing in the Carlsberg Group, *Administrative Science Quarterly*, 62(4), 657–97.

Hernes, T. (2014). *A Process Theory of Organization*, Oxford University Press.

Hernes, T. (2022). *Organisation and Time*, Oxford University Press.

Hernes, T., & Schultz, M. (2020). Translating the distant into the present: how actors address distant past and future events through situated activity, *Organization Theory*, 1, 1–20.

Howard-Grenville, J., & Rerup, C. (2016). A process perspective on organizational routines, in A. Langley & H. Tsoukas (eds), *The SAGE Handbook of Process Organization Studies* (pp. 323–39), Sage.

Huy, Q. N. (2002). Emotional balancing of organizational continuity and radical change: the contribution of middle managers, *Administrative Science Quarterly*, 47(1), 31–69.

Huyssen, A. (2003). *Present Pasts: Urban Palimpsests and the Politics of Memory*, Stanford University Press.

Jarzabkowski, P. (2003). Strategic practices: an activity theory perspective on continuity and change, *Journal of Management Studies*, 40(1), 23–55.

Kaplan, S., & Orlikowski, W. J. (2013). Temporal work in strategy making, *Organization Science*, 24(4), 965–95.

Kimberly, J. R., & Bouchikhi, H. (1995). The dynamics of organizational development and change: how the past shapes the present and constrains the future, *Organisation Science*, 6(1), 9–18.

Kunisch, S., Bartunek, J. M., Mueller, J., & Huy, Q. N. (2017). Time in strategic change research, *Academy of Management Annals*, 11(2), 1005–64.

Langley, A., Smallman, C., Tsoukas, H., & Van De Ven, A. H. (2013). Process studies of change in organization and management: unveiling temporality, activity, and flow, *Academy of Management Journal*, 56(1), 1–13.

Lasewicz, P. C. (2015). Forget the past? Or history matters? Selected academic perspectives on the strategic value of organizational pasts, *The American Archivist*, 78(1), 59–83.

Lubinski, C. (2018). From 'history as told' to 'history as experienced': contextualizing the uses of the past, *Organization Studies*, 39(12), 1785–809.

Mantere, S. (2008). Role expectations and middle manager strategic agency, *Journal of Management Studies*, 45(2), 294–316.

March, J. G. (1981). Footnotes to organisational change, *Administrative Science Quarterly*, 26(4), 563–77.

Mcgivern, G., Dopson, S., Ferlie, E., Fischer, M., Fitzgerald, L., Ledger, J., & Bennett, C. (2018). The silent politics of temporal work: a case study of a management consultancy project to redesign public health care, *Organisation Studies*, 39(8), 1007–30.

Midttun, A. (1995). Forhandlingsbasert omstilling fra plan til marked; det store hamskiftet i norsk kraftindustri, *Sosiologi i dag*, 25, 27–65.

Miller, K. D., Gomes, E., & Lehman, D. W. (2019). Strategy restoration, *Long Range Planning*, 52(5), 101855.

Munro, R. (1998). Belonging on the move: market rhetoric and the future as obligatory passage, *The Sociological Review*, 46(2), 208–43.

Nichols, T., & Beynon, H. (1977). *Living with Capitalism: Class Relations and the Modern Factory*, Routledge and Kegan Paul.

Pettigrew, A. M. (1990). Longitudinal field research on change: theory and practice, *Organization Science*, 1(3), 267–92.

Reissner, S. C. (2011). Patterns of stories of organizational change, *Journal of Organizational Change Management*, 24(5), 593–609.

Royal Ministry of Petroleum and Energy (1990). Proposition No. 43 (1989–90) to the Odelsting concerning an act relating to the generation, transmission, Trading and Distribution of Energy, etc. (The Energy Act). Recommendation from the Ministry of Petroleum and Energy 30 March 1990 (approved in the Council of State on the same day), Oslo, Norway.

Ramsey, C. (2005). Narrative: from learning in reflection to learning in performance, *Management Learning*, 36(2), 219–35.

Rouleau, L., & Balogun, J. (2011). Middle managers, strategic sensemaking, and discursive competence, *Journal of Management Studies*, 48(5), 953–83.

Schultz, M., & Hernes, T. (2013). A temporal perspective on organizational identity, *Organization Science*, 24(1), 1–21.

Schultz, M., & Hernes, T. (2019). Temporal interplay between strategy and identity: punctuated, subsumed, and sustained modes, *Strategic Organization*, 18(1), 106–35.

Strangleman, T. (1999). The nostalgia of organisations and the organisation of nostalgia: past and present in the contemporary railway industry, *Sociology*, 33(4), 725–46.

Suddaby, R., Foster, W. M., & Quinn Trank, C. (2010). Rhetorical history as a source of competitive advantage, in J. Baum & J. Lampel (eds), *The Globalization of Strategy Research* (pp. 147–73), Emerald Group Publishing.

Tucker, D. A., Hendy, J., & Barlow, J. (2012, January). Sensemaking and social accounts in middle managers, Academy of Management Annual Meeting, Academy of Management, Boston, MA.

Wadhwani, R. D., Suddaby, R., Mordhorst, M., & Popp, A. (2018). History as organizing: uses of the past in organization studies, *Organization Studies*, 39(12), 1663–83.

Ybema, S. (2004). Managerial postalgia: projecting a golden future, *Journal of Managerial Psychology*, 19(8), 825–41.

Ybema, S. (2010). Talk of change: temporal contrasts and collective identities, *Organization Studies*, 31(4), 481–503.

11 The role of organisational narrative in continuity and change of organisations

Frans Bévort

Introduction

This chapter discusses how organisational narrative is involved in organisations to create continuity, to enable (but also delimit) change and how narrative points to the way organisational continuity and change constitute each other. The chapter shows how narrative has a central role in understanding organisations by defining the collectively important tenets of the organisation. On the one hand, this view holds that narrative is fundamentally about continuity because it institutionalises distinctive lasting properties of the organisation, properties which define its identity. On the other hand, narrative is essential for the way organisations can conceive of the future and thereby also change.

From Ricœur's (1980, 1984) theory of time and narrative, we see that narrative both helps us make sense of organisational time as a chronological experience and at the same creates a more comprehensive understanding of the organisation's meaning that is not bound to time. But for narrative to support sensemaking of the future, it needs to establish a new connection to action in chronological time. While a narrative creates and maintains continuity it also provides material for alternative futures (Bartel & Garud, 2009; Kaplan & Orlikowski, 2014), thereby providing impetus for change. The relation between narrative and continuity/change, respectively, is discussed further. First, the point is made that continuity is far from being an automatic occurrence but rather is an accomplishment that takes much effort, when we look at organisations. Second, the central point is that change is not something that just happens in the future, but to a large extent is created in the present and rooted in the past. Thus, for instance, the commonplace view of change processes tends to be unidirectionally future-oriented and to disregard the importance of the past (Hernes & Schultz, 2020; Schultz & Hernes, 2013).

The central argument highlighted here is that the use of organisational narrative can provide a way to connect what is and what was with what could/should be and thus balance continuity and change processes. In other words, the chapter contributes to the theorising of the integration of continuity and change using narrative theory and to show how this theory can inform our understanding of how we make sense of organising and change (Ricœur, 1984, 1980; Hernes & Obstfeld, 2022; Hernes & Shultz, 2020; Schultz & Hernes, 2013; Czarniawska, 2004; Weick, 1995; Weick & Quinn, 1999; Kaplan & Orlikowski, 2014; Bartel & Garud, 2009).

The case of a small Danish retail bank, Lån & Spar Bank, is used to illustrate the use of narrative theory. The story of the development of the bank's narrative describes how the bank distances itself from and returns to the past in a series of change efforts. Interestingly, the bank renews its narrative by suppressing the historical relations to the trade unions that founded it, but then finds new material and drive by rediscovering and drawing on elements of the same past. The chapter concludes by giving ideas as to how this case can inform practice and ideas to future research in continuity and change using narrative theory.

Theory of narrative and time in relation to continuity and change

Seen from a narrative theoretical perspective (Ricœur, 1980, 1984; Hernes et al., 2015) and based on sensemaking theory (Weick et al., 2005; Weick, 1995), organisational continuity is seen as an accomplishment (Garfinkel, 1967) as much as organisational change is. Thus, continuity is the result of the ongoing efforts of actors to produce and organise social reality based on a comprehensive conception of organisational meaning developed from using a commonly accepted narrative of the past, present, and future of the organisation. To understand the power of narrative in relation to continuity and change, it is helpful to reflect upon the human experience of time. In *Time and Narrative*, Ricœur (1984) refers to Augustine's pondering upon the Skeptics'[1] claim of the nonexistence of the phenomenon time: 'The future has not yet occurred; the past is no more, and the present is but a moving point with no extension, how can we prove or measure the existence of time?' (my paraphrase).

Augustine (AD 354–430) resolves this paradox by pointing to the extension in the mind ('distentio animi' in Latin), as Ricœur notes in quoting from Augustine's *Confessions* (AD 397–400) of the 'threefold present':

> Augustine's inestimable discovery is, by reducing the extension of time to the distension [swelling] of the soul, to have tied this distention to the slippage that never ceases to find its way into the heart of the *threefold present* – between *the present of the future, the present of the past and the present of the present* [emphasis added]. In this way he sees discordance emerge again and again out of the very concordance of the intentions of expectation, attention, and memory. (Ricœur, 1984, p. 21)

That we stretch our minds in different temporal directions, past, present and future with similar intentions, and that this leads to heterogeneous and unexpected results, makes Ricœur point to the act of emplotment and narrative as central in the way humans make sense of the experience of time. Emplotment is the action that leads to the creation of a narrative. According to Ricœur, narrative can encompass both discordance and concordance, resembling change and continuity. The question is how.

Ricœur develops three narrative time dimensions: prefigurative, configurative and refigurative time (Ricœur, 1980, 1984; Hernes & Obstfeld, 2022). The prefigurative narrative time deals with events as they occur in chronological sequence. Events are ordered and made sense of in relation to the already existing narrative. This narrative mode is essentially describing an extension of the perceived continuity; 'following this event, that event happened'. However, besides ordering events chronologically, narrative has a 'configurational' property (Ricœur, 1980, p. 178). That is, a narrative not only describes the sequential course of events in time but also elicits a holistic meaning of the organisation of events that may even challenge a unidirectional conception of temporality:

> The configurational dimension, in turn, displays temporal features that may be opposed to these 'features' of episodic time. The configurational arrangement makes the succession of events into significant wholes that are the correlate of the act of grouping together. (Ricœur, 1980, p. 179)

Configuration means that a narrative is describing the significance of events for the organisation and their interrelations and not just the sequence and time in which they took place. In other words, Configuration is adding new sense to events in a comprehensive account that elevates the narrative from sequential time. Referring to the 'threefold present', the narrative expands its scope from conceiving the present as the most recent stage in a sequence to providing a holistic account that simultaneously connects the 'presents' of past, present and future.

The point is that the narrative process represents a collective 'memory' which recollects and reinterprets the history in reverse order from the end to the beginning and constructs the 'plot' of the narrative (ibid., p. 180). This process resembles the way individuals understand the course of their lives backward to make sense of the present situation and what possible futures may be.

In his essay 'Narrative Time', Ricœur writes: 'Repetition thus tends to become the main issue in narratives in which the quest itself duplicates a travel in space that assumes the shape of a return to the origin' (Ricœur, 1980, p. 185). He goes on to quote Mircea Eliade's description of Ulysses as a 'trapped voyager' on a journey back to the beginning, but also potentially to a truer self, and argues that this is a fundamental motif in human experience (ibid.). However, the circular movement back to the starting point, to gain forward movement, seems a productive view at making sense of the future, using action as the steppingstone.

Thus, Ricœur states that narrative creates *refiguration*, where 'the configured narrative is translated into action' (Hernes & Obstfeld, 2022, p. 6) to handle novel situations, but which at the same time refers back to the sequential perspective of the prefigurative narrative. This means that the configurative narrative is the resource that the refigurative narrative uses to describe change action in chronological time.

This description of the role of narrative and time stresses how the narrative link between the past and the present is critical to maintain continuity, but at the same time it stresses how the journey back becomes a process of finding a new and perhaps better future. Hernes et al. (2015) and Hernes and Obstfeld (2022) take issue with Weick's view that sensemaking is always retrospective in the sense that sensemaking is always directed towards acts that have already elapsed. This is, of course, basically a pragmatic notion, that is, that we can understand our world only through action and that understanding will inevitably follow the fact of execution of action. The Schutzian idea of *future perfect* – 'I have seen the future and it works' (Hernes et al., 2015) – seems to challenge this idea and point to a more future-oriented narrativity and sensemaking. But a simplistic version of future-oriented sensemaking, like the idea of 'sensegiving' (Gioia & Chittipeddi, 1991), is in danger of ignoring the pragmatic anchoring of sensemaking in action and thus leading to cognitivist speculation.

An organisational narrative is a description of the culturally embedded and commonly held beliefs, 'this is how we became who we are in this particular way', more than just a strategic management tool that can be manipulated easily (Hernes & Bévort, 2018). This is the constructive capacity of narrative, where the narrative builds the social reality of the organisation and its environment (Berger & Luckmann, 1966). Thus, the idea of 'change narrative' needs to be handled with care. The point for now is that narrative fundamentally makes it possible to make sense of continuity as well as change.

In the next two sections, the relation between narrative and continuity and change, respectively, is discussed at more length.

Narrative and organisational continuity

Continuity, or stability, is traditionally taken for granted as the default state of affairs when organisations are contemplating implementing change (Lewin, 1947). Even the more modern change literature often takes the position that continuity is the opposite of change and that this 'steady state' is more or less devoid of effort, almost as an automatic extension of the past and present into the future if left untouched. As if the continuity of organisational activity were an inevitable fact of life.

What, then, constitutes continuity in a social context like an organisation? Seen from a process perspective, continuity in social organisations is the result of ongoing interaction of the actors in and involved in the organisation. As mentioned above, continuity is an ongoing accomplishment, what Weick (1979) coined *organising*, a view that describes how actors enact the organisational reality that they inhabit:

> The organizing model is based on the view that [external] order is imposed rather than discovered, on the grounds that action defines cognition. The basic sensemaking device used within organisations is assumed to be talking to discover thinking. (Weick, 1979, p. 165)

This notion, that humans impose a notion of order and meaning on the environment by talking and telling stories, is key to understanding how narratives are essential to understand how organisational continuity is produced. As

Czarniawska (2004) points out, to understand human conduct and intentions, it is necessary to understand the settings in which they make sense:

> Such settings may be institutions, sets of practices or some other contexts created by humans – contexts which have a history, within which both particular deeds and whole histories of individual actors can be and have to be situated in order to be intelligible. (ibid., p. 4)

Thus, one role of narrative is to describe and render human contexts intelligible and to a large extent make such contexts real to the actors who enact the narrative. The narrative confirms the image that the organisational actors share about the nature and properties of the organisation. The narrative guides and creates direction in the ongoing construction of organisational identity (Albert & Whetten, 1985). This idea of how narrative is creating continuity relates to Weick's (1995) thinking about sensemaking in which 'identity' is the anchor of the process of sensemaking: 'I see the world from the perspective of who I am, and I act accordingly in order to enact a world that corresponds with who I am' [illustration]. When organisational actors enact a narrative, it connects and commits their individual identities to the identity of the organisation (Hernes & Bévort, 2018). And this process is to a large extent a process of establishing and guarding organisational continuity.

It is, however, not helpful to understand this continuity as in any sense a steady state. On the contrary, the narrative's role in establishing continuity is one of defending a recognisable continuity in the face of changes in conditions and potentially disruptive events. Interestingly, institutional theory, going back to its roots (e.g. Berger & Luckmann, 1966), has tried to explain the way social organisations become stable and recognisable as distinct social entities, that is, institutions. The question is what creates the enduring quality of social organisation if we cannot base it on functional (it is part of a larger whole) or rationalistic (it is the most effective) explanations. Selznick's (1957) observation was that an organisation begins as a solution, or a tool, to solve a problem but soon becomes 'infused with value' in the sense that the organisation takes on meaning in its own right, in the eyes of the stakeholders. A meaning that one could argue is represented by the narrative of the organisation and which entrenches the continuity of the organisation.

Neoinstitutional theory has further developed this focus on organisational continuity. Meyer and Rowan (1977) phrased the term 'rationalized myth' which resembles in institutional theory the way I understand the role of narrative in organisations. The idea is that a specific practice or technique becomes self-legitimising in a field (e.g. Human Resource Management) and as such does not need to refer to any other justification; for example, 'implementing health policies is good for organisations because it is an appropriate thing to do that proper organisations do'. And such narrative sensemaking (health policies) devices tend to become self-fulfilling prophecies because the actors who are committed to them, act to confirm them (Weick, 1995).

Also, later institutional theory has taken a processual turn with 'institutional work' (Lawrence & Suddaby, 2006) by pointing to the fact that the creation, maintenance and change of institutions demand that actors carry out the activities, processes and interactions that are necessary for their occurrence. In this context, enacting a narrative can be seen as the ongoing 'institutional maintenance work' that is critical for the existence of organisational continuity. Referring to the discussion of whether continuity is static or dynamic, the idea of 'institutional maintenance work' stresses the point that continuity in the face of environmental changes may make it necessary to constantly develop and change behaviour to accomplish the recognisable continuity which is called for. In this necessity, we can already see a link between how narrative can link continuity and change as well as change and continuity.

The idea from Ricœur (1984, 1980), that narrative describes temporality and historicality, enables broader sensemaking to help members make sense of future action (prefiguration, configuration and refiguration), all of which includes continuity but also implies change over time. Prefiguration and configuration, however, are the dimensions most preoccupied with continuity, but refiguration would not be possible without them. The paradoxical insight is that travelling through time implies change, but that it is difficult to recognise change if it is not contextualised by a notion of continuity and recognisable stability. In the next section, I will discuss organisational scholars who have explored the role of narrative in change and innovation.

How narratives are involved in and may drive change

In the management literature (Hagel, 2013; Kaplan & Orlikowski, 2014), narrative has become seen as instrumental for achieving management-driven change that can transform organisations' futures into their desired futures. However, the role of narrative in linking the past and present to the future is often neglected. The focus is predominantly on describing an attractive future state and not on how this state will create continuity with the past and present narrative. Often the past is seen as something that needs to be left behind or treated with forbearance.

What is the role of narrative in organisational change? We have seen above how narrative can be seen as critical in accomplishing organisational continuity. A number of different authors argue, like Hagel (2013), that narrative is a powerful change instrument in the hands of leaders. However, the danger is to overlook how an underlying narrative in many ways is central to the sensemaking of the organisation that creates continuity, as discussed above. Thus, in practice, a narrative can take effect as a change instrument only through the adoption of the narrative by organisational actors through their actions. This is precisely rendered in Hernes et al. (2015), where it is explained that an organisation becomes able to implement planned changes only when employees have the opportunity, through consecutive meetings, to discuss how the old and the new narrative could work out together. In their paper, they show how employee interaction leads to commitment to the new narrative. Still, Hernes et al. (2015) take a strong view on narratives as drivers of change:

> Thus, in a sensemaking view, it is not individuals who are assumed to be drivers of change, but the degree to which commitment evolves around certain narratives serving to hold activities and people together in a certain direction of change. (p. 122)

Other authors have pointed to the value of narrative as a 'strategic' device unlike the more traditional strategic tools. These authors tend to stress how narrative may be the link between future and past, change and continuity.

Kaplan and Orlikowski (2014) point at 'strategic narrative' as a way to connect past, present and future. It does this in a way that creates more strategic flexibility than the typical midrange future-directed strategic forecasting. And they make the point that in making the connection between past, present and future, organisations can both secure the necessary continuity, plausibility, and acceptability, but also develop the resources from the past and the present that may bring the organisation into a better future (Kaplan & Orlikowski, 2014). In this we see the influence of Weick's idea that organising is imposing one's own image on the environment rather than trying to discover the nature of the environment through forecasting. Narrative provides both figure and ground. It describes the actor, the context and how they are related and interdependent. The main point made by Kaplan and Orlikowski (2014) is that using a strategic narrative gives you much more space to imagine new futures than trying to analyse the environment in short-to-medium time into the future.

Bartel and Garud (2009) have a similar but more radical take on the role of narrative in change innovation. They discuss how narrative can further innovation in organisations and they use the concept innovation narratives.

Innovation narratives are either structured or provisional narratives. The former are narratives that create a plot, whereas the latter function by absorbing fragments of activity without a plot (p. 110).

> Unlike structured narratives that offer a particular point of view on past situations through the use of plots, provisional narratives are in-process speculations on situations that have not reached a conclusion. (Bartel & Garud, 2009, p. 112)

The provisional narrative thus is a proto narrative, which is emerging in action with the purpose of making sense of undefined occurrences and events.

Bartel and Garud (2009) argue in several ways how an innovation narrative can function as a bridge between an existing narrative and new possible narratives: as translators, as boundary objects, as coordinators (p. 110), or as a repertoire for future action (p. 114). The change enabling flexibility that Kaplan and Orlikowski (2014) pointed at is radicalised in a fragmented set of multiple emerging narratives that innovation can thrive from. Even in this view, the movement and link between the narrative as continuity (plot) or enabler of innovation or change is clear.

As mentioned, Ricœur uses the concept refigurative narrative to specify how the common meaning in the configurative narrative, as well as elements of the prefigured narrative, are (re-)connected to chronological time by action to make sense of the future, that is, to create and push forward change. In a similar vein, Pedersen (2009) shows how narratives and stories redefine and modify time in the sensemaking of change processes.

Above we have seen how narrative merges continuity and change in the sense that a narrative: 'keeps track of the order of events', it 'tells the story about why we are here; before, now and then' and it 'lines up options as to where we can go (based on the former two)' (paraphrase of prefiguration, configuration and refiguration from Ricœur, 1984; Hernes & Obstfeld, 2022). The important qualification here is that while the passing of time and events is inevitable, the meaning that we ascribe to the organisation and the choices of action we make, based on them, are not. This is the 'emplotment' role of narrative.

In the case illustration below, I will investigate how continuity and change are intersecting in the narrative elements that have framed the trajectory of the organisation.

Case illustration: finding out who to be by enacting parts of who you were

The main illustration is the story of a small Danish savings bank, Lån & Spar Bank ((LSB) Lend and Save Bank, in English), originally founded by civil servants in the late nineteenth century (1880), which became a disruptive player in Danish retail banking by reinventing and redeploying its narrative in the 1990s. And by reconnecting to the past by rediscovering the usefulness of its roots in the white-collar unions. LSB is interesting because it is a peculiar case of organisational change and continuity. For one thing, the bank grew from 15,000 to 150,000 customers within the first 10 years of the 'New LSB'. Simultaneously, it became in the 1990s a very vocal political player in the discussion of securing transparency in retail banking targeting private customers and even a first mover in applying ICT directly in the interphase with customers (the first PC/internet banks in Denmark, Bjørn-Andersen et al., 2004).

The story (1): a narrative and the configuration of a new narrative

When PS became CEO of what later became Lån & Spar Bank (LSB) in 1988, he came from a midsized regional savings bank in Denmark. In contrast, LSB was a small but national savings bank which targeted public sector employees as customers. Indeed, historically the bank was created as a lending and savings facility for civil servants and others holding public office ('Laane og Sparekassen for Offentlige Embeds- og Bestillingsmænd') back in 1880 having, for instance, offices at the Danish Navy headquarters (Holmen). It became the 'Lending and Savings Bank for Public Employees' in the 1970s. Following this genesis, the savings bank was, and is today, owned by a range of public sector white-collar and academic unions, together with a small group of private investors.

An important contextual factor, which coincided with PS's arrival at LSB, was that the regulation of the financial sector changed at the beginning of the 1990s. Along with a number of fundamental changes in the sector, the savings banks, which had been part of the cooperative movement, were allowed to change their status to banks and limited companies, and LSB, as most other savings banks in Denmark, became a bank and was listed on the stock exchange (Bévort, 1997).

The strategy scholar, Costas Markides has noted the extraordinary strategic change of LSB:

> Within three years, Lån & Spar emerged as the most profitable bank in Denmark and its market share had more than quadrupled. This success has continued through the 1990s – from 1991 to 1996, the bank was on average the most profitable of the top ten banks in Denmark. By 1997, when the direct bank had evolved into the world's first on-line real-time PC bank with internet banking also on offer, it had moved from number 42 in Denmark to number ten. All this without a single acquisition. (1999, p. 2)

What were the decisive strategic choices that LSB made which, according to Markides, were so successful?

1. Focusing on white-collar high-value customers: functionaries and academics.
2. Simplifying the product portfolio to fit this target client group.
3. Moving towards low-cost self-service (new products and technologies).
4. Offering non-negotiable prices on all services.
5. Creating a young and entrepreneurial culture around in-house development of services and technology. (1999, p. 2)

On the one hand, 'Lån & Spar Bank', with its new name that veiled its savings bank past, was heading for change that in many ways sought to remove the constraints of being a 'public sector employee bank'. Internally, the narrative in the bank was that LSB was a 'speedboat': agile and swift to adopt change, and the big competitor banks were 'super tankers'. The traditional affinity to the public sector, and unions even, was played down in the communicated narrative. Technological progress was highlighted and the fact the bank was a first mover with PC/internet banks was probably more a source of pride than profit for the bank. This was the change narrative that distanced the bank from its past and pointed into the future in a way that was not based on continuity.

On the other hand, many of the characteristics of the historical savings bank were retained and even made more explicit: Focusing on academics, functionaries and professionals and redesigning the service provided to these resourceful customers were in many ways the logical extensions of the past and what the owners in the white-collar and academic unions would care for. Later, LSB created 'private label' banks to serve several unions and thereby directly profited by drawing on its history and ownership. Here, continuity played a central role as a resource for reimagining the future and change.

In these ways, the story of LSB captures the complex interplay between continuity and change and the way narratives connect future and past. In the next section, we will see how different narratives are maintaining continuity and driving change in the case.

The story (2): competing narratives when new futures are developed[2]

In the middle of the 1990s, LSB needed to reinvigorate its narrative in order to find new ways to develop effective strategies both to consolidate earlier initiatives and to manage the low-interest market that emerged in the 1990s and which challenged the low-margin concept of the bank (Bévort, 2000).

The management invited all employees to a strategy process facilitated by Costas Markides from London Business School, called 'Magical Jump', with the purpose of analysing the bank's present situation and contributing to its future strategic decisions. The event was essentially about rethinking the bank's narrative and involving the staff in the process. This process engendered a lot of reflections and suggestions, many of which later became part of the new LSB (Bévort, 2000).

Two particular trends were emerging in the suggestions from the bank's employees.

First, there was a strong urge among employees, the majority of whom came from 'traditional' banks, to revert aspects of the bank's strategy and align it with 'normal' banks. Working with business customers is typically regarded as high status in banks and from a banker's perspective, it was natural to prefer a return to this model, even though it was in opposition to the idea of being the bank preferred by private wage-earning customers (Bévort, 2000).

Second, many of the ideas for services were focusing on utilising the historical relations to the white-collar unions more aggressively. For instance, offering banking services in satellite banks with the unions' own name/brand (private label). Using the fact that unions own the bank, many of these suggestions focused on how to use this direct access to unions' memberships, even though LSB's new narrative was focusing less on unions and was targeting private customers.

Today (2023) the bank has 387 employees and 20 branches. The bank cooperates with more than 50 unions (of academics and white-collar professionals).

In the story about LSB, several decisive narratives interact in ways which illustrate how continuity and change are enacted.

1. First, the old narrative about being a savings bank owned and used by a specific group of public employees, and how it seeks to fulfil their interests.
2. Second is a newer narrative of a modern bank that is catering for resourceful, that is, well-educated private wage-earning customers and a bank which is technologically progressive.
3. Third, the narrative of 'the normal and professionally appropriate bank', which is carried by the many new bankers hired in the 1990s.

The three narratives are pulling the bank in different directions, and they illustrate different aspects of continuity and change. The original narrative seems to resist the challenge from the other two narratives in the way that some of the characteristics of the old savings bank are reinterpreted and modified in, for instance, the renewed collaboration with unions in 'private label' banks and directly in the marketing of special services for members of the owner unions. A new slogan says: 'become a customer in a bank we own together'. This could also be seen as refiguration, in the sense that it is action for renewal that points to the narrative of the trade-union past.

Also, in the second (and main) narrative of being the bank for affluent academics and public sector professionals, this bank has a political voice in the customer protection debate in the financial industry (banks' customers are not covered by the normal customer protection provisions and laws in Denmark). This is a refiguration that leads to action that points to the union past but also to the newly configured middle-class segment who feels uncomfortable with the larger banks' elitist client practices.

In the context of the third narrative, the new image of a more generic retail bank for private customers is reinvigorated and the bank has expanded its physical presence with branches in areas where the target customers live and work. This is a part of the 'new LSB' from the 1990s but is also pointing back to the 'normal bank' narrative. Finally, the bank has started 'Lån & Spar Business', which is a return to the high-status business segment and in contradiction to the main narrative. However, it is still designed to cater to small enterprises based on personal professional service and ownership associations, and so on, that many of the bank's new core customers run and demand banking services to deal with.

All three narratives refer to different aspects of the prefigurative narrative of past events and experiences, while 'new LSB' could be seen as a configurative narrative, and the strategic activities point at what was and then propel it into the future. The LSB case has served to illustrate how the bank in its strategic renewal from the 1990s to 2023 has drawn actively on its past and connected it to the present and found resources to imagine new futures in the requisite organisational narratives in the bank and in the industry. In these ways, it demonstrates the interdependence between organisational continuity and change.

Discussion

When discussing narrative's role in the mutual constitution of continuity and change, we encounter problems in identifying the figure and ground roles of narratives and change narratives, respectively. If we look from the perspective of an imagined preferable future state, it may not be possible to understand valuable aspects of the history (Kaplan & Orlikowski, 2014), and we may end up as Ulysses, a trapped voyager (Ricœur, 1980). The past of LSB could in this perspective be seen as representing a limiting, socially destitute situation, illustrated by a portfolio of bad debts that LSB had in the 1990s, derived from a product offering loans on favourable terms (and credit scores) to members of the owner unions.

From another perspective, as we have seen, the journey back to the underlying narrative provided LSB with resources to see a new possible future (configuration – refiguration), building on the organisation's distinctive narrative (Schultz & Hernes, 2013), a narrative that could attract customers far beyond the traditional segment.

Another interesting question is how a new narrative can rearrange the context (ground) given by the existing narrative in a way that unlocks the regressive allure of the past we (figure) are captured by, releasing the trapped voyager as it were, and how this shift in perspective allows us to see the alternative possible futures in the same past. To paraphrase Ricœur (1980, 1984), move from configuration to refiguration and make sense of the existing narrative in a new way (Hernes & Obstfeld, 2022, p. 7).

Implications for management

The ambiguity of the relation between continuity and change remains because the need to preserve continuity can be adversarial to change efforts and other elements of continuity can be a central part of change, as we saw in LSB.

Engaging employees in narrative processes like the 'Magical Jump' event in LSB can help organisations exploiting the potential of change embedded in the continuity that constitutes the organisation (Hernes et al., 2015; Hernes & Bévort, 2018). Especially when many organisational cultures and narratives are brought together, as in the case of LSB, it is a very effective intervention to involve and commit the staff in processes of reimagining and rewriting the organisational narrative, a narrative which underpins the organisation's continuity, but which also is a potential resource for change and innovation.

Thus, the importance of focusing in this chapter on the role of continuity in change processes probably holds the most central implications for management. Change, like most events, does not emerge from nowhere. Change is something we do and make sense of. But the same can be said of continuity. Continuity is not what happens if we do nothing. Continuity is an ongoing accomplishment that involves action and sensemaking (Weick, 1995).

In this chapter I have argued that narrative is the way we make sense of organisational change as something that emerges from (elements of) organisational continuity and that organisational continuity is dependent on change to maintain and preserve continuity in the face of external contingencies. Fundamentally, it is impossible to think change if we are unable to specify the 'as is' that represents the present continuity (of past and present). A narrative is helpful in this respect because it creates a comprehensive image of this continuity, an image that 'change' needs as a contrast to define the 'to be' of the desired future. On an even more pragmatic note, understanding how organisational continuity is accomplished is bound to leave managers much better prepared to accomplish meaningful organisational change. And again, the organisational narrative is key in both instances (Bartel & Garud, 2009; Kaplan & Orlikowski, 2014). To act, we must be able to make sense of the past (from the vantage point of the present, and even the imagined futures) and this sensemaking in turn enables us to imagine and enact multiple possible futures. Such things are possible when we work with narrative.

Theoretical contribution to continuity/change

The contribution of this chapter is to theorise the interdependency of continuity and change by using narrative theory and to illustrate how this interdependency can be seen to happen in real-life organisations (Ricouer, 1984, 1980; Hernes & Obstfeld, 2022; Hernes & Shultz, 2020; Schultz & Hernes, 2013; Czarniawska, 2004; Weick, 1995; Weick & Quinn, 1999; Kaplan & Orlikowski, 2014; Bartel & Garud, 2009). The argument in the chapter dissolves the duality between continuity and change and shows how narrative constructs the interdependency between them, using time theory from Ricœur (1980, 1984). The paradoxical point in the relationship between continuity and change is that if we were to imagine an organisational change process that removed all continuity, the organisation would cease to exist – or at least would not be recognisable or sensible as such. Here we are getting close to Augustine's solution of the paradox about the existence of time: expanding the mind to understand the threefold present of past, present and future. Using Ricœur's notion of emplotment and narrative, we can see that organisational narrative 'expands our mind' to make it possible to make sense of continuity in the changed organisation.

Conclusion/further research

I have argued that narrative can connect continuity and change in organisations using Ricœur's theory of time and narrative. Continuity is as much an accomplishment as change is, and it is not possible to understand one without the other. We use narrative to create continuity, but narrative, in many forms, is also a driver of change. In the LSB case, we saw that even after a radical organisational change, elements that pointed to continuity with an older narrative persistently emerged in new guises. In this way, continuity became a resource and platform for change. Further research is called for on the ways organisations use narrative to build continuity and on how narrative influences the agency of managements in selecting new futures. Such research could help us understand better the interaction processes that create the narrative which sustains continuity and how they might engender change.

Notes

1. School of Greek philosophers that disputed the existence of reality (e.g. Xenophanes and Democritus are counted among them).
2. The author experienced the process personally. Thus this is, in part, an autoethnographic narrative.

References

Albert, S., & Whetten, D. A. (1985). Organizational identity, *Research in Organizational Behavior*, 7, 263–95.

Bartel, C. A., & Garud, R. (2009). The role of narratives in sustaining organisational innovation, *Organisation Science*, 20(1), 107–17.

Berger, P. L., & Luckmann, T. (1966). *The Social Construction of Reality: A Treatise in the Sociology of Knowledge*, Penguin.

Bévort, F. (1997). Vejen fra isolation til det åbne marked. Den finansielle sektors strategiske dilemma, in T. Andersen & K. Ronit (eds), *Den danske banksektor*, Systime.

Bévort, F. (2000). Kompetence mellem struktur-og kulturudvikling, in T. Andersen, I. Jensen & A. Prahl (eds), *Kompetence – i et organisatorisk perspektiv* (pp. 91–120), Roskilde Universitetsforlag.

Bjørn-Andersen, N., Andersen, K. V., Larsen, M. H., & Schou, P. (2004). Impact of IT in the Danish banking industry, with specific illustrations from the Nordea Group and Lån & Spar Bank, working paper, Department of Informatics, Copenhagen Business School.

Czarniawska, B. (2004). *Narratives in Social Science Research*, Sage.

Garfinkel, H. (1967). *Studies in Ethnomethodology*, Prentice Hall.

Gioia, D. A., & Chittipeddi, K. (1991). Sensemaking and sensegiving in strategic change initiation, *Strategic Management Journal*, 12(6), 433–48.

Hagel, J. (2013, October 1). The untapped potential of corporate narratives, Edgeperspectives, retrieved 30 January 2023 from http://edgeperspectives.typepad.com/edge_perspectives/2013/10/the-untapped-potential-of-corporate-narratives.html.

Hernes, T., & Bévort, F. (2018). *Organisering i en verden i bevægelse*. Samfundslitteratur.

Hernes, T., Hendrup, E., & Schäffner, B. (2015). Sensing the momentum: a process view of change in a multinational corporation, *Journal of Change Management*, 15(2), 117–41.

Hernes, T., & Obstfeld, D. (2022). A temporal narrative view of sensemaking, *Organisation Theory*, 3(4), https://doi.org/26317877221131585.

Hernes, T., & Schultz, M. (2020). Translating the distant into the present: how actors address distant past and future events through situated activity, *Organisation Theory*, 1(1), https://doi.org/2631787719900999.

Kaplan, S., & Orlikowski, W. (2014). Beyond forecasting: creating new strategic narratives, *MIT Sloan Management Review*, 56(1), 11–21.

Lawrence, T. B., & Suddaby, R. (2006). Institutions and institutional work, in S. R. Clegg, C. Hardy, T. B. Lawrence & W. R. Nord (eds), *The Sage Handbook of Organization Studies* (pp. 215–54), Sage.

Lewin, K. (1947). Concept, method and reality in social science: social equilibria and social change, *Human Relations*, 1(1), 5–41.

Markides, C. (1999). Six principles of breakthrough strategy, *Business Strategy Review*, 10(2), 1–10.

Meyer, J. W., & Rowan, B. (1977). Institutionalized organisations: formal structure as myth and ceremony, *American Journal of Sociology*, 83(2), 34–63.

Pedersen, A. R. (2009). Moving away from chronological time: introducing the shadows of time and chronotopes as new understandings of narrative time, *Organization*, 16(3), 389–406.

Ricœur, P. (1980). Narrative time, *Critical Inquiry*, 7(1), 16–90.

Ricœur, P. (1984). *Time and Narrative* (volume 1), University of Chicago Press.

Schultz, M., & Hernes, T. (2013). A temporal perspective on organizational identity, *Organization Science*, 24(1), 1–21.

Selznick, P. (1957). *Leadership in Administration*, University of California Press.

Weick, K. E. (1979). *The Social Psychology of Organizing*, Addison-Wesley.

Weick, K. E. (1995). *Sensemaking in Organisations*, Sage.
Weick, K. E., & Quinn, R. E. (1999). Organisational change and development, *Annual Review of Psychology*, 50(1), 36–86.
Weick, K. E., Sutcliffe, K. M., & Obstfeld, D. (2005). Organizing and the process of sensemaking, *Organization Science*, 16(4), 409–21, https:// doi.org/ 10 .1287/ orsc .1050 .0133.

12 Approaches to studying continuity and change

Ann Langley

Introduction

Increasingly, scholars of time, process and organizational change view change and continuity as an intertwined duality, rather than a dualism or contradiction. Farjoun (2010) explicitly theorized the ways in which stability (a form of continuity) can enable change (e.g. by ensuring access to resources), while change can enable stability (e.g. as improvisational adjustments allow routines to be maintained over time). Weick and Quinn (1999) contrasted "episodic change" with "continuous change," to distinguish between radical and planned restructuring efforts (Greenwood & Hinings, 1996) and incremental adjustments in ways of doing things that emerge naturally and inevitably every day (Tsoukas & Chia, 2002). Yet, a common finding about so-called "episodic change" efforts is that despite intentions, they too are subject to continuous incremental shifts that reorient them in situ (MacKay & Chia, 2013; Orlikowski, 1996). Moreover, ongoing and more continuous types of change can accumulate and turn into a radical transformation that might appear to be episodic when seen from a distance (Hernes, Hussenot, & Pulk, 2021; Plowman et al., 2007).

This chapter will review the methodological implications of studying continuity and change considered as a co-constructed duality, focusing on qualitative methodologies, and drawing on my own experience and on other published research. Specifically, I will consider, in turn, three different research foci (on *change*; on *reproduction*; on *narrative*) that contribute to illuminating the duality. Discussion of each of the three foci involves first summarizing the type of research design, data and analysis the approach implies, and then examines, by drawing on examples, how the duality between continuity and change manifests itself when using each approach.

Focusing on *change*; revealing continuity

In the very first volume of the *Organization Science*, a journal whose mission at that time was defined as "breaking out of the normal science straitjacket" (Daft & Lewin, 1990), Van de Ven and Huber (1990) edited a special collection of seven methodological articles (e.g. Leonard-Barton, 1990; Pettigrew, 1990) intended to break away from the dominant approaches to studying organizational change at that time by introducing "process" organizational perspectives focusing on the question "How does an organizational change emerge, develop, grow or terminate over time?" rather than on questions oriented around the antecedents and consequences of change. That special issue, along with several classic book-length empirical studies produced around that time (Hinings & Greenwood, 1989; Johnson, 1987; Pettigrew, 1985; Van de Ven, Angle, & Poole, 1989/2000) gave impetus to a burgeoning body of qualitative longitudinal research that took as its key focus the processes of organizational change (especially planned change), and that laid the groundwork for other methodological contributions as well, including my own work (Langley, 1999; Van de Ven, 1992). These methodological contributions proposed the qualitative longitudinal case study as the ideal research design for capturing long term organizational change, and for theorizing about it. I will now briefly summarize the basic methodological considerations scholars encounter in studying change using the classic longitudinal case study, before reflecting on how these methods mobilize, reveal and problematize notions of continuity and change.

Focusing on change: design, data collection and analysis

Longitudinal case studies explicitly designed to study organizational change typically begin from the premise that some formally intended organizational change either has occurred or been proposed. The study is then aimed at understanding how change actually happens over time, through an analysis of ongoing activities in relation to that project, possibly extending over several years. For example, with colleagues (Cloutier, Denis, Langley, & Lamothe, 2016; Denis, Dompierre, Langley, & Rouleau, 2011; Denis, Lamothe, & Langley, 2001) I have been involved in several studies of planned change processes in health care, beginning at the point where a significant structural change decision had been made. My focus was specifically on the roles of senior leaders, but scholars may also focus on middle managers or on change recipients at operational levels (Balogun & Johnson, 2004; Huy, 2002), and they may include consideration of a variety of different phenomena such as cognition, emotions, power dynamics, leadership, and so on.

Studies of this type may be designed to study processes retrospectively and/ or prospectively (Langley, 2009; Leonard-Barton, 1990). The advantage of studying change retrospectively is that one can already assess to some degree what has happened, and know whether and to what degree some kind of change has or has not occurred. Data collection may also be more efficient than with prospective research. The disadvantage of this approach is that such studies are inevitably oriented partly by hindsight, and result in thinner and less detailed stories. This is avoided by studying processes forward in real time resulting in a richer and potentially more complete dataset, something that I personally see as more desirable. Yet, the open-endedness of studies of this type and the unpredictability of future events may be a source of insecurity for the researcher, and sometimes lead to a reorientation in research questions, as we will illustrate later.

A second important design choice is the number of cases. Cases of organizational change are so rich that there may be plenty to see and understand within a single case, especially if it extends over long periods of time. Yet studying processes running in parallel for different cases enables scholars to better understand the dynamics underpinning different outcomes. Such cases need to be comparable however, for this approach to make any sense. Thus, Inger Stensaker and I examined how the same change process was taken up by three different divisions of the same energy company (i.e. controlling for the overall context) and, showing how change was diluted in all three cases, but following quite different pathways depending on the change strategies adopted (Stensaker & Langley, 2010). Studying multiple cases enables both literal replication (revealing similar patterns across cases) and theoretical replication (revealing different patterns and the mechanisms behind them) within the same study (Yin, 2013). However, it is important to be aware that presenting multiple longitudinal case studies within the same journal article is a challenging endeavor, because it requires both a depth of evidence across time and across cases (Berends & Deken, 2021). Although I have tried to avoid this because I believe in the power of case replication, it is not rare to find that cases may need to be dropped for publication purposes.

A third important design choice concerns data sources. Longitudinal case studies generally draw on what has been known as the "big three": interviews, observations and documents (Langley, 2009). While many scholars rely very extensively on interviews, date stamped archival data or observations are particularly useful to mitigate hindsight bias, and compensate for the limitations of interviews in capturing chronology. At the same time, interviews are irreplaceable for researchers to access not just the facts of what happened but also the cognitions (Balogun & Johnson, 2004; Monin, Noorderhaven, Vaara,

& Kroon, 2013) and emotions (Huy, 2002; Huy, Corley, & Kraatz, 2014) surrounding them that might have important implications. Other sources may be used too, such as diaries and focus groups (Balogun & Johnson, 2004), and emails or video recordings (Liu & Maitlis, 2014).

Finally, what kinds of analysis tools are most appropriate for longitudinal case studies? In my own methodological work, I have suggested a variety of techniques and angles that generate different types of theorizing. However, the two approaches that I almost always come back to are "temporal bracketing" and "visual mapping" (Langley, 1999). Temporal bracketing involves decomposing event chronologies into time segments or phases separated by "discontinuities." In relation to the topic of this volume, note how I use the word "discontinuity" here – what I am referring to is specific events that have a particularly significant impact on the trajectory of change. In my experience, discontinuities that shift trajectories are often (though not always) changes in key leaders, or structural moves that reorient power relations. Once, temporal brackets or phases have been defined, they become units of analysis with which grounded theory coding can be used to understand how discontinuities alter patterns of action, and how those patterns of action in turn contribute to creating a new context for further action in the future. This kind of analysis involves what I call "longitudinal replication" in which studied theoretical mechanisms can be seen to carry greater weight and credibility because they repeat themselves across different time periods. Visual mapping is a complementary technique that involves representing data visually using flow charts of other displays that can illustrate how particular events influence each other and can also capture interruptions and discontinuities in event flows (Langley & Ravasi, 2019; Langley & Truax, 1994).

I find the two analytical devices of temporal bracketing and visual mapping to be highly generative for theorizing, and come back to them regularly in my own work (Bucher & Langley, 2016; Denis et al., 2011; Denis et al., 2001; Kouamé, Hafsi, Oliver, & Langley, 2022). I see that others find them useful as well (Gehman, Treviño, & Garud, 2013; Howard-Grenville, Metzger, & Meyer, 2013; Wright & Zammuto, 2013). They work best to make sense of change when data is spread over fairly long periods punctuated by easily recognizable discontinuities and interruptions. For example, in their study of identity resurrection in Eugene Oregon, Howard-Grenville et al. (2013) created temporal brackets to represent three successive periods of community identity dynamics focused on Oregon's "Tracktown USA" historical identity. The temporal brackets corresponded to the tenure of three different track coaches over 30 years. By analyzing data on events occurring within each period and representing them with a visual map linking tangible and intangible resources with lived experiences, the authors were able to understand how and why the Tracktown USA identity first declined, then virtually disappeared, but was subsequently resurrected.

In addition to temporal bracketing and visual mapping, grounded theorizing methods (Gioia, Corley, & Hamilton, 2013), narrative perspectives (Pentland, 1999), and holistic comparative case studies (Eisenhardt, 1989, 2021) offer alternative analytical tools. These may also be productively combined together within a given study as I have noted elsewhere (Langley, 1999). Smith's (2002) description of the multiple analytic methods she developed for her comparative study of the trajectories of the Baby Bell companies created by the breakup of AT&T offers a rich example of how these various approaches can work together. Another example is given by Chiles, Meyer and Hench's (2004) complexity theory-based study of the origin and transformation of musical theaters in Branson, Missouri.

Encountering continuity while studying change

Having explained the methods issues involved in focusing a study on deliberate organizational change through longitudinal case studies, I now identify the various ways in which the continuity–discontinuity duality manifests itself in these studies, and examine their implications. First, as indicated above, qualitative cases studies of deliberate organizational change, including my own, are most often driven by an interest in what will happen following or leading up to major *discontinuities*. These may be occasioned by organizational crises, or in many cases, by structural shakeups such as mergers (Cloutier et al., 2016; Monin et al., 2013), deregulation (Balogun & Johnson, 2004; Jarzabkowski, Lê, & Van de Ven, 2013) or other forms of reorganization that are intended to achieve significant improvements in organizational efficiency, effectiveness, or competitiveness (Currie, Lockett, Finn, Martin, & Waring, 2012; Hinings & Greenwood, 1989; Huy, 2002). Restructuring of this type implies discontinuity because it often involves assigning new responsibilities, reorienting incentive schemes, and disrupting established relationships as people are moved around organizations. Moreover, restructuring, though taking time to plan and decide on, may appear to happen very quickly at least in formal terms. It really does seem to take on the character of discontinuity, with a clear and distinct before and after.

Yet at the same time, the motivation for studying planned change and major discontinuities such as this is almost always related to their problematic and non-obvious nature. There are two complementary elements that tend to contribute to this. First, apparent structural discontinuities do not instantaneously produce change in behaviors. Even when concrete moves are made that seem to shift roles and relationships, this is never achieved in a day, and will involve multiple micro-events. Change is notoriously seen as difficult, and may often be "resisted" (Ford, Ford, & D'Amelio, 2008; Huy et al., 2014). While resistance may well be constructive, in order for change to occur and to deliver expected outcomes, it is likely that forces of "inertia" (driving continuity) (Hinings & Greenwood, 1989), need to be overcome.

Secondly, most organizations, even those that engage in radical structural change, need to keep their operations going even as roles and relationships may shift, sometimes radically – in other words, maintaining another form of continuity in routine activity is also essential for the success of planned change, immediately revealing the duality between continuity and change (Farjoun, 2010). In other words, while key research questions or puzzles turn around the *how of change*, issues of continuity (considered positively in terms of avoidance of disruptive chaos, or negatively in terms of resistance and inertia) rapidly come to the fore.

Many of my own studies have thus focused on the tensions created by this duality between continuity and change. For example, in a study of leadership and change in pluralistic settings characterized by multiple value systems and diffuse power (Denis et al., 2001), we showed how substantive change occurred in fits and starts, punctuated by the effects of leaders' actions on their ability to maintain their political positions in the face of disaffection from constituents. In a study that examined four types of institutional work (structural work, conceptual work, operational work, relational work) (Cloutier et al., 2016) involved in implementing reform in four health care settings, we identified sources of "slippage" or friction with respect to intentions associated with each form of work, resulting in modest shifts in operational functioning despite apparently dramatic structural reorganization. Currie et al. (2012) found similar forms of slippage in a study of health care networks, as powerful actors were able to reorient changes in ways that enabled them to sustain or enhance existing privileges, despite reformative intentions. None of these studies suggests that change or changing does not occur. However, change *changes* even as it is enacted (Langley & Denis, 2006). Actions to achieve change interact with and are influenced by ongoing practices grounded in prior cognitions and power relationships as well as unexpected events. The result is that what may be described on paper as transformational "episodic change" is inevitably renegotiated in practice in ways that are situated and incremental – that is, in ways that correspond in then end, quite closely to Weick and Quinn's (1999) concept of "continuous change."

Indeed, in relation to studies focusing on planned organizational change, a research drama that I have personally encountered, especially with prospective designs, is that what was supposed to be a major change can dissipate into nothing, or take so long to produce its expected effects that research funds and energy run out before the supposed change takes off. When this happens, a study originally aimed at explaining change may turn into a study aimed at explaining its apparent reverse, continuity. For example, I and my colleagues (Denis et al., 2011) wrote an article about the phenomenon of "escalating indecision" when faced with exactly this. After initiating a real-time study of merger implementation, we found that the organization was seemingly unable to move from decision-making towards substantive action, because every "decision" it ostensibly made embedded the need to revisit that decision all over again at a later date. This process of perpetual decision-making with no final decision went on for the eight years of our data collection, and beyond. Rather than explaining change, our study drew attention to what is in fact quite a common phenomenon ("escalating indecision"), and to elucidate how and why it occurs.

So far, we have implied that organizational change is often less radical than expected or intended, and that this happens through a process of dilution influenced by inertial forces embedded in existing practices and relationships. Many studies of organized efforts to address societal issues such as responding to climate change have revealed some of these very same processes of progressive dilution (Grodal & O'Mahony, 2017; Schüssler, Rüling, & Wittneben, 2014; Wright & Nyberg, 2017), that is, reversion to continuity with the past (otherwise labeled "business as usual"). Yet, some scholars have also shown that ongoing and continuous but non-deliberate activities in the day-to-day might conceivably *amplify* processes of changing in positive ways rather than dampen them (Plowman et al., 2007). Indeed, theorizing and researching ways for organizations to harness continuous activities to achieve positive radical change over time would seem urgent, at least in the particular area of climate change.

Focusing on *reproduction*; revealing change

While achieving positive change is, of course, important, achieving continuity can be equally critical, from a practical perspective. One has only to consider the ramifications of COVID-19 pandemic which disrupted almost every aspect of society and the economy (Brammer, Branicki, & Linnenluecke, 2020). The challenge has been to sustain over time the routines and practices that keep key institutions such as health care system, businesses, the education system, and all other activities going. This requires effort and new approaches to doing things, revealing again how change is fundamental to continuity as well. The more general point is that maintenance, or the ability to continuously produce and reproduce order – is just as critical a research topic in organization and management theory as understanding how to achieve change. It may however, seem less obvious since continuity is often taken for granted and unquestioned, until something like a crisis (a pandemic, or other disruption) renders it suddenly more fragile.

Nevertheless, organizational scholars adopting a strong process or practice ontology (Feldman & Orlikowski, 2011; Tsoukas & Chia, 2002), have become interested in the dynamics underpinning organizational routines, generally seen as sources of order, continuity and stability. In a similar vein, institutional scholars have pointed out the importance of understanding the micro-foundations of institutions, and the way in which they are produced and sustained over time (Powell & Rerup, 2017). Indeed, from a practice perspective, an institution cannot be said to exist unless it is reproduced every day through action and interaction (Barley, 2017; Smets, Aristidou, & Whittington, 2017; Zilber, 2020). Both routines and institutions are concepts that imply continuity and stability almost by definition. The understanding of how this continuity and stability is (or not) achieved, perhaps even when shaken by disruptions is the focus of a different stream of research, which tends to adopt more fine-grained ethnographic methods than those we discussed earlier as we now describe.

Focusing on reproduction: design, data collection and analysis

Organizational ethnography is a methodology that is aimed at understanding organizational practices and cultures from within (Van Maanen, 2011), gaining access to the meanings participants give to their work through prolonged engagement with and direct observation of the practices and cultures studied (Lincoln & Guba, 1985). Ethnographies may sometimes be designed to investigate organizational change processes over time explicitly (Barley, 1986; Kellogg, 2011), in which case aspects of the discussion offered in the previous section apply equally well. However, in this section, I focus more in the use of ethnography to study what Van Hulst et al. (2017, p. 225) call the "noun-like qualities of organizational life" in which ethnographers "become immersed in the day-to-day, the business-as-usual, the constant reproduction of yesterday." In doing so however, they remain sensitive to the idea that reproduction is never perfect, and often needs to be worked on.

The study of organizational routines is exemplary of the ethnographic focus on reproduction because the very definition of routines as "repetitive, recognizable patterns of interdependent actions, carried out by multiple actors" (Feldman & Pentland, 2003, p. 95) implies repetition, reproduction and continuity; and second, because as Dittrich (2021) points out, the vast majority of existing research on routine dynamics has drawn on ethnographic methods, beginning with Feldman's (2000) seminal article on routines in a university housing office. That article led to a theorization of routines as composed of two aspects: the ostensive aspect (how people describe a routine in the abstract), and a performative aspect (the specific activities performed on a given occasion). These two aspects are seen as mutually constitutive, enabling continuity and stability over time, but also allowing flexibility, as people adjust their specific everyday actions to the contingencies of the moment. To appreciate the design choices involved in studying continuity and reproduction, I will draw on the routines literature for many of the examples below.

A first design choice involved in studying routines or indeed any process of reproduction over time using ethnographic methods concerns establishing the unit of analysis. How to draw boundaries around what is and what is not considered to be a focal routine or a practice being reproduced? Often, the unit of analysis will only be identified after an initial exploration of the various activities taking place in the research site (Dittrich, 2021). Choices may also be based on the way in which individuals in the site themselves refer to particular practices or routines. Finally, in studying reproduction and continuity, the more interesting units of analysis may well be those activities where it appears that some effort is required to keep things on track due to potential disruptions (e.g. as in hospital emergency rooms) (Wright, Meyer, Reay, & Staggs, 2021).

A second design choice involves the approach used to document the routines or practices being reproduced. While interviews are useful to appreciate people's abstract conceptualizations of what they do (e.g. reflecting the "ostensive" aspect of routines), they are generally limited in their ability to capture specific everyday activities, because this kind of knowledge is embedded in the practice itself and not readily accessible to the conscious mind (Nicolini, 2009). Rather, in-depth observations of everyday performances appear to be the best way to capture the processes of reproduction, and adaptation in situ, and this is where the approaches traditionally associated with ethnography come into play. These activities might involve shadowing people during their workdays (Feldman, 2000), sitting in meetings (Bucher & Langley, 2016; Deken, Carlile, Berends, & Lauche, 2016; Howard-Grenville, 2005), hanging out in places where routines play out on shop-floors, laboratories or hospital wards (Danner-Schröder & Geiger, 2016; Kellogg, 2011; Wright et al., 2021), video-taping people at work (Spee, Jarzabkowski, & Smets, 2016), and even participating in the activities themselves to better understand what the experience is like (Lok & Rond, 2013). Feldman (2000) reports 1,750 hours of observation over four years and Dittrich (2021) reports on documenting over 80 iterations of the same routine in order to understand its dynamics. While these examples may be exceptional, capturing the reproduction of routines and practices in sufficient detail to understand what is involved in performing them requires prolonged effort, and generates vast amounts of data, which leads to the next question – how to deal with it?

Analyses of routines necessarily require fine-grained and detailed tracking of how specific activities contribute to the reproduction and adaptation of patterns over time. Visual mapping may be a useful tool here too (Dittrich, 2021). This may take the form of tracing "narrative networks" that indicate how activities chain themselves together (Danner-Schröder & Geiger, 2016; Pentland & Feldman, 2007). While their overall analysis process may cover multiple incidences of routines and practices, scholars have generally presented their work by taking what I label "deep dives" (Fachin & Langley, 2018) into their data, focusing on a small number or incidences (two to five) within their dataset that appear representative of the overall processes they wish to illuminate, and developing narrative vignettes (a form of "thick description") to elaborate in detail on the events surrounding them and the theoretical mechanisms associated with reproduction and adaptation they reveal. These may include descriptive ethnographic data on who did what, but also quotes from interviews and conversations. The "first order" narratives are then abstracted in a comparative and conceptual way in a "second order" more theorized account. An innovative way of representing data (that reflects the "reproductive" or repetitive and generic nature of the practices considered) has been developed by Paula Jarzabkowski and colleagues (Jarzabkowski, Bednarek, & Lê, 2014; Spee et al., 2016): the "composite narrative" based on a thick description integrating multiple incidents involving different people, but oriented around a single story with a fictitious key protagonist. This device has the advantage of preserving confidentiality for individuals while including rich data that offers insight into the dynamics studied.

Encountering change while studying continuity (as reproduction)

While the study of routines and other apparently stable phenomena such as institutions essentially emphasizes the maintenance of continuity, the richness of the ethnographic approach adopted also indirectly illuminates change as well. Martha Feldman, who initiated the stream of research on routines as generative systems discussed above, notes that it was the phenomenon of continuity and stability that first drew her to this topic. However, she was surprised to find that what she was seeing did not fit with her initial assumptions:

> Because I study phenomena ethnographically for the most part, I could contribute to our understanding of stability in organizational routines by exploring the microprocesses that produced this stability. (...) During the course of the research I began to notice that I had a problem. The mechanisms of stability were not the only thing I would have to explain. Indeed, every one of the routines I was following was exhibiting some change and several of them exhibited considerable change over the period of observation. (Feldman & Orlikowski, 2011, p. 1244)

Based on these observations, she and Brian Pentland developed the work that became the foundation for a more general theory of routines as generative systems (Feldman, 2000; Feldman & Pentland, 2003). As Feldman points out, other scholars had of course noted that routines do change through exogenous shocks (i.e. more strictly "episodic" forms of change). However, what Feldman and Pentland (2003) revealed in their studies and theorizing was how routines might shift and change *endogenously* through everyday adaptation as people engaged in performing them. This is most likely to occur when everyday shifts in performances are widely communicated and incorporated into the ostensive aspect of the routine that subsequently guides future performance. In other words, routines are in many ways the means by which organizations sustain a form of order while continuously undergoing change, expressing the duality between change and continuity we began with. Subsequent scholars on routine dynamics have elaborated and enriched these ideas (e.g. Deken et al., 2016; Howard-Grenville, 2005).

In a different approach to juxtaposing continuity and change, Danner-Schroeder and Geiger (2016) show how crisis intervention teams rely on routines to deal with unexpected, chaotic and highly "discontinuous" situations (e.g. earthquakes and other disasters). Some of these routines are executed through standard procedures that rely on artifacts and training aimed at reproducing exactly the same processes in very different situations. Others embed flexibility, but this flexibility and the range of responses that might be developed are again oriented beforehand through artifacts, training programs (e.g. simulations) that specifically encourage selection and recombination. This study shows how routines can inject stability into unstable situations.

Finally, other studies have begun to consider how routines or practices that are disrupted by unforeseen external events may be recreated in situ to enable a form of continuity. Feldman et al. (2022), for example, show how mental health practitioners recreated their ways of working following hurricane Katrina, building patterns in their interventions that drew on the past, but eventually coalesced with the patterns of others to generate new ways of working. Lok and De Rond's (2013) study of the Cambridge boat race rowing team illustrated how breaches of acceptable practices by rowers or others might be reinterpreted to sustain institutional norms through "containment work," or alternatively, when they were too extreme to be recognized as acceptable minor deviations, lead to disciplinary action or other forms of "restoration work" that more forcefully re-established the norms that had sustained the Cambridge rowing establishment for 175 years. The authors conclude that the stability of institutions (like that of routines) over long periods of time is maintained by the acceptance of a degree of plasticity that accommodates to minor deviations. In other words, the maintenance of continuity through reproduction is possible only if institutions and routines are flexible enough to accommodate change.

Focusing on *narrative*: socially constructing the continuity–change duality

As we saw in the previous sections, studies that focus specifically on change or on reproduction over time tend nevertheless to draw attention to the opposite pole of the continuity-chain duality. The third research focus we discuss here – on *narratives* – offers another approach to capturing continuity and change. Indeed, Vaara et al. (2016, p. 499) argue that narratives (i.e. the way in which people or organizations make sense of phenomena through storytelling about the linkages between past, present and future) is intimately tied up with understandings of both continuity and change as they are constructed or brought into being:

> At one level, people's accounts or researchers' narratives provide descriptions of sequences of events, which frame these events as change or stability. At another level, organizational narratives can also be influential in organizational processes, thereby changing the trajectory of events that unfold, which in turn may change the organization or reproduce the status quo.

This quotation reveals the dual role of narratives: as representations of experience, but also as "performative" (i.e. a means of influence, that can contribute to bringing the elements expressed in them to pass). From this perspective, the narrative perspective is intimately tied up with theories of sensemaking and communication in organizations, and involves different sets of methodological tools from those presented above, as we now describe.

Focusing on narrative: design, data collection and analysis

While case study research and ethnography sometimes draw on a narrative sensibility (Balogun, Bartunek, & Do, 2015; Zilber, 2020) at the analytical stage, research that emphasizes, above all, a narrative approach has some distinctive features concerning the types of data and modes of analysis mobilized. The two most common forms of research that exploit narratives are based on in-person interviews in which individuals offer stories that incorporate explicit or implicit constructions of change and/or continuity in identity, strategy or other dimensions (Brown, 2006; Dunford & Jones, 2000; Rhodes, Pullen, & Clegg, 2010; Sonenshein, 2010), or on organizational-level communications (e.g. reports, speeches, other forms of managerial communication), and that consider narrative representations of organizational trajectories (Chreim, 2005; Dalpiaz & Di Stefano, 2018; Maclean, Harvey, Golant, & Sillince, 2021).

In terms of units of analysis, narrative studies take many different forms. Some scholars focus on clearly defined and highly specific stories that involve an identifiable beginning, middle and end with a clear message or plot (Gabriel, 1995). However, most researchers adopt a somewhat looser understanding of the notion of narrative as including any form of sensemaking that involves elements of coherence and temporality, even though this may be expressed in a somewhat fragmented manner (Vaara et al., 2016). Scholars may also reconstruct coherent collective narratives by pulling together fragments from a variety of different sources that reflect a degree of convergence around the way in which people construct the situation in which they find themselves (Brown, 2006; Hardy & Maguire, 2010).

Yet, narrative perspectives are also distinctive in the way in which they can richly illuminate polyphony and diversity in understandings of continuity and change (Brown, 2006; Vaara et al., 2016), something that is often less visible in the outputs of case study and ethnographic work where scholarly outputs tend to take the form of a singular monolithic account that is intended to capture the essence of what occurred. Narrative studies have revealed, for example, that the stories people tell, especially in situations of organizational change are likely to differ in systematic ways as a function of their experience and social position (Boje, 1995; Currie & Brown, 2003; Dunford & Jones, 2000). Moreover, the ways in which different narratives interact and potentially coalesce (or not) to form collective understandings (Brown, 2006; Rhodes et al., 2010; Vaara & Tienari, 2011) can be of crucial interest, as is the way in which certain narrative constructions may be delegitimized or suppressed (Balogun et al., 2015; Boje, 1995). Some scholars have argued that researchers interested in organizational change and continuity should themselves be more open in their writing to recognizing the multiplicity of narratives that might be constructed to explain the same phenomena (Buchanan & Dawson, 2007).

When a narrative perspective is adopted, the analytic tools drawn on may also be quite diverse, grounded in a rich body of theorizing that lies beyond the field of organization studies (sociology, philosophy, linguistics and communication). For example, some scholars draw on forms of literary structural analysis (Greimas, 1987) to identify characters qualified as heroes, villains, helpers or bystanders in the underlying plot of a particular narrative, and the way in which they interact (Gertsen & Søderberg, 2011). This is the approach used by Hardy and Maguire (2010) in their study of the different narratives produced about the role of the chemical insecticide DDT in discussions of the Stockholm Convention. Others inductively identify narrative "themes" that reflect common labels, synonyms and descriptors of organizations or their identities to analyze narratives and their evolution over time (Chreim, 2005). Scholars have also drawn on Gergen and Gergen's (1997) notion of "narratives of the self" as taking progressive, regressive or stable forms (Sonenshein, 2010). Finally, Ricœur's (1984) theorizing of narrative has also served as inspiration to organizational scholars. For example, Rhodes et al. (2010) draw on Ricœur's sequence of narrative practices called prefiguration, configuration and refiguration to show how employee narratives about downsizing in a large company, although dissimilar in some ways, nevertheless converged around a similar understanding of the organization's ethical identity that constrained future ethical questioning, and that would likely orient its future decisions.

It is important to note also that narrative analysis usually requires more than simply analyzing the narrative "text" but also the "context" in which narratives are produced (Bruner, 1991). The question of who authors narratives, who is the audience, and in which particular setting makes a difference to how these narratives are received and understood. Thus, most studies reach beyond a purely textual analysis and collect complementary data on context as well. Beyond the different specific analytical approaches, a focus on narrative also suggests different approaches to considering time and temporality, and thus continuity and change as we see next.

Socially constructing continuity and change

The longitudinal case studies and ethnographies we discussed earlier feature attention to time as linear, and punctuated by events that are observable in the empirical world. Moreover, longitudinal cases focusing on change are mostly about explaining the past, while ethnographic studies are more oriented towards understanding the ongoing construction of an evolving present

(Langley & Tsoukas, 2010). Narrative studies have the potential to capture different conceptions of temporality (subjective, objective, emphasis on not only the past and present but also the future), and thus offer some quite different insights into the continuity–change duality.

First, *within* specific narratives, time is represented and constructed as *subjective and experiential*, rather than objective and abstract. Thus, narratives produced at a single point in time incorporate interpretations of the linkages among past, present and future, potentially articulating continuity and change in the way they are framed. For example, Sonenshein (2010) showed how within the same interview, managers of a retail organization offered almost contradictory narratives about how the change they were engaging in was both radical and important, but would not involve much change at all, expressing the duality by juxtaposing different stories which might then be taken up differently by employees, depending on which of these narratives they found more acceptable or more challenging. In a study of Proctor and Gamble, Golant et al. (2015) showed how in their speeches executives built on values from the past to legitimize change by reorienting the meanings of key identity labels that could achieve resonance with employees.

At the same time, many studies that take a narrative perspective consider not only narratives produced at a single point in time, but also how narratives may differ or evolve from one timepoint to the next. For example, Currie and Brown (2003) examined the narratives told by senior managers and middle managers at two time points during change at a hospital. On a much broader scale, Dalpiaz and Di Stefano (2018) examined narrative constructions of change and continuity as expressed in a series of 25 books produced by leaders and stakeholders of Alessi between 1979 and 2010. By examining how the narratives were constructed over time, they identified three narrative practices by which Alberto Alessi was able to "harness the tension between narrative familiarity and novelty" to create attractive transformational change over multiple years. In my own recent work, I have been analyzing narratives of change and continuity generated by a large cooperative bank over 80 years, as expressed in an internal house organ (Basque & Langley, 2018). Specifically, we focused on the way in which the founder's memory is invoked in communications over the years. We showed how "conservative invocations" in early years (which suggest that the founder's original articulation of identity issues should be fully respected) gave way in later periods to "progressive invocations" (in which it is no longer the founder's words, but rather his innovative vision and persona that are lauded and used to legitimize change). The commonality over all these years is, however, one of continuity. The founder figure is sustained as an important identity symbol, yet his role is reconstructed over time.

A third dimension of temporality that comes to the fore with the focus on narrative, but that was largely absent when we discussed the previous research foci is the emphasis on the *future*, as manifested in the potentially performative nature of narratives. This is revealed, for example, in Hardy and Maguire's (2010) study of the Stockholm convention, where we see that subject positions (or identities) created and legitimized in earlier narratives influenced groups associated with those subject positions to take on more proactive roles and to reorient subsequent narratives in ways that better conformed to their interests. Similarly, Sergeeva and Winch (2021) show how project narratives perform and change the future, by assigning responsibilities, roles and accountabilities that orient future action (Deuten & Rip, 2000).

Overall, a focus on narrative emphasizes the way in which links between past, present and future are socially constructed. Narratives may sometimes project important transformations or breaks with the past (Dalpiaz & Di Stefano, 2018; Ybema, 2010), sometimes express and reaffirm continuity (Golant et al., 2015), and sometimes both at the same time (Basque & Langley, 2018; Sonenshein, 2010). Continuity or change and their mutual relationship is at least in part in the eye of the beholder, or at least, in the words of the narrator. In organizational settings, both continuity and change may be perceived as valuable and important. The emphasis placed on these in narrative will vary depending on judgements of their legitimacy at specific points in time.

Conclusion

In this chapter, we explored three different research foci relevant to the change-continuity duality, and sketched the methodological issues associated with each. We showed how studies of change tend to reveal forces of continuity, manifested potentially in resistance to change, but also in the need to preserve ongoing operations. Conversely, studies that focus on reproduction (such as those oriented towards understanding routines), inevitably reveal that stability and continuity can only be sustained through constant change. Finally studies that focus on narrative reveal the subjective and socially-constructed nature of both continuity and change, and the way in which people, deliberately or not, may articulate stories that orient others' understandings in ways that preserve valued aspects of the past, while adapting to the challenges of the future. The three research foci offer different perspectives on the continuity-change duality, and are likely to lead to different kinds of research outputs. They are, however, quite clearly complementary. Future research might address how they might be combined, and consider whether there might be other ways for researchers to engage with the continuity–change duality in productive ways. Underpinning this duality are the Scylla and Charybdis of stasis and chaos. For their own survival, organizations (and indeed humanity itself) need to navigate continually between these poles. There is still much to learn about how this can be achieved.

References

Balogun, J., Bartunek, J. M., & Do, B. (2015). Senior managers' sensemaking and responses to strategic change, *Organization Science*, 26(4), 960–79.

Balogun, J., & Johnson, G. (2004). Organizational restructuring and middle manager sensemaking, *Academy of Management Journal*, 47(4), 523–49.

Barley, S. R. (1986). Technology as an occasion for structuring: evidence from observations of CT scanners and the social order of radiology departments, *Administrative Science Quarterly*, 31(1), 78–108.

Barley, S. R. (2017). Coalface institutionalism, in R. Greenwood, C. Oliver, T. B. Lawrence & R. E. Meyer (eds), *The Sage Handbook of Organizational Institutionalism* (pp. 338–64), London: Sage Publications.

Basque, J., & Langley, A. (2018). Invoking Alphonse: the founder figure as a historical resource for organizational identity work, *Organization Studies*, 39(12), 1685–708.

Berends, H., & Deken, F. (2021). Composing qualitative process research, *Strategic Organization*, 19(1), 134–46.

Boje, D. M. (1995). Stories of the storytelling organization: a postmodern analysis of Disney as "Tamara-Land", *Academy of Management Journal*, 38(4), 997–1035.

Brammer, S., Branicki, L., & Linnenluecke, M. (2020). COVID-19, societalization and the future of business in society, *Academy of Management Perspectives*, 34(4), 493–507.

Brown, A. D. (2006). A narrative approach to collective identities, *Journal of Management Studies*, 43(4), 731–53.

Bruner, J. (1991). The narrative construction of reality, *Critical Inquiry*, 18(1), 1–21.

Buchanan, D., & Dawson, P. (2007). Discourse and audience: organizational change as multi-story process, *Journal of Management Studies*, 44(5), 669–86.

Bucher, S., & Langley, A. (2016). The interplay of reflective and experimental spaces in interrupting and reorienting routine dynamics, *Organization Science*, 27(3), 594–613.

Chiles, T. H., Meyer, A. D., & Hench, T. J. (2004). Organizational emergence: the origin and transformation of Branson, Missouri's musical theaters, *Organization Science*, 15(5), 499–519.

Chreim, S. (2005). The continuity–change duality in narrative texts of organizational identity, *Journal of Management Studies*, 42(3), 567–93.

Cloutier, C., Denis, J.-L., Langley, A., & Lamothe, L. (2016). Agency at the managerial interface: public sector reform as institutional work, *Journal of Public Administration Research and Theory*, 26(2), 259–76.

Currie, G., & Brown, A. D. (2003). A narratological approach to understanding processes of organizing in a UK hospital, *Human Relations*, 56(5), 563–86.

Currie, G., Lockett, A., Finn, R., Martin, G., & Waring, J. (2012). Institutional work to maintain professional power: recreating the model of medical professionalism, *Organization Studies*, 33(7), 937–62.

Daft, R. L., & Lewin, A. Y. (1990). Can organization studies begin to break out of the normal science straitjacket? An editorial essay, *Organization Science*, 1(1), 1–9.

Dalpiaz, E., & Di Stefano, G. (2018). A universe of stories: mobilizing narrative practices during transformative change, *Strategic Management Journal*, 39(3), 664–96.

Danner-Schröder, A., & Geiger, D. (2016). Unravelling the motor of patterning work: toward an understanding of the microlevel dynamics of standardization and flexibility, *Organization Science*, 27(3), 633–58.

Deken, F., Carlile, P. R., Berends, H., & Lauche, K. (2016). Generating novelty through interdependent routines: a process model of routine work, *Organization Science*, 27(3), 659–77.

Denis, J.-L., Dompierre, G., Langley, A., & Rouleau, L. (2011). Escalating indecision: between reification and strategic ambiguity, *Organization Science*, 22(1), 225–44.

Denis, J.-L., Lamothe, L., & Langley, A. (2001). The dynamics of collective leadership and strategic change in pluralistic organizations, *Academy of Management Journal*, 44(4), 809–37.

Deuten, J. J., & Rip, A. (2000). Narrative infrastructure in product creation processes, *Organization*, 7(1), 69–93.

Dittrich, K. (2021). Ethnography and routine dynamics, in M. S. Feldman, B. T. Pentland, L. D'Adderio, K. Dittrich, C. Rerup & D. Seidl (eds), *Cambridge Handbook on Routine Dynamics* (pp. 103–29), Cambridge: Cambridge University Press.

Dunford, R., & Jones, D. (2000). Narrative in stractegic change, *Human Relations*, 53(9), 1207–26.

Eisenhardt, K. M. (1989). Building theories from case study research, *Academy of Management Review*, 14(4), 532–50.

Eisenhardt, K. M. (2021). What is the Eisenhardt method, really? *Strategic Organization*, 19(1), 147–60.

Fachin, F. F., & Langley, A. (2018). Researching organizational concepts processually: the case of identity, in C. Cassell, A. Cunnliffe & G. Grandy (eds), *SAGE Handbook of Qualitative Management Research Methods* (pp. 308–27), London: Sage Publications.

Farjoun, M. (2010). Beyond dualism: stability and change as a duality, *Academy of Management Review*, 35(2), 202–25.

Feldman, M. S. (2000). Organizational routines as a source of continuous change, *Organization Science*, 11(6), 611–29.

Feldman, M. S., & Orlikowski, W. J. (2011). Theorizing practice and practicing theory, *Organization Science*, 22(5), 1240–53.

Feldman, M. S., & Pentland, B. T. (2003). Reconceptualizing organizational routines as a source of flexibility and change, *Administrative Science Quarterly*, 48(1), 94–118.

Feldman, M. S., Worline, M., Baker, N., & Lowerson Bredow, V. (2022). Continuity as patterning: a process perspective on continuity, *Strategic Organization*, 0(0), https://doi.org/14761270211046878.

Ford, J. D., Ford, L. W., & D'Amelio, A. (2008). Resistance to change: the rest of the story, *Academy of Management Review*, 33(2), 362–77.

Gabriel, Y. (1995). The unmanaged organization: stories, fantasies and subjectivity, *Organization Studies*, 16(3), 477–501.

Gehman, J., Treviño, L. K., & Garud, R. (2013). Values work: a process study of the emergence and performance of organizational values practices, *Academy of Management Journal*, 56(1), 84–112.

Gergen, K. J., & Gergen, M. M. (1997). Narratives of the self, in L. Hinchman & S. Hinchman (eds), *Memory, Identity, Community: The Idea of Narrative in the Human Sciences* (pp. 161–84), Albany: State University of New York.

Gertsen, M. C., & Søderberg, A.-M. (2011). Intercultural collaboration stories: on narrative inquiry and analysis as tools for research in international business, *Journal of International Business Studies*, 42(6), 787–804.

Gioia, D. A., Corley, K. G., & Hamilton, A. L. (2013). Seeking qualitative rigor in inductive research: notes on the Gioia methodology, *Organizational Research Methods*, 16(1), 15–31.

Golant, B. D., Sillince, J. A., Harvey, C., & Maclean, M. (2015). Rhetoric of stability and change: the organizational identity work of institutional leadership, *Human Relations*, 68(4), 607–31.

Greenwood, R., & Hinings, C. R. (1996). Understanding radical organizational change: bringing together the old and the new institutionalism, *Academy of Management Review*, 21(4), 1022–54.

Greimas, A. (1987). *On Meaning*, Minneapolis: University of Minnesota Press.

Grodal, S., & O'Mahony, S. (2017). How does a grand challenge become displaced? Explaining the duality of field mobilization, *Academy of Management Journal*, 60(5), 1801–27.

Hardy, C., & Maguire, S. (2010). Discourse, field-configuring events, and change in organizations and institutional fields: narratives of DDT and the Stockholm Convention, *Academy of Management Journal*, 53(6), 1365–92.

Hernes, T., Hussenot, A., & Pulk, K. (2021). Time and temporality of change processes: applying an event-based view to integrate episodic and continuous change, in M. S. Poole & A. Van de Ven (eds), *Oxford Handbook of Organizational Change and Innovation* (pp. 731–50), Oxford: Oxford University Press.

Hinings, C. R., & Greenwood, R. (1989). *The Dynamics of Strategic Change*, Oxford: Basil Blackwell.

Howard-Grenville, J. (2005). The persistence of flexible organizational routines: the role of agency and organizational context, *Organization Science*, 16(6), 618–36.

Howard-Grenville, J., Metzger, M. L., & Meyer, A. D. (2013). Rekindling the flame: processes of identity resurrection, *Academy of Management Journal*, 56(1), 113–36.

Huy, Q. N. (2002). Emotional balancing of organizational continuity and radical change: the contribution of middle managers, *Administrative Science Quarterly*, 47(1), 31–69.

Huy, Q. N., Corley, K. G., & Kraatz, M. S. (2014). From support to mutiny: shifting legitimacy judgments and emotional reactions impacting the implementation of radical change, *Academy of Management Journal*, 57(6), 1650–80.

Jarzabkowski, P., Bednarek, R., & Lê, J. K. (2014). Producing persuasive findings: demystifying ethnographic textwork in strategy and organization research, *Strategic Organization*, 12(4), 274–87.

Jarzabkowski, P., Lê, J. K., & Van de Ven, A. H. (2013). Responding to competing strategic demands: how organizing, belonging, and performing paradoxes coevolve, *Strategic Organization*, 11(3), 245–80.

Johnson, G. (1987). *Strategic Change and the Management Process*, Oxford: Basil Blackwell.

Kellogg, K. C. (2011). Hot lights and cold steel: cultural and political toolkits for practice change in surgery, *Organization Science*, 22(2), 482–502.

Kouamé, S., Hafsi, T., Oliver, D., & Langley, A. (2022). Creating and sustaining stake-holder emotional resonance with organizational identity in social mission-driven organizations, *Academy of Management Journal*, 65(6), 1864–93.

Langley, A. (1999). Strategies for theorizing from process data, *Academy of Management Review*, 24(4), 691–710.

Langley, A. (2009). Studying processes in and around organizations, in D. Buchanan & A. Bryman (eds), *The Sage Handbook of Organizational Research Methods* (pp. 409–29), London: Sage Publications.

Langley, A., & Denis, J.-L. (2006). Neglected dimensions of organizational change, in R. Lines, I. G. Stensaker, A. Langley & J.-L. Denis (eds), *New Perspectives on Organizational Change and Learning* (pp. 136–61), Bergen: Fagbokforlaget.

Langley, A., & Ravasi, D. (2019). Visual artifacts as tools for analysis and theorizing, in T. B. Zilber, J. Amis & J. Mair (eds), *The Production of Managerial Knowledge and Organizational Theory: New Approaches to Writing, Producing and Consuming Theory* (Research in the Sociology of Organizations) (vol. 59, pp. 173–99), Bingley: Emerald Publishing.

Langley, A., & Truax, J. (1994). A process study of new technology adoption in smaller manufacturing firms, *Journal of Management Studies*, 31(5), 619–52.

Langley, A., & Tsoukas, H. (2010). Introducing perspectives on process organization studies, in S. Maitlis & T. Hernes (eds), *Process, Sensemaking, and Organizing* (vol. 1, pp. 1–27), Oxford: Oxford University Press.

Leonard-Barton, D. (1990). A dual methodology for case studies: synergistic use of a longitudinal single site with replicated multiple sites, *Organization Science*, 1(3), 248–66.

Lincoln, Y. S., & Guba, E. G. (1985). *Naturalistic Inquiry*, Newbury Park, CA: Sage Publications.

Liu, F., & Maitlis, S. (2014). Emotional dynamics and strategizing processes: a study of strategic conversations in top team meetings, *Journal of Management Studies*, 51(2), 202–34.

Lok, J., & Rond, M. d. (2013). On the plasticity of institutions: containing and restoring practice breakdowns at the Cambridge University Boat Club, *Academy of Management Journal*, 56(1), 185–207.

MacKay, R. B., & Chia, R. (2013). Choice, chance, and unintended consequences in strategic change: a process understanding of the rise and fall of NorthCo Automotive, *Academy of Management Journal*, 56(1), 208–30.

Maclean, M., Harvey, C., Golant, B. D., & Sillince, J. A. A. (2021). The role of innovation narratives in accomplishing organizational ambidexterity, *Strategic Organization*, 19(4), 693–721.

Monin, P., Noorderhaven, N., Vaara, E., & Kroon, D. (2013). Giving sense to and making sense of justice in postmerger integration, *Academy of Management Journal*, 56(1), 256–84.

Nicolini, D. (2009). Articulating practice through the interview to the double, *Management Learning*, 40(2), 195–212.

Orlikowski, W. J. (1996). Improvising organizational transformation over time: a situated change perspective, *Information Systems Research*, 7(1), 63–92.

Pentland, B. T. (1999). Building process theory with narrative: from description to explanation, *Academy of Management Review*, 24(4), 711–24.

Pentland, B. T., & Feldman, M. S. (2007). Narrative networks: patterns of technology and organization, *Organization Science*, 18(5), 781–95.

Pettigrew, A. (1985). *The Awakening Giant*, Oxford: Basil Blackwell.

Pettigrew, A. M. (1990). Longitudinal field research on change: theory and practice, *Organization Science*, 1(3), 267–92.

Plowman, D. A., Baker, L. T., Beck, T. E., Kulkarni, M., Solansky, S. T., & Travis, D. V. (2007). Radical change accidentally: the emergence and amplification of small change, *Academy of Management Journal*, 50(3), 515–43.

Powell, W. W., & Rerup, C. (2017). Opening the black box: the microfoundations of institutions, in R. Greenwood, C. Oliver, T. B. Lawrence & R. E. Meyer (eds), *The Sage Handbook of Organizational Institutionalism* (pp. 311–37), London: Sage Publications.

Rhodes, C., Pullen, A., & Clegg, S. R. (2010). 'If I should fall from grace …': stories of change and organizational ethics, *Journal of Business Ethics*, 91(4), 535–51.

Ricœur, P. (1984). *Time and Narrative, Volume 1*, Chicago, IL: University of Chicago Press.

Schüssler, E., Rüling, C.-C., & Wittneben, B. B. (2014). On melting summits: the limitations of field-configuring events as catalysts of change in transnational climate policy, *Academy of Management Journal*, 57(1), 140–71.

Sergeeva, N., & Winch, G. M. (2021). Project narratives that potentially perform and change the future, *Project Management Journal*, 52(3), 264–77.

Smets, M., Aristidou, A., & Whittington, R. (2017). Towards a practice-driven institutionalism, in R. Greenwood, C. Oliver, T. B. Lawrence, & R. E. Meyer (eds), *The Sage Handbook of Organizational Institutionalism* (pp. 384–411), London: Sage Publications.

Smith, A. D. (2002). From process data to publication: a personal sensemaking, *Journal of Management Inquiry*, 11(4), 383–406.

Sonenshein, S. (2010). We're changing—Or are we? Untangling the role of progressive, regressive, and stability narratives during strategic change implementation, *Academy of Management Journal*, 53(3), 477–512.

Spee, P., Jarzabkowski, P., & Smets, M. (2016). The influence of routine interdependence and skillful accomplishment on the coordination of standardizing and customizing, *Organization Science*, 27(3), 759–81.

Stensaker, I. G., & Langley, A. (2010). Change management choices and trajectories in a multidivisional firm, *British Journal of Management*, 21(1), 7–27.

Tsoukas, H., & Chia, R. (2002). On organizational becoming: rethinking organizational change, *Organization Science*, 13(5), 567–82.

Vaara, E., Sonenshein, S., & Boje, D. (2016). Narratives as sources of stability and change in organizations: approaches and directions for future research, *Academy of Management Annals*, 10(1), 495–560.

Vaara, E., & Tienari, J. (2011). On the narrative construction of multinational corporations: an antenarrative analysis of legitimation and resistance in a cross-border merger, *Organization Science*, 22(2), 370–90.

Van de Ven, A. H. (1992). Suggestions for studying strategy process: a research note, *Strategic Management Journal*, 13(S1), 169–88.

Van de Ven, A. H., Angle, H. L., & Poole, M. S. (1989/2000). *Research on the Management of Innovation: The Minnesota Studies*, Oxford: Oxford University Press.

Van de Ven, A. H., & Huber, G. P. (1990). Longitudinal field research methods for studying processes of organizational change, *Organization Science*, 1(3), 213–19.

Van Hulst, M., Ybema, S., & Yanow, D. (2017). Ethnography and organizational processes, in A. Langley & H. Tsoukas (eds), *The Sage Handbook of Process Organization Studies* (pp. 223–36), London: Sage Publications.

Van Maanen, J. (2011). Ethnography as work: some rules of engagement, *Journal of Management Studies*, 48(1), 218–34.

Weick, K. E., & Quinn, R. E. (1999). Organizational change and development, *Annual Review of Psychology*, 50(1), 361–86.

Wright, A. L., Meyer, A. D., Reay, T., & Staggs, J. (2021). Maintaining places of social inclusion: Ebola and the emergency department, *Administrative Science Quarterly*, 66(1), 42–85.

Wright, A. L., & Zammuto, R. F. (2013). Wielding the willow: processes of institutional change in English county cricket, *Academy of Management Journal*, 56(1), 308–30.

Wright, C., & Nyberg, D. (2017). An inconvenient truth: how organizations translate climate change into business as usual, *Academy of Management Journal*, 60(5), 1633–61.

Ybema, S. (2010). Talk of change: temporal contrasts and collective identities, *Organization Studies*, 31(4), 481–503.

Yin, R. K. (2013). *Case Study Research: Design and Methods*, Thousand Oaks, CA: Sage Publications.

Zilber, T. B. (2020). The methodology/theory interface: ethnography and the microfoundations of institutions, *Organization Theory*, 1(2), https:// doi .org/ 10 .1177/ 2631787720919439.

Index